THE 25 MINDSETS

The 25 Mindsets

UNDERSTAND ANYONE, EVEN YOURSELF

KAREN WHITTEN

LIONCREST
PUBLISHING

THE 25 MINDSETS
Understand Anyone, Even Yourself
First Edition

ISBN 978-1-5445-4313-0 *Hardcover*
978-1-5445-4312-3 *Paperback*
978-1-5445-4311-6 *Ebook*

CONTENTS

PART 3. UNDERSTANDING THE 25 MINDSETS

PART 4. LIVING IN ALIGNMENT WITH YOUR MINDSET

INTRODUCTION

"Knowing yourself is the beginning of all wisdom."

—ARISTOTLE

Tell me what irritates you about others, and I'll tell you what your passion and purpose are. Are you most irritated when someone takes credit for another's work? Your passion and purpose are to strengthen yourself and others so people feel supported. It's that simple. While I don't have telepathic superpowers, what I do know is that your triggers, passion, and purpose are deeply interconnected.

This book is a step-by-step guide to help you get clear on who you are so that you can align with that truth. It challenges the false notion that you are so complex you can't possibly figure yourself out. Once you determine which of the 25 Mindsets you relate to, you will understand yourself in a new way. You'll be positioned to pursue a life that honors your incredible gifts—gifts you've very likely taken for granted.

To use your gifts most effectively, you'll need to know your passion and purpose. But don't worry, this won't be a daunting task. Passion and purpose need not remain a great mystery. They seem like nebulous concepts only because we haven't defined them for what they truly are. Passion, for instance, is often assigned to a specific activity, such as tennis, knitting, volunteering, or gardening. But your passion is more than that. It's not the *activity* that holds the key to finding your passion; it's what your actions *accomplish*. When you align with your passion by doing what you're innately motivated to do, something shifts. Your actions bring about a desired outcome. Someone or something is better off as a direct result of your actions. If you are someone who experiences a natural high after checking things off your to-do list, your actions shift a task that was incomplete to a task that has been completed. This points to a passion for completing new tasks and challenges. By examining the underlying *shift* that occurs when you do what innately motivates you, you will unveil your true passion.

My own desperation to discover my passion led me down a winding road to decipher order in the chaos that is me—and you. After spending almost two decades in Corporate America, most of those years at Microsoft, I found myself burned out and miserable, despite my outward appearance of a happy and successful life. The discoveries I share in this book helped me overcome burnout, find my passion and purpose, pursue work that energizes me, overcome insecurities, and strengthen my relationships. It's been my greatest honor to help businesses, couples, professionals, and people like you to do the same.

Achieving all this is possible when you align with who you are. Yet to align with who you are, you must first know who you are, which brings us to the age-old question: *Who am I?*

That's where the 25 Mindsets come in.

THE 25 MINDSETS

Your mindset influences how you perceive the world around you. It includes your expectations of how people should and shouldn't behave and what you are and aren't motivated to do. It affects your learning style, career aspirations, relationships, and interests. Your mindset touches nearly every aspect of your life, yet for the most part, you don't realize it exists, or that most people come equipped with a different mindset than you.

Consider that some people enjoy being the center of attention, while others prefer working behind the scenes. Some stick with what's been proven over time, while others seek out the latest innovations. And some make the rules, while others break them. These differences arise because there are different mindsets.

You see the world through your particular mindset, while others see the world through theirs. Each of us aligns with one of 25 Mindsets, and each mindset has traits that distinguish it from other mindsets. Every day, we observe distinguishing traits in other people: Elon Musk is an outside-the-box thinker. Serena Williams is competitive. Björk is eccentric. Gabriel Iglesias is hilarious. Jane Goodall respects all life. Simon Cowell is direct.

You have traits that set you apart from others too. There are things that are blatantly obvious to you that are not, in fact, apparent to everyone else. For example, maybe you believe people should read the directions before they start a project. Or maybe to you, people should act with a sense of urgency, or look for opportunities to make improvements. When people don't meet your basic expectations, it's baffling that someone can disregard something so obvious to you. You're left wondering: *How can people behave in a way so clearly unacceptable?*

The answer has everything to do with your mindset, and theirs.

Your mindset is fundamental to who you are: it's what you know deep down to your core and why you do what you do. Like an operating system, it runs in the background and guides your decisions, interactions, and how you interface with the world around you.

Perhaps the most perplexing part about your mindset is that it feels universal. You believe that, surely, everyone experiences the world as you do. Only they don't.

Herein lies our challenge.

Because we don't acknowledge different mindsets, our differences become an underlying source of conflict and frustration. We perceive the world through our own mindset lens and assume others should also see our perspective. Meanwhile, others see the world through their mindset lens and expect us to see the world as they do.

Without a common means to understand each other, we're limited to a single perspective. So when disagreements arise, we're quick to assume we're right and others are wrong. When people "overreact," we're apt to view them as demanding, unreasonable, or too sensitive.

Along with lacking a way to understand others, we don't have an easy way to understand ourselves. If we follow an accepted narrative of who we "should" be, we may land a high-paying job only to find it comes at the cost of happiness. We rationalize work as something we must do, as opposed to something we're motivated to do. Many of us continue down this path even though it drains us—a path where success is materialized, passion is unrealized, and burnout is normalized.

This lack of understanding—of both ourselves and others—causes angst, frustration, and even suffering. The alternative is a simple, comprehensive way to understand ourselves and each other.

The 25 Mindsets celebrate individual strengths by acknowledging our differences. Understanding the mindsets awakens you to the reality that your mindset is one of many and that each mindset is vital to humanity's collective success and well-being. We were never meant to be like each other. Instead, we're perfectly designed to complement one another. This elevated perspective brings clarity, eases tension, and provides each of us the opportunity to live a more fulfilling life.

A LITTLE BACKSTORY

You may be wondering, *Why twenty-five mindsets? Why not sixteen mindsets? Or nine? Or just two?*

The 25 Mindsets is a product of observation. It's the culmination of thirty-seven years of clinical research, patient observation, and unrelenting persistence, bringing together my research with the original work of Dr. Carolyn Mein.

Dr. Mein observed twenty-five distinct types of people through her work as a chiropractor. Using applied kinesiology, she identified common patterns in her patients to better understand and serve their needs. Working with thousands of patients in the United States and around the world, she evaluated people to determine whether they aligned with a previously discovered type or a new one. After identifying the twenty-fifth type in 1985, she found that every person over the next three and a half decades aligned with one of her previously identified types.

I first came across Dr. Mein's work after seeing a book lying on my friend's coffee table. In *Different Bodies, Different Diets*, Dr. Mein detailed observations she witnessed in her patients. At the time, she offered a practitioner certification, and having just left my corporate career, I took the opportunity to explore this new interest. With a certification in hand, I worked with friends and family, yet found it difficult to determine someone's type given my lack of applied kinesiology skills.

I decided to pursue other work and projects, but I carried a nagging sense that there was more to discover. I wanted an easy method to understand myself and others. I wanted to bring understanding to the corporate world. And despite our complexities, I wanted to structure this awareness to make it easy for people to digest. But how?

I knew I was on to something the moment I realized that our triggers aren't random. One afternoon, I read a blog where the writer revealed his lifelong mistrust of people and his frustration with the way others behaved. It struck me that his source of irritation (what I refer to as his *trigger*) was the direct opposite of his core value (what I refer to as his *principle*). He was most irritated with people "not doing things right" because he valued "doing things right."

I then saw the same phenomenon in myself and others who share my mindset. I'm triggered when people are inconsiderate, and my core principle is rooted in a need for people to be considerate of others' experiences.

It struck me: I feel more strongly about being considerate than 96 percent of people. Twenty-four out of twenty-five people feel more strongly about a different principle, such as being prepared, being kind, or being accountable. Though there are eight billion people on the planet, we do not uphold eight billion different principles. There are only twenty-five core principles, and we each fit neatly within one of the 25 Mindsets. This meant that the principle so very important to me was not equally valued by most everyone else.

This epiphany was exhilarating. In a moment, so much made sense. I had newfound compassion for myself and others. I understood how other people could show up contrary to how I "needed" them to behave because they protected a different principle. For example, I expect people to be considerate (my principle) and am triggered when people are inconsiderate (my trigger), but my friend Kathryn expects people to be prepared and is most irritated when people are unprepared. She does not share my same mindset, so she upholds a different principle.

Just as people with different mindsets uphold different principles, they also have different passions and purposes. Conversely, people who share your mindset uphold the same principle and share your passion and purpose.

While *The 25 Mindsets* helps you distinguish various personality traits, it's more than a personality profile: it's also a tool for alignment. In other words, it's not enough to *know thyself*. You must take the next step and *be thyself* by honoring the inherent values and motivations that are central to who *you* are. Aligning with who you are holds the key to your satisfaction and fulfillment. This book will give you the tools to do just that.

WHAT TO EXPECT

The 25 Mindsets is divided into the following four sections:

- Part 1: Understanding the Multifaceted Nature of Mindsets
- Part 2: Discovering Your Mindset
- Part 3: Understanding the 25 Mindsets
- Part 4: Living in Alignment with Your Mindset

In Part 1, "Understanding the Multifaceted Nature of Mindsets," you'll gain a thorough understanding of the key facets of your mindset—principle, passion, and purpose—and their respective opposites—trigger, void, and hurt. This will give you the foundation you need to understand anyone.

Part 2, "Discovering Your Mindset," will lead you through a process where you will narrow the list of 25 Mindsets to find *your* mindset. Here you will discover if you are an Accomplisher, Achiever, Adviser, Authenticator, Balancer, Captivator, Connector, Cultivator, Envisioner, Harmonizer, Inquisitor, Integrator, Intuitor, Observer, Optimizer, Pathfinder, Perceiver, Producer, Progressor, Protector, Risktaker, Sensor, Stabilizer, Supporter, or Synthesizer mindset.

Part 3, "Understanding the 25 Mindsets," comprises over half of this book. It includes twenty-five chapters, one for each mindset. Since your initial focus will be on finding your mindset, you will skip most chapters in this section. Consequently, you'll likely find this book is a quick read. The intention is *not* for you to understand all twenty-five mindsets, but to start with your mindset, while also recognizing that others bring their own perspective. In the future, as you discover the mindsets of other people in your life, you can return to this section to learn more about them.

Finally, Part 4 focuses on "Living in Alignment with Your Mindset." Coupled with your newfound self-awareness, this section provides you with valuable tools to help you align with your mindset when you are misaligned. It is arguably the most important part of the book. When you align with your mindset, you can improve relationships, overcome burnout, dissolve insecurities, and feel how you've always yearned to feel. It is this section that will show you how to live the life you've always wanted to live and find satisfaction in being who you truly are.

You are far more extraordinary than you have allowed yourself to believe. Every mindset is important, valuable, significant, and equipped with incredible gifts. Our world would not be as enjoyable, beautiful, or productive without any one mindset. You deserve to know your passion and purpose and to experience the aliveness that comes from living in alignment with who you are. You aren't a jumbled assortment of traits and characteristics. On the contrary, the various aspects of your being are sublimely interconnected.

I invite you to transform your self-understanding and live a fulfilling life by honoring the gifts of your mindset.

PART 1

UNDERSTANDING THE MULTIFACETED NATURE OF MINDSETS

"Who in the world am I?
Ah, that's the great puzzle."

—LEWIS CARROLL, *ALICE IN WONDERLAND*

MINDSET POLARITIES

"The lens we look through will determine what we see."

—RENEE SWOPE

On December 7, 2012, I sat in a conference room on the twenty-sixth floor in one of the Petronas Towers in Kuala Lumpur, Malaysia. The meeting was the culmination of a yearlong project to create role clarity and consistency across a global team of three thousand Microsoft employees. I'd been at Microsoft for twelve years, at the time as an engineering manager. My job was to lead a team of technical professionals working with the company's large enterprise customers, while my role in this project team revolved around curating tools to support our field engineers. The project was on the verge of a global rollout. But on the third day, sitting at a boardroom table with nine colleagues from around the world, I sensed a shift in our executive sponsor, a seasoned Microsoft leader.

Throughout the week, we all spent long days in face-to-face meetings to ensure our work landed consistently across diverse geographies. Yet, on day three, the executive sponsor cut the meeting short and dispassionately proclaimed the rollout would be handled through a few emails and conference calls. After my initial pushback, I quickly recognized what was not being said: an organizational change was on the horizon, thus the project would never land.

I'd poured myself into this project because I'd witnessed employees demoralized through the company's stack ranking performance review process, which, fortunately, has long since been retired. Back then, the process ranked people on a forced curve and effectively reduced people to a number: 1 if you rose to the small subset at the top of the heap, and 5 if you landed at the bottom. Too often, weaknesses were emphasized, while unparalleled talents and achievements were minimized. Our project team had taken a giant step in addressing these issues and celebrating each employee's unique gifts. I, along with others, had worked days, late nights, and weekends to support this effort. But now it was all for nothing.

At that moment, sitting in a conference room almost ten-thousand miles from home, I knew I was going to end my career with Microsoft.

With my heart and mind at odds, my decision was clear, yet it felt irrational. From an outsider's view, my life looked perfect. I had a thriving career working for one of the world's most sought-after employers. I lived among world-renowned ski resorts in the heart of Colorado. I took once-in-a-lifetime vacations every year.

At the same time, I was miserable.

Over the previous two years, I'd grown more drained, depleted, and disengaged. As I held the corporate line, I watched the trust I had built within my team vanish. Rather than feeling praised for their accomplishments, many employees felt diminished during the review process. It didn't matter what I said; all people heard was a number.

On top of that, I spent much of my time putting out fires or, like the meeting in Malaysia, investing time in projects that turned out to be a waste, which are things that drain my energy most as a Synthesizer mindset. I would think about the once-vibrant manager I had been and wondered if she still lived somewhere within me.

To top it all off, I felt ashamed for feeling this way. How could I have so much and appreciate it so little? I questioned where I had gone wrong. I had thought if I followed the path to success and arrived there, I'd feel a sense of satisfaction. I was wrong.

Instead, I felt burned out, and my burnout extended well beyond my career: I had neglected my personal needs, ignored my social needs, numbed my emotions, and magnified my insecurities.

This story is my own, but it's not unique.

At times, all of us find ourselves feeling out of sorts—at work, school, in our relationships, and life. We find ourselves *misaligned.*

You know the feeling of being misaligned, though you may call it by a different name. You feel "off." You don't quite feel yourself because you're going against your nature in some way. In caveman terms, it often feels like *Ugh!*, *Grr!*, or *Argh!* In more modern terms, it's characterized as WTF.

We've all been there. The discomfort can last a moment, or it can consume you for hours, days, weeks, months, or years. It can feel temporary, or it can feel like it might never end.

Misalignment refers to the uncomfortable state of going against your nature.

Just about anything can spur feelings of misalignment: a bad hair day, a bad face day, not being understood, feeling excluded, not being able to find your people, or not knowing what you want to be today, tomorrow, or in retirement. It could result from going to a job or class you hate, feeling you've failed, or feeling bored, exhausted, different, or trapped. Often, it feels like something is missing, but you're not sure what.

If you find yourself feeling out of sorts, like I was, it doesn't mean you're flawed. It means you're *misaligned.*

The solution is *alignment.*

When you're aligned, the friction you feel internally and externally dissipates. Balance returns, and you feel fulfilled. It's as if, in honoring your essence, you effortlessly function as designed.

Alignment refers to the satisfactory state of living congruently with your nature.

Aligning with who you are requires you to forgo any belief that we are one-size-fits-all. We're not. Some people are peacekeepers; others are agitators. Some love to socialize and work a crowd; others crave solitude. Some seek thrills; others choose a more cautious path.

Alignment for one person can feel like a misalignment for someone else with a different mindset.

Your satisfaction doesn't come by doing what brought satisfaction to someone else. And it won't come from chasing a fabricated image of who you should be, even if that image is smart, sexy, and successful. Your satisfaction comes from aligning with who *you* are.

Yet, to align with who you are, you must be clear about who you are. So let's explore: Who are you?

To find out who you are, you must also see who you are *not.*

Think back to when you were in grade school. How did you identify a cheetah? It's fast, of course. An elephant? It's big. And a giraffe? Tall. By acknowledging what something was, you also implied what it was not: a cheetah is fast, not slow; an elephant is big, not small; a giraffe is tall, not short.

It's as if you cannot know what something is without knowing what it's not. When you say someone is "nice," you not only observe them being nice, but you also recognize they aren't mean.

Your mindset works the same way. It distinguishes who you are, while at the same time pointing to who you are not. You possess traits that set you apart from others. Perhaps you are neat, not sloppy; generous, not selfish; or a good listener who doesn't talk over people. Most likely, you can think of several distinctions that differentiate you from others. In doing so, you are identifying *polarities.*

A polarity distinguishes two opposing attributes.

When you examine polarities within yourself, they may seem trivial, even obvious, like the animal characteristics noted above. If you're empathetic, you're not callous. If you're charismatic, you're not dull. If you methodically think things through, you don't impulsively jump to conclusions.

The 25 Mindsets relies on the concept of polarities to help you better understand yourself.

Likewise, when you notice a trait in someone else, it points to a polarity that distinguishes them from other mindsets. Kelly Clarkson is expressive, not reserved. Dwayne Johnson is hardworking, not lazy. Comedian JP Sears is self-directed, not conforming.

Malala Yousafzai is strong-willed, not passive. Simon Sinek is optimistic, not pessimistic.

That's not to say there are lazy and pessimistic mindsets but to acknowledge that some mindsets value being strong-willed *more than* having a strong work ethic. Other mindsets value being self-directed *more than* being optimistic. You can be hardworking, optimistic, and self-directed, yet feel more strongly about one than others.

The polarities within you differentiate you from others and help answer the age-old question: *Who am I?*

Mindsets distinguish "who you are" by recognizing the polarities that exist within each of us. By understanding the polarities, you can better understand yourself, and others.

Your mindset helps you understand *who* you are by understanding the *How, What, and Why* aspects within you. There are three mindset polarities:

1. **The How Polarity**: The first polarity distinguishes *how* you expect people to behave, and how you expect people to not behave.
2. **The What Polarity**: The second polarity distinguishes *what* you are naturally motivated to do, and what you are not motivated to do.
3. **The Why Polarity**: The third polarity distinguishes *why* you do what you do (to realize a desired state of being), and the consequence if you do not (which would result in an undesirable state of being).

Your *How, What, and Why* characterize how you experience the world. The three polarities work together synergistically to make up your *mindset.*

A mindset is an innate disposition governing *how* you expect people to behave (and not behave), *what* you are motivated to do (and not do), and *why* you do what you do (and the consequence if you do not).

You might think of yourself as an antenna tuned into a specific frequency, while the other twenty-four mindsets are tuned into different ones. When you're rocking out to the oldies on 99.9 FM, you don't hear today's hits on 102.3 or classical music on 88.1. It doesn't mean the other stations don't exist or that they don't play great music; it just means you're not tuned into them. Mindsets operate similarly: what you're naturally tuned into—and energized by—isn't what others automatically tune into or enjoy.

Because certain things are so very clear to you, you naturally believe they're apparent to others too. It seems that everyone else would experience the world as you do and value what you value. Only it's not true.

Different people have different expectations of *how* people should behave: Sensor mindsets expect people to be supportive, not unsupportive; Authenticators expect people to be well-intentioned, not ill-intentioned; Achievers expect people to be accountable, not unaccountable.

People view life through their mindset lens, so most others feel differently than you do about *how* people should behave, *what* they are motivated to do, and *why* they do what they do.

At the same time, you're not alone in your worldview: one in twenty-five people share your mindset. Other people with your mindset view life through a similar lens because the same polarities that distinguish you exist within them. You share, for example, the same expectations of how people should and should not behave.

Our differences, resulting from different polarity distinctions, make people complementary in nature. Every mindset is important to the greater whole; each creates a connection to some larger ecosystem that could be as small as one family or group, or as large as all of humanity. Because of our differences, we have people motivated to enter a variety of roles and professions, including teachers, farmers, plumbers, musicians, managers, first responders, inventors, healers, landscapers, and everything else necessary to ensure our collective success and well-being. There are even people motivated to do the very things you dread doing, which means if those people can happily take those tasks off your plate, you are free to do what you are motivated to do. That's why the world needs you to be exactly who you are.

THE MINDSET FRAMEWORK

"Attention is key; for where man's attention goes, there goes his energy, and he himself can only follow."

—COUNT OF ST. GERMAIN

A few years ago, I came across the "Deep Relating Workshop," led by author and transformational journalist Neil Strauss. Strauss planned to host the workshop for a handful of couples at his home in Malibu, California. I was ecstatic. I admired Strauss for boldly facing personal challenges and being a catalyst for change. I promptly replied to his email and expressed "our" interest, and then told my husband, Scott, about the exciting opportunity.

Scott didn't need long to think about this so-called opportunity. He had no interest in being a part of this workshop. He hated the idea and was suspicious of my motivations. Was I going to make him fly to California, only to publicly humiliate him by breaking the news that I was a lesbian, pregnant with someone else's baby, or about to join a cult that Neil had lured me into?

Unable to rationalize how Scott came to his conclusion, I was speechless. *What the hell just happened?*

Even with the best of intentions, we sometimes find ourselves thrust into a misaligned state. In one moment, we are on top of the world. In the next, we are baffled and misunderstood. We assume people will share our perspective because it's so clear to us.

Through the lens of my mindset, I could justify my perspective as the most favorable and rational one. After all, I wanted to invest in our relationship. Scott didn't. I was open-minded. He was short-sighted. I'm right. He's wrong. End of story.

Except, what if my perspective wasn't right, and his wasn't wrong? What if our views were just different?

When we compare opposing perspectives, we typically look at both viewpoints through one mindset lens: our own. Naturally, we conclude that our perspective is the superior one.

The trick is to see both perspectives through each individual's mindset lens.

Once you do this, you can make sense of just about everyone.

Personally, I like to improve upon things. If things are fine, then by golly, that's no excuse not to make them better! Two weeks before the "Deep Relating Workshop" debacle, I attended Jack Canfield's "One Day to Greatness" workshop in Denver with my teenage son and walked away feeling enlivened. When I heard about a new workshop, it presented a similar opportunity for me to invest time doing something worthwhile. In my mind, this workshop would be so much fun.

However, Scott didn't attend the Canfield workshop, nor did he want to. He craves an interactive dialogue. Being talked at isn't his thing. Though the Strauss workshop would be interactive, Scott believed couples only attend relationship workshops if the relationship was all but sunk. Since we didn't have any glaring issues, he concluded I must be hiding something from him, with plans of springing it on him in the company of strangers. With such a backstory, it made perfect sense that, for him, a "Deep Relating Workshop" was akin to slow torture and humiliation.

When we see others' perspectives solely through our own mindsets, things can turn ugly fast. We end up deciding he doesn't care about the marriage, or she is keeping secrets, because we assume people view the world as we see it.

The key to understanding others is to broaden our lens enough to see another's perspective. In seeing through another's mindset lens, not our own, different perspectives make sense.

Synthesizer mindsets, like mine, thrive on investing time in doing things that pay off. In my mind, a few days attending a workshop translated to an even stronger relationship for decades to come. Scott, a Connector mindset, requires favorable outcomes. Thus, he's not about to walk naively into a situation he knows nothing about.

The 25 Mindsets provide a framework to understand each other and open us to see others' perspectives in a new way. To fully understand mindsets, we need to delve into the six facets within the three polarities of *How, What, and Why*. The six facets represent the opposing ends of the three polarities: principle and trigger, passion and void, and purpose and hurt.

Principle represents *how* you expect people to behave. **Trigger** represents your expectation of *how* people should *not* behave.

Passion tells us *what* you are innately motivated to do. **Void** points to *what* you are *not* motivated to do because it drains your energy.

Purpose represents an underlying intention and *why* you do what you do. **Hurt**, in contrast, results in an undesired state and underscores *why* it's detrimental if you don't align with your principle and passion.

The Mindset Framework acknowledges each mindset's three polarities (*How, What, and Why*) and their respective facets: principle and trigger, passion and void, and purpose and hurt.

The opposing attributes—principle and trigger, passion and void, purpose and hurt—exist within each of us and lay the foundation of the Mindset Framework, as shown below.

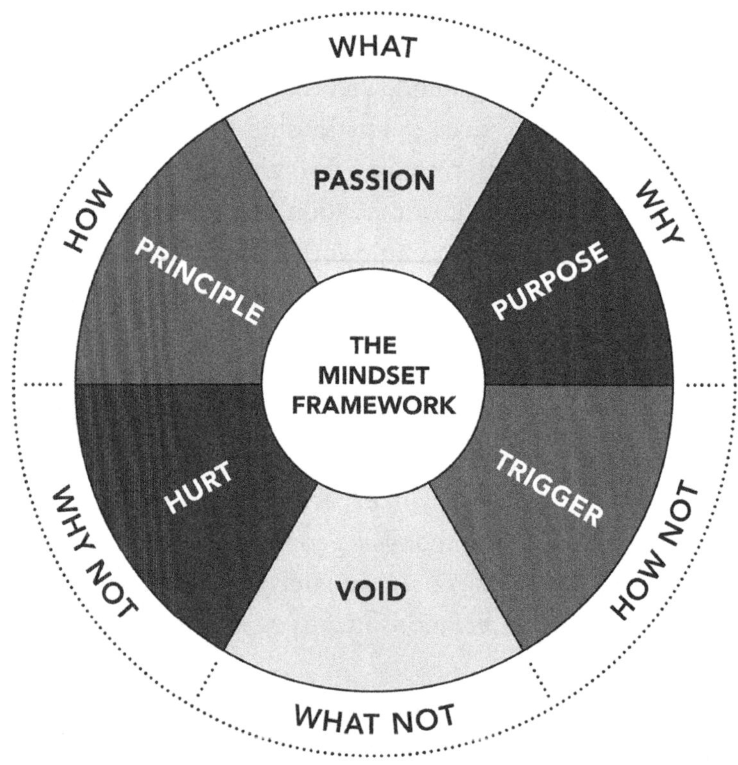

The six facets work together to create the perfectly orchestrated whole that is you.

But while all six facets are core to your mindset, you don't occupy these facets simultaneously. For example, you could be feeling invigorated doing something you're passionate about, then get interrupted and become annoyed. In an instant, you leap from the *passion* facet to *trigger*.

Every day, each of us move between various facets. Consider Patti, a Pathfinder and fifth-grade schoolteacher. When teaching motivated students, Patti is aligned with her **passion**. When working with a student who just wants the answers and refuses to learn, she feels drained and falls into her **void**. When she speaks to students about the importance of treating each other with respect, she's upholding her **principle**. But when she witnesses a student mistreating another, she's instantly **triggered**. As she thinks about a student shamed by another, she feels **hurt**. Then, when she goes out of her way to support the shamed student, Patti is aligned with her **purpose**.

In this sense, mindsets are multifaceted. Like Patti, your experience differs based upon what facet you reside in—principle, trigger, passion, void, purpose, or hurt. Whatever facet you place your attention upon determines the facet in which you currently reside.

> The multifaceted nature of mindsets acknowledges that, while your mindset is made up of six facets, your attention does not reside in all six facets simultaneously.

It's our multifaceted nature that has made it so darn difficult to understand ourselves, let alone others. We tend to simplify ourselves: am I *this*, or am I *that*? The reality is, we're more complex than that. Ironically, it is when we acknowledge our complexity and resist the urge to make things black and white that we can finally make sense of ourselves and others. *The 25 Mindsets* allow for the complexity of each person while simultaneously presenting a straightforward way of understanding yourself and others.

The Mindset Framework takes something extremely complex—a means of understanding eight-billion distinct individuals—and makes it remarkably simple. The framework and its respective polarities and facets help us see, and make sense of, our multifaceted nature. Because of your multifaceted nature, you can be both patient and impatient, introverted and extroverted, serious and playful, or stubborn and accommodating. We are living, breathing oxymorons. We all show up quite differently when ensnared by our trigger as opposed to when we engage in our passion.

My mom, for instance, can be both patient and impatient. When I was a kid, she spent several hours a day for weeks helping me and my sister learn how to sew—a blanket, jacket, pair of shorts, prom dress—whatever we decided to make. She stuck with us, day after day, until we were competent, then continued to be there whenever we had a question with a new technique or needed help ripping out a seam after we made a mistake. Her patience was unparalleled. But show up ten minutes late for the family Christmas dinner, and you won't see any resemblance of patience. She told us dinner was at 5:00, and it's now 5:08. If that clock strikes 5:12, and you haven't arrived yet, you'll have officially ruined Christmas.

So is my mom patient or not?

The answer is: it depends on what facet she resides in. She's extraordinarily patient when she's aligned with her passion. She's impatient when she's misaligned, irritated by people who are late or fail to appreciate her well-laid plans.

Just like my mom, at any given time, we are either aligned or misaligned, based on where our attention lies. Principle, passion, and purpose represent the aligned facets of a mindset. Their respective opposites—trigger, void, and hurt—make up the misaligned facets.

Because the six facets of your mindset are so tightly integrated, when you determine any one facet, it will make learning the other five facets much easier. Your trigger tends to be the easiest to identify because we all seem to know what infuriates us about others. In Part 2, when you go through the process of discovering which of the 25 Mindsets is *your* mindset, you'll start by identifying your triggers.

But before you discover your mindset, it's important to understand the intricacies of each mindset facet. Understanding the facets is key to self-understanding and knowing how to realign when you become misaligned. The following six sections will help you better understand each of the six facets: principle, trigger, passion, void, purpose, and hurt. With this foundation, you'll glean insight into yourself, make sense of others' perspectives, and ultimately strengthen your relationships.

Speaking of relationships, remember the "Deep Relating Workshop"? My husband soon came around to the idea when he understood my reason for wanting to attend and how it aligned with my passion. That said, we never went. The workshop logistics were being worked out in November 2018, a time when the hills surrounding Malibu, California, caught on fire. Strauss lived nearby, and while his home remained intact, many of the homes on his street had burned. Given the major devastation in the area, the workshop never took place. In our own way, Scott and I still grew from the experience. He was able to understand my eagerness to attend by acknowledging my mindset, and I was able to understand his hesitation by acknowledging his. I wasn't right. He wasn't wrong. We brought different perspectives that made sense when we looked through the other's lens.

PRINCIPLE

"Policies are many; principles are few. Policies will change; principles never do."

—JOHN C. MAXWELL

I remember, as a kid, watching a Coca-Cola commercial where a diverse group of people sang the song, "I'd Like to Teach the World to Sing (In Perfect Harmony)." The commercial displayed faces and races different from each other and sent a clear message: we can be different yet be tolerant of one another and all live in harmony.

This message of tolerance is consistent with the Harmonizer mindset's *principle*. This principle is a rule they abide by and wish others to abide by too: to be harmonious, tolerant, and accepting of differences.

Like Harmonizers, every mindset has a rule—a principle—they adhere to.

Perhaps you want everyone to be personable and kind. Maybe you expect everyone to work hard to build competence. Perhaps you just wish people used common sense.

Whatever is true for you, this rule represents your expectation of appropriate behavior. It's a moral principle you fiercely uphold and need others to uphold too. If it were up to you, everyone in the whole world would abide by this rule.

> A principle represents your innate expectation of how people should behave.

Though you may value many principles, there is *one* you instinctively uphold above all others. This principle is a foundational facet of your mindset because it directly impacts your expectations of yourself, your expectations of others, how you treat people, and how you want to be treated. Your mindset principle shapes much of how you view the world and the people in it.

Interestingly, no one had to teach you this principle. You may credit your grandma for her wisdom, "Grandma always said, 'If you don't have anything nice to say, don't say anything at all.'" Meanwhile, your cousin remembers Grandma saying, "If you start something, finish it." You remember certain adages because they resonate with you. Grandma said something that highlighted this principle already engrained in you.

While all 25 Mindset principles are within you, you do not value each principle equally. Your mindset principle represents the single value you protect most. The twenty-five principles we collectively uphold are simple, pure, and straightforward. As a whole, we expect others to be:

- Accountable
- Beneficial
- Caring
- Clear
- Competent
- Considerate
- Decent
- Diligent
- Disciplined
- Dynamic
- Effective
- Improving

- Insightful
- Kind
- Persistent
- Prepared
- Self-Directed
- Sensible
- Supportive
- Thorough
- Thoughtful
- Tolerant
- Truthful
- Useful
- Well-Intentioned

As if by design, the twenty-five principles work together harmoniously. No two principles oppose another. There is a principle to be *clear*, but no principle to be unclear; a principle to be *thoughtful*, but no principle to be rash; a principle to be *self-directed*, but none to conform. Yes, people can be unclear, rash, and conforming, but these characteristics show up as defense mechanisms when people are misaligned, not as a principle that drives their actions.

Seeing the list of principles, it may feel impossible to choose just one. That's because you have learned what's important to your parents, teachers, and friends. You've learned to uphold their values too. Though you value and uphold many principles, you are brilliantly biased to safeguard just one above all others. Each principle is too essential to humanity not to have a group of people protecting it most. Together, we preserve these human virtues, ensuring no principle gets neglected. And while some principles may seem similar, such as *kind* and *caring*, each principle has specific and unique characteristics, which we'll delve into in the respective mindset chapters.

Your mindset principle, whatever it is, leaves you feeling psychologically safe and balanced when it's upheld. However, you don't give it much thought until someone has compromised it. Just as you don't notice the room temperature until it's too hot or too cold, you don't think about your principle until it gets knocked out of balance. When it comes to your principle, you want to maintain a steady and balanced state: homeostasis. If you uphold the mindset principle to be *diligent*, you will feel balanced as long as people act responsibly. If people are instead *negligent* and fail to think things through, you'll quickly find yourself in an unbalanced state.

Because you need your mindset principle to be honored to feel at ease, you are likely to project this need onto others. If you are diligent and think things through, you will expect others to be diligent and think things through as thoroughly as you do. Meanwhile, everyone around you assumes you automatically value and act based on *their* principle, which is where conflict often arises. All of us desperately try to make sure people uphold what's important to us, generally unaware others adhere to different principles. By learning about others' mindset principles, we can learn to honor what is important to others and help others understand what is important to us, and ultimately create a more peaceful and respectful world.

TRIGGER

"Everything that irritates us about others can lead us to an understanding of ourselves."

—CARL JUNG

My brother, Paul, a Supporter mindset, is as laid back and easygoing as they come. I've never seen him get too worked up about anything, and he's had plenty thrown his way. That changed when he told me about Corey. Corey had asked Paul to help him move into a new apartment in Fargo, North Dakota. Always one to help, Paul willingly agreed. However, on moving day, as Paul loaded the truck, Corey made himself a sandwich and leisurely ate it. When snack time was over, Corey moved slowly, hauling half as many boxes to the truck as Paul. Then, with several loads yet remaining, Corey sat on the couch and turned on the PlayStation. Once a cool cucumber, Paul became irate. Paul values being useful, and when people don't make themselves useful or, worse, sit idly and watch others work, he feels triggered.

Your trigger encompasses those things that irritate you *most* about others. The things you find irksome aren't random; they reveal that someone failed to uphold your principle.

Looking closely at the things that provoke you tells a great deal about the principle you uphold.

A trigger refers to a behavior that contradicts your expectation of how people should behave.

We aren't all triggered by the same things, but we feel the effects of triggers similarly. Your trigger brings about a "*Grr!*" sensation within you as your inner caveman activates. Your heart rate goes up, and your fight response kicks in. You feel angry, irritated, and defensive. You instinctively step into action, even before consciously realizing *why* you feel as you do.

This reflex takes hold because someone violated the principle you inherently uphold above all others.

Each of us unconsciously assess people's behavior according to our mindset principle. In this way, your mindset behaves much like a thermostat, but instead of monitoring temperature, it monitors behavior. As soon as someone acts inappropriately, according to your mindset, you're immediately provoked. This happens in an instant because to you, upholding your principle is as natural as blinking. It's automatic. You don't need to give it conscious thought.

As a result, you're likely to feel astonished, even baffled, that others could overlook something so obvious to you. Of course, they uphold a different mindset principle, so the things that trigger you don't trigger them in the same way.

It's true that many different things can trigger you. As mentioned, my mom, a Stabilizer mindset, gets aggravated when people are late. But Stabilizers aren't the only mindset bothered when people are late. It's also irritating to Accomplishers and Balancers, among others. But if I ask Accomplishers what irritates them *most,* lack of punctuality won't be the first thing that comes out of their mouth. They're more likely to share an example of someone making a mess and not cleaning it up. And Balancers are likely to be bothered when people are late, but then they'll admit they are sometimes late themselves—something Stabilizers will never do if they can help it. Balancers are more irritated when people surprise them or cause them to have to reshuffle their plans.

What is it that irritates you the most? What gets you worked up, even before you consciously know exactly why you're triggered?

Consider the examples below, which are prominent triggers for just five of the mindsets.

- Progressors feel most triggered when people tell them what to do or what to think.
- Integrators feel most triggered when people don't do their fair share and consequently hinder others.
- Optimizers feel triggered when people make baseless claims that can't be backed up by truth or facts.
- Connectors feel triggered when people cause setbacks or delays that could have been avoided.
- Authenticators feel triggered when people lack empathy for others and are manipulative, malicious, or dishonest.

Very likely, you relate to some statements more than others. As you imagine a friend telling you what to do—"You can't vote for him"—you may feel a strong charge, a medium charge, or no charge at all. The things that irk you *most* tell you about your trigger and, therefore, the principle you protect.

To further illustrate these varying charges, imagine a number line ranging from negative ten (–10) to positive ten (+10) with zero as neutral. The negative numbers reflect the charge you experience from a trigger, and the positive numbers represent how much you value the principle.

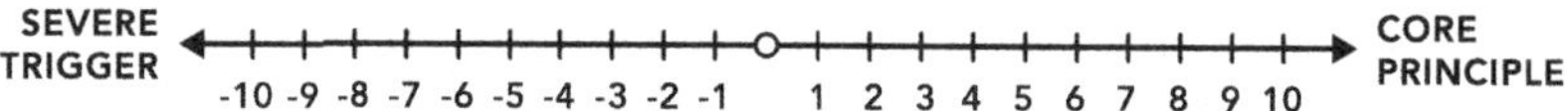

The further you move away from zero in either direction, the greater the charge. My brother, a Supporter, would rate people who do not make themselves useful as a –10 and usefulness as +10. He isn't all that bothered when people make baseless claims, so he would rate being untruthful as a –5 and being truthful as a +5.

Optimizers, however, would score much differently. If someone is untruthful, it carries the maximum charge at –10, and being truthful is easily a +10 in their book.

You can be irritated by multiple things, yet you'll find you are *most* irritated by some things more than others.

Because people don't universally uphold your principle, defending it often feels like a burden, which causes you to feel frustration and anger. You may even try to convince yourself your feelings are irrational or that you shouldn't care—except you do care, because upholding your principle operates at a far deeper level than logic or self-control.

Though triggers may feel unpleasant, they serve a purpose. If some people weren't triggered by lateness, we'd all waste time waiting for appointments. If other people weren't triggered by rudeness, we'd be surrounded by a bunch of jerks. If people weren't triggered by liars, we wouldn't get to the truth. In this way, the things that trigger you serve us all.

PASSION

"Don't ask yourself what the world needs; ask yourself what makes you come alive. And then go and do that. Because what the world needs is people who have come alive."

—HOWARD THURMAN

What is my passion?

When I walked away from a successful corporate career in 2013, it was this unanswered question that burned within. Feeling passionless, I committed to finding the answer, whatever it took. Along the way, I pursued skiing and snowboarding as hobbies. I tried fly-fishing, sailing, and paragliding. I went trail running, scuba diving, and stand-up paddleboarding. I rafted, and I golfed. I dove into creative pursuits, like photography, scrapbooking, sewing, and even soapmaking. I decorated and remodeled. I read and wrote. I pumped my fists at concerts. I volunteered.

Still, I couldn't answer the question. Unable to find the same level of joy in things that "normal" people liked, I felt like there was something wrong with me.

What I discovered is: passion becomes fuzzy and nebulous when we confuse it—or reduce it—to a mere activity, though it's common to do so.

When we ask others, "What is your passion?" we might hear answers like traveling, writing, or painting, because we've relegated passion to an activity. Unfortunately, when we search for that one overriding activity that will bring us joy, we set ourselves up for disappointment because passion is more than just an activity.

To truly understand passion, we need to redirect our focus from the activity to what the activity accomplishes. While the activities we love bring us joy, they oftentimes cease feeling like our passion when they no longer bring about the desired outcome we crave. When a specific activity we once enjoyed loses its luster or fails to give us a long-term sense of satisfaction, we often fall into a confused state, thinking we've lost our passion. What's really happened is we've just inaccurately defined what passion is.

Unaware of this misidentification, most people continue to search for their passion through a host of other activities. But in a world of infinite activities and possibilities, this can feel like trying to find a Skittle in a pool filled with M&M's; suddenly, passion seems nebulous and unobtainable.

But finding your passion is possible. The part of you that led you to pick up this book already believes that's true. It's just a matter of looking beyond the activity and seeing what the activity accomplishes.

When I moved to Colorado in 2001, I thought snowboarding was my passion. Yet once I proved to myself that I could ride switch and take on any terrain, I started losing my enthusiasm for snowboarding. If I was getting better, snowboarding motivated me. Once I achieved my desired level of mastery, it didn't excite me as much. What truly motivated me was seeing my efforts pay off, which was evident only when I was improving.

When we examine what an activity accomplishes, we can begin to truly understand passion. The activity, snowboarding, allowed me to achieve the desired outcome. Before, I was a novice snowboarder, and after, I was a skilled snowboarder, so my efforts paid off. If my efforts feel worthwhile, which relates to my underlying passion, an activity motivates me.

Understanding the outcome that comes about as the result of your actions is the critical piece we've been missing; it can enable everyone to know, and align with, their passion.

> Your passion represents what you are innately motivated to do, and by doing it, you bring about a desired outcome.

When you are aligned with your passion, you are motivated to take action, which, as we've seen, often comes through activities. Passion is never passive. It requires action, and this action shifts a less-ideal state to a more-ideal state; it shifts an opportunity to a desired outcome. My opportunity to witness my efforts pay off came through snowboarding, as well as through researching, writing, and numerous other activities.

My friend and favorite chef, Justin Peterson, loves to cook. But as you now know, cooking is not his passion. When Justin aligns with his passion, he first envisions what he wishes to create. On a Saturday morning when he has the day off from his executive chef duties at Copper Mountain Resort, he may envision serving his family light and fluffy Belgian waffles topped with pillowy whipped cream and sliced strawberries. With this vision in mind, he eagerly mixes, bakes, chops, and whips to progress his idea until, finally, his creation is plated and served to his eagerly awaiting family. Justin, an Envisioner, has shifted his vision into a reality.

When we align with our passion, there is a transformative *shift* that transpires because of our actions.

While Envisioners shift a vision to a reality, the underlying shift for each mindset differs from one mindset to the next. Sensors shift a curiosity to discover what is currently unknown to having discovered something new. Supporters shift an uncompleted task to a completed task. Pathfinders shift from being not yet self-sufficient to being independently competent.

You are motivated by things that allow you to make a similar shift—a shift that aligns with you and your mindset. The Passion Shift diagram that follows illustrates this concept.

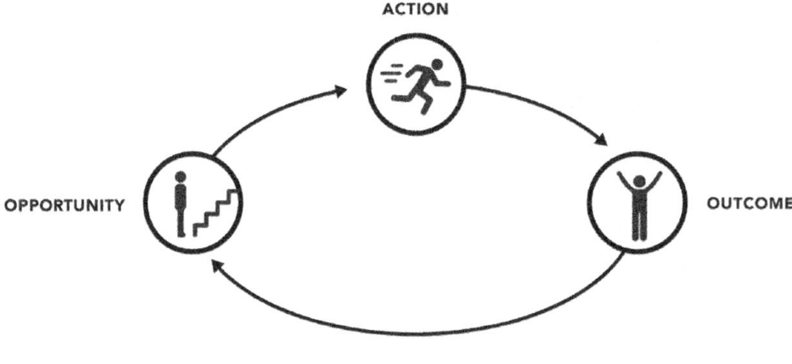

THE PASSION SHIFT

The three steps—opportunity, action, and outcome—play out when you align with your passion. You recognize an opportunity that motivates you. You take action. Then, because of your actions, you bring about the desired outcome. It's at this moment—when you see evidence of the desired outcome—that you experience a natural high.

> The Passion Shift depicts a transformation from a less-ideal state (opportunity) to a more-ideal state (outcome), which transpires when you take action that aligns with your passion.

The Passion Shift begins by identifying an **opportunity**. This is the less-ideal or "before" state—before you have instigated a shift. The opportunity can be anything—making dinner, helping a friend, or planning an event—provided it motivates *you*. With our Envisioner, the opportunity was Justin's idea to serve his family the perfect Belgian waffle.

Whatever the opportunity, it requires **action** to bring about a shift. Action is where the magic happens because only action can bring about a more-ideal state. For my Envisioner friend, the action involved getting out his waffle maker, flour, sugar, and eggs, mixing everything in a bowl, whipping up the cream, and slicing strawberries.

Finally, the **outcome** is when you see evidence that your actions have brought about a more-ideal state. At this moment, you experience a surge of energy, a high, which rewards you for completing the Passion Shift. For our Envisioner, the desired "after" state was seeing his waffle vision brought to life.

These three steps—opportunity, action, and outcome—repeat each time you align with your passion and complete the Passion Shift. The Passion Shift recognizes passion as a series of engaging pursuits, each with a distinct beginning and end. Making waffles is but one passion pursuit. Justin may have many passion pursuits in play—creating a new restaurant menu, planning a family vacation, improving a process—all of which invite the opportunity to align with his passion for bringing his visions to life.

When aligned with your passion, you feel energized, engaged, and eager to get out of bed. To pinpoint your passion, reflect on those moments when you experienced a natural high. That high offers a wealth of information about what drives you because it signifies you've completed the Passion Shift. Accomplishers, for example, experience a high after checking things off their to-do list. For them, the checkmark signifies they've completed a challenge, which is their passion. Sensors experience a high when they reveal something previously unknown to them, as they are passionate about making discoveries.

By examining your highs, you learn more about the shift that results from your actions, which can help you identify your true passion.

Understanding the underlying shift behind your passion helps explain why some things motivate you more than others, be it golfing, volunteering, researching, or cooking. Certain activities allow you to achieve your desired outcome more fully than others. Some people volunteer at a food bank and experience a high that lasts for days. For others, the experience is underwhelming, because the food bank doesn't allow them to complete the Passion Shift. There's no better or worse, just different.

To complete the Passion Shift and experience a high, your actions must bring about a more-ideal state that aligns with *your* mindset.

Of course, multiple mindsets can be motivated by similar activities, like dancing, provided the activity allows them to make a shift that aligns with their mindset. For an Authenticator, dancing elicits a sense of aliveness. For an Advisor, dancing presents an opportunity to achieve mastery. They're each motivated, but for different reasons.

What are you motivated to do? Your innate motivations and your natural highs will lead you to understand your passion. It need not remain an enigma. When you find your passion—and you will—you can then align with it and focus more energy on doing it. When aligned with your passion, you do your best work, think most clearly, get the most done, and feel a strong sense of self-worth.

Your passion is your gift. Passion is the secret ingredient that motivates people to learn new skills, share their knowledge, solve problems, create art, start new businesses, and live a fulfilling life. Your gift is essential because when you align with your passion, you bring about a more-ideal state. Because of you, something, or someone's experience, improves.

VOID

"A weakness is an activity that makes you feel weak. Even if you're good at it, if it drains you, that's a weakness."

—MARCUS BUCKINGHAM

A few years before leaving Microsoft, I charged into my office each day, eager to jump in and get to work. I loved being part of a global team. I loved working with so many intelligent people.

So when my enthusiasm dissipated, I couldn't help but think there was something wrong with me. I even went to the doctor, but she told me I was just fine.

Except I didn't feel fine. I went from enthusiastically working twelve-hour days to dodging phone calls from colleagues. I worked far fewer hours, yet each workday felt like an eternity. The work was easy, relative to other things I'd done, so why was it so difficult for me?

Sure we had just gone through a reorganization, but my position hadn't changed. I was still a manager. I still had a team of rock stars who could address the most gnarly technical issues for the largest customers around the globe. What I failed to acknowledge was even though my title did not change, my job description did. Gone were my days of proactively removing obstacles for my team. After the reorganization, I had to react and put out fires. At one point, I had over fifty employees reporting to me, and issues were constantly popping up. My job resembled a game of whack-a-mole, but rather than excite me, it drained me.

I was in my void.

Passion and void reside on opposite ends of the *What* polarity. Passion refers to what you're motivated to do, and void is what you're least motivated to do. If you're motivated by positivity, you'll be drained by negativity. If you're motivated by being proactive, you'll be drained when reacting. While your passion gives you energy, your void sucks the life force out of you like a vampire, leaving you feeling depleted and disengaged. In your void, five minutes can feel like an hour. You feel as though you're walking through wet cement. Your void is the reason you procrastinate, rebel, dig your heels in, or resist.

Your void represents what you are *not* motivated to do because it depletes your energy when you do it.

Your void is not enjoyable, but it is a normal part of who you are—or more accurately, who you aren't. Your void tells you what you are *not* designed to do. Even seemingly easy tasks require substantial effort when they're in your void because they go against the fabric of your being, which creates friction. For some, the simple task of returning a hammer to Home Depot can feel so utterly boring, they all but refuse. When in your void, you'd rather be doing something else—anything else.

One of the biggest challenges surrounding the void is that we haven't acknowledged its existence. But it's real. Everyone has a void. We all have activities that demotivate us. Yet, by failing to admit the void exists, we can misinterpret the draining effects and think there's something wrong with us. When we face an undesirable task, such as returning a hammer to the store, it's difficult to rationalize the friction we experience. After all, others don't seem to dread the same things we dread. We question ourselves. Why is it so easy for some people to complete the very tasks we run from?

Understanding the void helps us make sense of these differences. The fact is we're not individually wired to do it all. No one is—though some may try, only to find it eventually takes a toll on their well-being. That's what happens when you spend too much time in your void.

Like passion, void is not one-size-fits-all. Remarkably, what demotivates one mindset motivates another. As I grew disengaged with my career, my coworker, Mikel, flourished. When issues popped up, he'd enthusiastically whack 'em down. Meanwhile, I'd begrudgingly fix an issue when, really, I wanted to find the root cause of the problem and avoid the fire drills in the first place—my norm before the reorganization.

After the reorganization, I no longer brought my A game. Meanwhile, managers like Mikel shined. Why? Because we are motivated—and demotivated—by different things. Whereas I dread reacting to crises, Integrators like Mikel thrive under pressure. We all shine when we are aligned with our innate motivations. Conversely, we don't bring our best self forward when in our void; we are neither productive nor positive. If you stay in your void, you'll feel irritable and impatient.

There's a good chance you're spending too much of your day in your void if you dread going to work, want to quit what you're doing, or lack a sense of self-worth. While you can't fully escape the void and will inevitably need to do things you aren't particularly motivated to do, building a career around it is a mistake. The difference between loving your job or hating it revolves around how much time you spend aligned with your passion, or how much time you're misaligned, in your void. If you chronically inhabit your void, burnout is a predictable consequence.

Being aware of your void helps you recognize when you're in it, so you can take action to realign. In this way, your void acts as a valuable indicator, urging you to do more of what motivates you and stop doing things that drain you.

PURPOSE

"I call this place, this state that we're longing for, 'the perfect and beautiful world.'"

—SUSAN CAIN

When I was in high school, I earned a Congressional Award for completing almost a thousand hours of voluntary public service, personal development, and physical fitness. I participated in after-school sports, attended leadership training, picked up trash along the highway, worked with mentally disabled adults, taught classes, and served community dinners. Through volunteer work, I served my community regularly.

As a high schooler, I acted in service to others, something we often associate with purpose. But as it turns out, I hadn't found my purpose.

Purpose isn't *what* you do. Purpose is your reason for doing something. It's the *why* behind what you do.

So *why* was I volunteering back then? Was I trying to bring joy to those who needed it most or aiming to help people live a rich and fulfilling life?

As much as I'd love to say yes, the truth of the matter is those extracurricular activities helped me build a resume, earn scholarships, and please my parents. Though my actions served others, the primary *intention* behind my actions focused on serving myself. As a result, I was not aligned with my purpose.

If I think about who has a definite purpose, some names come to mind: Malala Yousafzai, Martin Luther King Jr., Mahatma Gandhi, Jane Goodall, Andre Agassi, and Tony Robbins. Each of these individuals serves a cause that extends beyond themselves. I sense their underlying intention is to benefit others, rather than just themselves.

When Tony Robbins shows up for one of his fourteen-hour-a-day, four-day events, I believe he's there to better the lives of the people in the room, not to serve himself. When Andre Agassi invests in education, I sense his heartfelt concern for the students in Nevada, not a desire to see his name on the school.

All of the individuals mentioned have differentiated themselves by aligning with their purpose. It's not merely their actions—educating girls, motivational speaking, or studying chimpanzees—that are significant. Their actions are backed with an intention to benefit others.

Your purpose is not a task, a goal, or a project. Purpose is not something you do. It's a quintessential state of existence you yearn for and aspire to bring to others.

To align with your purpose, you don't have to be a celebrity or national activist. You just need to set your sights on something you're passionate about that benefits someone or something outside of yourself, and then go about it in a way that's meaningful to you.

Purpose represents a heartfelt intention to bring about a more desirable state of being that is focused on someone or something beyond yourself—the *Why* behind what you do.

While passion is *action*-oriented, purpose is *intention*-oriented. In general, we put extraordinary emphasis on our actions and little-to-no emphasis on the intention behind our actions. Because intention cannot be seen, it's generally minimized, neglected, or unacknowledged. Most of us take this underlying intention for granted, never giving it a conscious thought. You may even wonder, *If my actions are the same, does intention matter?*

Does it matter, for instance, if a restaurant server intends to earn a big fat tip or deliver an enjoyable experience? Does it matter if a donor's intention behind giving $10,000 to a nonprofit is to see her name embossed on a brick or advance the organization's mission? Does it matter if a dancer intends to win a competition or emotionally stir the audience?

While you can't *see* a person's intention, you can *feel* its subtle and powerful influence. Aligning with purpose can be the difference between a transactional and a transformational experience. *Why* you do something matters.

Purpose involves *why* you do what you do. You do what you are motivated to do (passion) *so that* people can experience a more desirable state of being (purpose). For example:

- Katie, a Protector and commercial airline pilot, enjoys developing and demonstrating extraordinary competence (her passion) so that people will be protected in the face of uncertainty and risk (her purpose).

- Elon, an Inquisitor and engineer, is motivated to push the limits and pursue original ideas (his passion) so that people can enjoy life and feel happy (his purpose).
- I am motivated to invest time doing worthwhile things (my passion) so that people can be who they are and do what they do best (my purpose).

Your reason for doing what you do—your purpose—won't suddenly strike you like a lightning bolt. On the contrary, your purpose is something that, deep down, you already know. It's familiar to you. Most likely, you just haven't recognized your purpose because it's such a natural part of who you are.

Purpose is heartfelt, benevolent, and personally meaningful to *you*. It's a state of being that you desire for yourself, yet you recognize its importance in the world, and you want it for others too. It doesn't need to be hard to find your purpose. To find your *Why*, you must ask the right question: what do I yearn for most? Your purpose is a state of being you yearn for. It's not material or gluttonous, but heartfelt and ethereal. It's why you care. It's your personal *I Have a Dream* speech or a song that resides in your soul. Its chorus varies based on your mindset, and it sounds like one of the following:

I just want people to...

- Live a rich and fulfilling life.
- Be happy.
- Live life to the fullest.
- Be free to be their genuine selves.
- Realize their potential and see their greatness.
- Feel seen and understood and know that they matter.
- Feel content and have inner peace.

- Experience peace and harmony.
- Feel safe being their authentic selves.
- Feel safe.
- Have the support they need to thrive in life.
- Enjoy life.
- Feel good.
- Feel supported.
- Have stability in life.
- Feel secure.
- Have a good experience and outcome.
- Be protected in the face of uncertainty and risk.
- Be successful.
- Have wealth that affords them the freedom to live the life they want.
- Achieve their full potential.
- Be comfortable and positioned for success.
- Move forward in a worthwhile direction.
- Have what they need to flourish in life.
- Be who they are and do what they do best.

Purpose often feels like longing because it's an undying aspiration for something that can never be fully completed. Like hunger, purpose is never satisfied once and for all. Even if you eat sixteen sandwiches today, eventually you'll feel hunger pangs and eat again. Similarly, there is always more to do when it comes to serving your purpose. Consider that world peace is never "done." Realizing success is never "done." Bringing happiness into the world is never "done." And though our work may not ever be "done," we all can experience more peace on earth because of Harmonizers, greater success because of Risktakers, and more happiness because of Inquisitors.

While purpose revolves around an intention that extends beyond yourself, it stems from your innermost desire for yourself. Harmonizers wish for peace on earth, and they yearn to experience peace within themselves. Risktakers wish for others to realize success, and they aspire toward personal success. Inquisitors want others to be happy, and they long to experience happiness within themselves too.

When you align with your purpose—when your intention expands beyond yourself—you create movement that reverberates like a ripple in the water. And most miraculously, it is when you align with your purpose that you not only create a more desirable state of being for others, but you also experience it for yourself.

HURT

"People go through so much pain trying to avoid pain."

—NEIL STRAUSS

Several years ago, my husband and I saw Moby perform at Belly Up, a music venue in Aspen, Colorado. Moby kicked off the evening by telling us there would be two sets: an acoustic performance followed by an intermission and then a DJ set. He clarified that audience chatter would not be tolerated and joked that those who brought something to take to enhance their rave experience should wait until intermission.

Moby and the extraordinarily talented female vocalist, Mindy Jones, filled the room with powerful vocals and a heartfelt sound. A few songs in, a young woman behind us began yakking it up with a friend. As Mindy was melodically bellowing, Moby stopped mid-song and visually zeroed in on the blabbermouth, saying, "Excuse me! Do you mind? She is *pouring* her heart out up here!"

Moby and Mindy promptly resumed their intimate performance as the young woman looked down sheepishly.

Moby had been triggered. He had set clear expectations, yet an audience member chose to disregard his clearly articulated guidance.

We get triggered for a reason: unacceptable behaviors cause undesired consequences. The blabbermouth was the source of the trigger. Her unacceptable behavior caused an undesired consequence—if someone is disrespectful, then Mindy would feel hurt. Moby, presumably an Optimizer mindset, likely spoke out to prevent Mindy and the audience from experiencing an adverse consequence. Our triggers are not only frustrating to us, but if allowed to carry on, they inevitably cause an undesired outcome for others.

When we react to our triggers, we're often trying to curtail or prevent a looming consequence. We don't just feel irritated; we also want to protect people from being negatively impacted because of the wrongdoer's behavior. We find ourselves stepping in to keep *others* from experiencing an unbearable state of being that is hurtful to *us*.

If your purpose represents a dream to create a more desired state of being, then you can expect to find your nightmare at the other end of the polarity. The opposite of purpose is hurt. It represents your undesired state of being.

For a Harmonizer, who yearns for peace, hurt shows up as conflict. For a Protector, who yearns for safety and protection, hurt means being vulnerable. For a Cultivator, who yearns for peace of mind, hurt emerges as worrying.

> Hurt represents an agonizing state of being that you can't stand to experience—and can't stand for others to experience.

Whether we feel triggered or hurt depends upon where we direct our attention. When we focus our attention on wrongdoers and their unacceptable actions, we feel triggered and angry. When we place our attention on the individual negatively impacted by the wrongdoer's actions, we experience hurt.

There is a cause-and-effect relationship between each mindset's trigger and hurt. When people fail to uphold your mindset principle, hurt is the consequence. You can think of it like this:

If people don't behave as I want them to behave (trigger), then others will experience an undesired state of being (hurt).

Captivators are triggered when people are not straightforward (trigger) because if people don't say what they mean, people won't get their needs met and will have to go it alone (hurt).

Protectors are triggered when people are unprepared (trigger) because when people don't ready themselves in advance, they will be vulnerable in the face of danger (hurt).

The void works similarly:

If people don't do what they are motivated to do (void), then others won't experience the desired state of being (hurt).

If Captivators don't help others and bring people joy (void), then people won't get their needs met and will have to go it alone (hurt).

If Protectors don't develop and demonstrate competence (void), then people will be vulnerable in the face of danger (hurt).

Our desire to steer clear of both triggers and the void is rooted in wanting to avoid our undesired state of being: hurt.

Just as we don't want others to experience our undesired state of being, we most certainly don't want to experience it ourselves.

In fact, this undesired state is at the root of our insecurities. When our core insecurity comes to light, it causes us to experience our intolerable state of being. We desperately want people to treat us in a particular way so that we can avoid the adverse outcome. Consequently, we put an extraordinary amount of effort into avoiding it.

Your insecurity represents how you cannot stand for people to perceive you or treat you because it causes you to experience hurt—an agonizing state of being.

Just as your triggers and void cause hurt, so too do your insecurities. It looks like this:

If people don't treat me how I want to be treated (insecurity), then I will experience the undesired state of being (hurt).

For example:

- If people criticize me (insecurity), then I'll feel like I don't matter (hurt).
- If people disapprove of me (insecurity), then I won't feel safe to let my guard down (hurt).
- If people think I'm unessential (insecurity), then I won't feel secure (hurt).

People of the same mindset share the same insecurity and hurt. This can help us understand how our own insecurity can feel so unbearable to us, yet other people remain unphased by such things—because they have a different mindset.

No matter our mindset, we all go to extraordinary lengths to hide or prevent our insecurities, doing anything necessary to avoid criticism, rejection, disappointment, humiliation—or our underlying insecurity—because we can't bear to experience our undesired state of being.

As much as we may want to hide them, insecurities are perfectly normal, in the sense that everyone deals with an underlying insecurity. There is a very specific and very logical reason for your insecurities, which you'll soon discover. More importantly, you'll be able to take steps to dissolve your insecurities.

THE NEXT STEP

The next step in your journey involves determining which of the 25 Mindsets is *your* mindset. You are brilliantly designed to uphold a principle, feel motivated by a passion, and serve a purpose. By determining your mindset, you will be better equipped to know how to align with your mindset and unlock the key to feeling fulfilled. So let's dive in and determine your mindset now.

PART 2

DISCOVERING YOUR MINDSET

"It would be so nice if something made sense for a change."

—LEWIS CARROLL, *ALICE IN WONDERLAND*

WHAT MINDSET ARE YOU?

I get it. You're eager to know: *which mindset is* my *mindset?* And soon, you'll have your answer. But this isn't like other personality tests you may have taken where you answer a series of questions and then—*voilà*—out pops your personality type. It is through a process of self-recognition, not a rigid formula, that you will identify your mindset.

In this section, you will complete two assessments and tally your answers, but that alone will not determine your mindset. Reading one or more of the mindset chapters after completing the assessments is where you'll get your true validation, and know, "Yes, that's me!"

Plan to spend thirty to sixty minutes completing this process. If it takes you longer, that's okay. Remember, some people travel the world for a year or more to find out who they are, while others move from job to job or relationship to relationship in search of their true selves. At the end of this book, you will understand your principle, passion, and purpose. The great news is you don't have to do all the work of defining them on your own; you just need to recognize them within yourself. And after you discover your mindset, you'll be equipped with the tools to enjoy the satisfaction of aligning with who you are. Taking all the time you need to find the one mindset that represents you is well worth it.

You have two options to help narrow down your mindset. You can complete the assessment in this book, or you can complete the assessment online.

1. **Book Assessment**: Follow Steps 1–5, as detailed in the following chapters. If you choose this option, go to the next chapter now.

2. **Online Assessment**: Complete an online assessment at *25Mindsets.com/Assessment.* If you choose this option, complete the assessment online, make note of the results, and then return to Part 3.

ASSESSMENT OVERVIEW

Five steps usher you through the process of determining your mindset:

- Step 1: You will identify your triggers by thinking about what irritates you.
- Step 2: You will rate the principle and trigger for each mindset on a scale of 1 to 5.
- Step 3: You will reflect on what motivates you and what drains you.
- Step 4: You will rate mindset passions and voids.
- Step 5: You will narrow the list of mindsets and read the mindset chapters that most represent you to ultimately determine your mindset.

To help you track your assessment ratings, you can print a tally sheet at *25Mindsets.com/Discover*, use the one below, or just grab a blank sheet of paper to track your answers.

So if you're ready, jump in.

Mindset	Principle & Trigger Assessment	Passion & Void Assessment	Total
Mindset 1	1 2 3 4 5	1 2 3 4 5	1 2 3 4 5 6 7 8 9 10
Mindset 2	1 2 3 4 5	1 2 3 4 5	1 2 3 4 5 6 7 8 9 10
Mindset 3	1 2 3 4 5	1 2 3 4 5	1 2 3 4 5 6 7 8 9 10
Mindset 4	1 2 3 4 5	1 2 3 4 5	1 2 3 4 5 6 7 8 9 10
Mindset 5	1 2 3 4 5	1 2 3 4 5	1 2 3 4 5 6 7 8 9 10
Mindset 6	1 2 3 4 5	1 2 3 4 5	1 2 3 4 5 6 7 8 9 10
Mindset 7	1 2 3 4 5	1 2 3 4 5	1 2 3 4 5 6 7 8 9 10
Mindset 8	1 2 3 4 5	1 2 3 4 5	1 2 3 4 5 6 7 8 9 10
Mindset 9	1 2 3 4 5	1 2 3 4 5	1 2 3 4 5 6 7 8 9 10
Mindset 10	1 2 3 4 5	1 2 3 4 5	1 2 3 4 5 6 7 8 9 10
Mindset 11	1 2 3 4 5	1 2 3 4 5	1 2 3 4 5 6 7 8 9 10
Mindset 12	1 2 3 4 5	1 2 3 4 5	1 2 3 4 5 6 7 8 9 10
Mindset 13	1 2 3 4 5	1 2 3 4 5	1 2 3 4 5 6 7 8 9 10
Mindset 14	1 2 3 4 5	1 2 3 4 5	1 2 3 4 5 6 7 8 9 10
Mindset 15	1 2 3 4 5	1 2 3 4 5	1 2 3 4 5 6 7 8 9 10
Mindset 16	1 2 3 4 5	1 2 3 4 5	1 2 3 4 5 6 7 8 9 10
Mindset 17	1 2 3 4 5	1 2 3 4 5	1 2 3 4 5 6 7 8 9 10

Mindset 18	1 2 3 4 5	1 2 3 4 5	1 2 3 4 5 6 7 8 9 10
Mindset 19	1 2 3 4 5	1 2 3 4 5	1 2 3 4 5 6 7 8 9 10
Mindset 20	1 2 3 4 5	1 2 3 4 5	1 2 3 4 5 6 7 8 9 10
Mindset 21	1 2 3 4 5	1 2 3 4 5	1 2 3 4 5 6 7 8 9 10
Mindset 22	1 2 3 4 5	1 2 3 4 5	1 2 3 4 5 6 7 8 9 10
Mindset 23	1 2 3 4 5	1 2 3 4 5	1 2 3 4 5 6 7 8 9 10
Mindset 24	1 2 3 4 5	1 2 3 4 5	1 2 3 4 5 6 7 8 9 10
Mindset 25	1 2 3 4 5	1 2 3 4 5	1 2 3 4 5 6 7 8 9 10

STEP 1

IDENTIFY YOUR TRIGGERS

The secret to understanding yourself begins with acknowledging the things that irritate you the most about others. **This is an imperative step you shouldn't skip** because it alerts you to what you find *most* irritating—a critical nuance—and only takes a couple of minutes to complete.

Write down at least three examples of when you experienced an instantaneous *"Grr!"* sensation. What was it that someone did, or didn't do, that severely triggered you? Did they not follow the rules? Did they beat around the bush? Were they rude? Did they tell you what to do? You can list triggers that are personal or professional, recent or past, significant or trivial. Write your responses here so you're primed to complete the assessment in Step 2.

1.

2.

3.

That was easy enough, right?

STEP 2

PRINCIPLE AND TRIGGER ASSESSMENT

In this step, you will read twenty-five summaries describing the mindset principle and trigger. After reading each statement, assign a value of 1 to 5, with a 5 representing statements most like you.

Each summary includes four statements. The first bullet relates to the mindset principle. The next three represent triggers for that mindset.

Your objective is to rate the mindset as a whole, identifying those mindsets where *all* statements strongly resonate with you.

This may be challenging. There will be some mindsets that "click" and feel right, but they may be the first ones you read or the last. Honor the process and keep going until you have read all twenty-five.

When reviewing the triggers, pay attention to how severely they *automatically invoke a response in you.* Resist any urge to scrutinize every bullet, and instead keep an eye out for triggers you read and then think, *Argh, yes, I hate that!* As you read, *feel* the triggers, then notice if they ignite you, and if so, determine whether it is mild, moderate, or profound.

Remember, a trigger activates your "fight" response. You're ready to argue, defend, and face the wrongdoer—even if you resist the urge to outwardly act. This "*Grr!*" response is key to identifying your triggers and should not be confused with a flight, freeze, or fawn response. You will read multiple behaviors you dislike or have been taught are inappropriate, but do your best to identify those that truly put you on the defensive.

If you start reading a summary and it's clear it's *not* you, rate it low and move on—you don't need to read every bullet. If you're not sure if something resonates or not, you can trust it's not your mindset. If it's a "maybe," it's a "no," so rate it low. If you find you agree with the initial mindset principle statement but don't strongly agree with the triggers, or vice versa, also rate it low. Reserve the 4 and 5 ratings for those mindsets that you suspect could be *your* mindset and ring most true to you.

Use the full scale of answers, 1 to 5, drawing on the following statements as general guides:

1. Not highly representative of me.
2. Uncertain if it represents me or not.
3. Somewhat like me; the triggers ignite a *moderate* charge in me.
4. Highly representative of me; the triggers ignite a *significant* charge in me.

5. Spot on, just like me; the triggers ignite an *instantaneous* and *intense* charge in me.

You can begin rating each mindset statement now.

MINDSET 1

- I am solution-oriented and want people to look for opportunities to make improvements.
- It irritates me when people lack common sense or do something inefficiently because "it's always been done that way."
- It triggers me when people continually complain about their situation, yet they won't do anything to make it better.
- I tend to arrive at solutions quickly and get irritated when people can't see the solution, even after I've thoroughly explained it to them.

Rating: ______

MINDSET 2

- I expect people to use common sense and act appropriately for the circumstances (for example, drive slowly when kids are at play; drive fast when on a wide-open road).
- I am especially irritated when people put rules, restrictions, or limitations in place that are unnecessary or don't make sense.
- It irritates me when people claim there is only one right way to do something.
- I am triggered by people who are deceitful or who abuse their power or authority.

Rating: ______

MINDSET 3

- I'm careful to fit everything in and keep it all in balance, so I want people to do their part to make sure things go as expected.
- I am most irritated when people surprise me or spring things on me with little to no notice.
- It triggers me when people commit to doing something and then bail at the last minute (i.e., they flake).
- I get triggered if someone lies to me about something big or small.

Rating: ______

MINDSET 4

- I expect people to think for themselves and come to their own conclusions.
- I am most irritated when people tell me what to do.
- I'm triggered by people who don't think for themselves but blindly do everything they're told (i.e., sheeple).
- I'm irritated by people who claim to have all the answers and know what is best for me and everyone else.

Rating: ______

MINDSET 5

- I have a strong intuition and want others to honor their inner sense of knowing rather than relying solely on external sources of information.
- It irritates me most when people belittle intuition because they don't understand it or have not developed it within themselves.
- I'm triggered by people who must see something to believe it and need every statement to be backed with proof and evidence.
- It aggravates me when people don't discern the difference between the truth and a false statement that's been presented as truth.

Rating: _____

MINDSET 6

- I want people to show concern for all people and to care about how others feel.
- It triggers me when people lack awareness, care, and concern for other people and life in general.
- It irritates me when someone obliviously overlooks other people and treats them like they don't matter (for example, they take two pieces of cake, so someone gets none).
- I get irritated when people don't seem to notice or care about their adverse impact on other people or their surroundings.

Rating: _____

MINDSET 7

- It's important to me that others be good and honest people who are friendly, personable, and kind to others.
- It irritates me when people don't listen or pay attention when they're having a conversation with someone.
- I am most irritated when people lack kindness and are instead mean, rude, hurtful, or condescending.
- I get triggered when people make sarcastic comments that are more hostile than witty.

Rating: ______

MINDSET 8

- It's important to me that people are respectful of people who are different from themselves.
- It irritates me when people present a dominating, my-way-or-the-highway attitude.
- I get triggered when people are intolerant of people different from themselves (for example, people who are racist or sexist).
- I get very irritated when people make waves, instigate conflict, or unnecessarily upset the peace.

Rating: ______

MINDSET 9

- I expect people to have good intentions and be tuned in to others' emotional needs.
- I am most irritated when people don't have good intentions but are manipulative.
- I get triggered by people who lack empathy for others and don't seem to care about causing others pain.
- I get agitated by people who are charming in their interactions but cunning in their intentions.

Rating: ______

MINDSET 10

- I want people to be supportive and to uplift others by offering encouragement.
- I am most irritated when people lack sensitivity and warmth and are instead discouraging and disapproving.
- It irritates me when people tear others down by pointing out everything that's wrong with them.
- I get triggered when people make others feel bad by degrading them rather than offering reinforcement.

Rating: ______

MINDSET 11

- I expect people to express themselves in a clear, straightforward, and direct manner.
- I am most irritated when people beat around the bush and won't just say what they need to say.
- It upsets me when people speak indirectly because they're afraid of hurting someone's feelings.
- I'm frustrated when people say they'll do something, but don't do it.

Rating: ______

MINDSET 12

- I expect people to have common human decency—be a good human and do their part to contribute.
- I'm triggered when people don't do their part or do less than their fair share.
- I am irritated by people who lack common human decency and consequently hinder others.
- I get very irritated when someone doesn't contribute to a group effort, causing me to have to pick up their slack or do poorly.

Rating: ______

MINDSET 13

- I expect people to make themselves useful and help out when work needs to be done.
- I am most irritated when people don't chip in and help when there are things that need to get done and instead sit around and watch others work.
- I'm triggered by people who are lazy, idle, unhelpful, and unproductive.
- I get irritated by people who are negative, instigate conflict, or create drama.

Rating: _____

MINDSET 14

- I expect people to help others, not because there's something in it for them, but because it's the right thing to do.
- I'm triggered by people who are selfish and "me" centric, seeming to care only about getting their own needs met, even if it means hurting others.
- It irritates me when people hoard information or resources that could benefit others.
- I get very irritated when someone takes all the credit for something that was a group effort.

Rating: _____

MINDSET 15

- I expect people to be on time and to uphold their commitments to others.
- I am most irritated when people are late.
- It irritates me when people don't follow the plan.
- It triggers me when people ignore the rules and do whatever is convenient rather than doing what is right.

Rating: ______

MINDSET 16

- I expect people to get things done and do their part to focus on and achieve the desired result.
- I get very irritated when people under-communicate or don't share the details needed to get things done.
- It irritates me when people think they're right, but I know they're wrong.
- It irritates me when people put outcomes at risk or cause things to not run smoothly.

Rating: ______

MINDSET 17

- I need people to keep things moving forward and act with a sense of urgency.
- I get very irritated when people are unprepared and cause setbacks that could have been avoided.
- I'm triggered by perfectionists who resist taking action or making a decision until every detail is buttoned up.
- It irritates me when people cause delays or keep things at a standstill.

Rating: ______

MINDSET 18

- I expect people to anticipate the risks ahead of them and be prepared for what's to come.
- I am most irritated when people are unprepared.
- It irritates me when people head out on an adventure and fail to bring the appropriate gear or don't dress appropriately for adverse conditions.
- I'm triggered by people who use untested tactics that could fail and then put myself or others at risk.

Rating: ______

MINDSET 19

- I expect people to be willing to learn and to work hard to become good at something.
- It bothers me when people mess up the play or compromise success because they didn't train or work as hard as others.
- It strongly triggers me when people waste time on things that don't matter.
- I'm irritated by people who refuse to do anything outside their job description.

Rating: ______

MINDSET 20

- I expect people to get their tasks done, do their job, and do it well.
- I get very irritated when people know what they're expected to do but don't execute.
- I'm strongly triggered when people threaten me, my family, or my friends.
- I'm triggered by people who have a clear task to perform, but then deviate from their responsibilities and do something else.

Rating: ______

MINDSET 21

- I expect people to do things to the best of their ability and take pride in all they do.
- I am most irritated when people make a mess and don't clean it up (for example, letting dirty dishes stack up on the counter).
- I'm triggered by people who procrastinate, have a poor work ethic, or perform below their potential.
- It irritates me when people broadcast their flaws as if they are trying to intentionally make themselves look bad.

Rating: _____

MINDSET 22

- I expect people to be responsible and to think things through.
- I get very irritated when people are shortsighted and don't think through the consequences of their impulsive actions or careless decisions (i.e., foolhardy).
- I'm triggered by people who see potential hazards but don't bother to do anything about them.
- It upsets me if people delay a project I'm part of because they didn't take a few minutes to first read the directions.

Rating: _____

MINDSET 23

- I expect people to be truthful, honest, accurate, and to do what's right.
- I get very irritated when people make baseless claims that can't be backed up with proof or evidence.
- I feel most triggered when people do or say things that have the potential to cause harm.
- It bothers me when people make recommendations when they haven't done their homework.

Rating: _____

MINDSET 24

- It's important to me that people consider the downstream impact of their decisions and how they will impact others.
- I get very irritated when people make rash decisions and don't think about others' needs.
- I'm triggered when people bulldoze others to do what's good for themselves.
- It irritates me when people jump to conclusions and make uninformed, emotionally driven decisions.

Rating: _____

MINDSET 25

- I want people to be considerate and take care to not hurt or trigger others.
- It irritates me when people brag and boast while directly or indirectly slighting others.
- I feel triggered when people are not authentic but, rather, present themselves in a fake manner to try to elicit a particular reaction.
- I am triggered when people belittle others or speak in a demeaning or dehumanizing tone.

Rating: ______

STEP 3

IDENTIFY YOUR MOTIVATIONS

The next step involves identifying what you're motivated to do. What were you doing when you last experienced a natural high? What do you most enjoy doing? List three things that come to mind.

I am motivated to...

1.

2.

3.

Next, think about the things that drain your energy. What things bring about an "*Ugh!*" feeling when you must do them? What makes you procrastinate, rebel, or dig in your heels?

List three things you avoid doing:

1.

2.

3.

Keep it up—you're over halfway there and well on your way to discovering your mindset!

STEP 4

PASSION AND VOID ASSESSMENT

Now it's time to review the passion and void summaries for each mindset. The summaries follow the same order as the previous assessment's mindsets, so you can skip the mindsets you rated lowest on the Principle and Trigger Assessment, because those low ratings indicate they are not your mindset. Therefore, cross out the mindsets with a low rating on your tally sheet, and proceed to rate the mid- and high-scoring mindsets (for example, if Mindsets 7 and 8 were given a 1 or 2 on the previous assessment, you don't have to read the summary for Mindset 7 and 8). Ultimately, your mindset will rate high across *both* assessments—this one and the previous one.

Using the same rating system, assign a value of 1 to 5, with 5 representing statements most like you. You can begin reviewing the mindsets now.

MINDSET 1

- I am a problem solver and am eager to help others overcome challenges.
- I feel most excited when I bring my ideas and visions to life.
- It's important to me to make progress, advance good ideas, and make a difference.
- It would devastate me to take action, then discover it made things worse for someone.
- I love visually observing progress and seeing everything come together or seeing someone happy.

Rating: ______

MINDSET 2

- I'm an outside-the-box thinker and like to imagine new ways of doing things.
- I'm a kid at heart—curious and constantly intrigued, amazed, fascinated, and in wonder of things.
- I feel most excited when pursuing something interesting and there's learning involved.
- If things are uninteresting or boring, I'm apt to procrastinate.
- My rebellious side shows up when I'm restricted from doing things in new or original ways.

Rating: ______

MINDSET 3

- I need new adventures, new experiences, and new things coming into my life.
- I love to explore new places, meet new people, and travel to unfamiliar locations.
- I'm easily bored.
- I like to take qualified risks and do things I'm not certain I can do, and then prove to myself I can do them.
- I want to have fun, do it all, and live life to the fullest.

Rating: ______

MINDSET 4

- I'm motivated to do things contrary to what is typical, normal, usual, orthodox, or expected.
- I enjoy proving people wrong and doing what people say cannot be done.
- I enjoy engaging with others and doing things that positively impact how people feel.
- I like to explore new ideas or ways of doing something, even if only in my mind, and enjoy the freedom to dream.
- It's draining for me to express myself in a way that's not truly genuine (for example, selling something I don't believe will help someone).

Rating: ______

MINDSET 5

- I most enjoy the freedom to live in the moment, doing what I want, when I want, how I want, and with whom I want.
- I feel most enlivened when following my inner knowing wherever it leads me.
- I seek out quiet, peaceful environments where I can get centered, connect with source, meditate, or go within.
- It pains me to be a minion and take orders from people when it runs contrary to what I am internally led to do.
- I have little desire to work in conventional environments that limit my connection, freedom, and inner knowing.

Rating: ______

MINDSET 6

- I am a lifelong learner, eager to learn from others, including those who are ahead-of-the-curve or ahead-of-their-time.
- I feel most excited when expanding horizons–my own or someone else's.
- I love the moments when my message resonates and the light bulb goes off in someone's mind, and they suddenly see what they previously did not see.
- I'm motivated to explore unconventional ideas and serve audiences whose needs have been neglected.
- I'm motivated to bring beauty, delight, and understanding into the world.

Rating: ______

MINDSET 7

- I am attentive to the needs of others and will gladly go out of my way to do things for people I care about.
- I feel most enlivened when spending quality time with the people I care about or giving attention to the activities that I enjoy most.
- I enjoy being there for others to help, listen, or offer my assistance.
- It drains me when I'm disconnected from the people in my life.
- I deeply cherish the moments when everyone is together, people are happy, and all feels right in the world.

Rating: ______

MINDSET 8

- It severely drains me to spend time around negative people who focus on everything wrong in the world.
- I enjoy bringing kindness, encouragement, laughter, and optimism into my surroundings.
- I feel most enlivened when I'm a positive influence or when I'm positively impacting myself, others, nature, or the environment.
- I'm likely to lose sleep or feel bothered by unresolved conflicts and misunderstandings.
- It's important for me to make others feel good and focus on the good in life.

Rating: ______

MINDSET 9

- I most enjoy spending time with people I know and trust, in settings where people feel safe to let their guard down and be authentic.
- It severely drains me to have to "play the part" and present myself in an inauthentic manner.
- I'm inspired to make people feel alive and positively impact how people feel (for example, through experiences, nature, beauty, art, music, connections, or words).
- I feel most enlivened when I'm emotionally engaged in whatever I'm doing or igniting others' emotions.
- Forced social interaction and small talk with strangers drain me.

Rating: ______

MINDSET 10

- I take great pleasure in the simple joys of life: the taste of food, the sound of music, and the visual intrigue of color and design.
- I love making discoveries and coming up with clever ideas (for example, discovering a solution to a problem or finding a new way of doing something).
- I enjoy working in service professions where I can engage with others and make people happy.
- I find myself feeling "off" when my surroundings feel unwelcoming (for example, being in gloomy weather).
- I enjoy stretching my known reality and expanding my awareness.

Rating: ______

MINDSET 11

- I feel most enlivened when bringing joy to others.
- I am quick to use humor and laughter to lighten stressful situations.
- I'm motivated to help people and give them the support they need.
- It hurts me deeply to see people whose needs are not being met (for example, seeing an abandoned child or animal).
- It drains me to take life too seriously and experience life as all work and no fun.

Rating: _____

MINDSET 12

- I thrive under the pressure of a deadline, stress, or time constraints.
- I love having the freedom and flexibility to choose how I get to spend my whole day.
- I can't stand working for micromanagers.
- If something is boring, monotonous, or unexciting, I'll likely procrastinate.
- I'm highly motivated to share enjoyable experiences with friends and family and be there for them when they're in need and I can help.

Rating: _____

MINDSET 13

- I am motivated to take steps to progress projects, goals, and tasks.
- I have relatively no interest in management positions.
- I love it when I get more done in a day than expected or when things get done ahead of schedule.
- I feel most excited when all goes smoothly, and things go better than expected.
- I'm motivated to do essential work and jobs that are necessary to keep homes and businesses running.

Rating: _____

MINDSET 14

- It's important to me to teach people "how to fish" so they can develop life skills and be self-sufficient.
- I enjoy strengthening and developing my skillset to become more competent and independent.
- It drains me to work in unsupportive environments where people don't contribute to one another's success.
- I enjoy teaching—whether formally or casually—by sharing information that supports people in practical ways.
- It pains me to give people the answer when I know they didn't learn something they will need to know.

Rating: _____

MINDSET 15

- I am motivated to make a positive and significant impact on people's lives.
- It drains me when my efforts are taken for granted or are not appreciated.
- I enjoy finding creative ways to make experiences special, enjoyable, and meaningful.
- I am motivated to serve others or a purposeful cause where I can make a valuable contribution.
- I feel most excited when I know that my efforts were impactful and appreciated by others.

Rating: ______

MINDSET 16

- I'm motivated to be an invaluable asset to people and projects.
- It drains me to be underutilized as a resource.
- I enjoy working on teams that get a lot done, get results, and get along.
- It excites me to know that my efforts were impactful and appreciated by others.
- I'm motivated to ensure everything runs smoothly and goes as planned.

Rating: ______

MINDSET 17

- I love to connect, converse, socialize, interact, and circulate in a crowd.
- I love talking to interesting people and finding out what other people know.
- I want to be in the know, but I don't want all the details–just give me enough information so I can share it with someone else.
- I don't care for one-way communication (i.e., being talked at).
- I feel most excited when making connections, such as listening to interesting people or sharing compelling information.

*Rating:*_____

MINDSET 18

- I'm motivated to take on and conquer personally meaningful challenges that include an element of risk.
- I enjoy taking on big challenges and persevering until I prove myself competent.
- I hate feeling like I can't keep up and am behind the eight ball or at a disadvantage.
- I enjoy taking calculated risks and putting my capabilities to the test.
- I feel enlivened when putting myself in consequential situations and then demonstrating competence.

*Rating:*_____

MINDSET 19

- I'm motivated to take risks that will pay off.
- I get impatient when things become too routine or move too slowly.
- I'm motivated to win, succeed, and help others do the same.
- I feel most excited when taking bold action and making an impact.
- I'm usually the one to address the elephant in the room and say what others are too scared to say.

Rating: ______

MINDSET 20

- I feel most excited when I pursue a challenge and then accomplish that challenge.
- I am motivated to rise to the challenge and succeed at difficult tasks.
- I enjoy testing myself and achieving whatever I set my mind to.
- I wholeheartedly devote myself to pursuits and fuel my achievements with intense determination, focus, and desire.
- It drains me to fail to achieve what I set out to achieve or have it take longer than expected.

Rating: ______

MINDSET 21

- I love checking things off my to-do list (but hate it when I can't get them all done).
- I don't want to start something if I know I can't finish it—I'm either all in or all out.
- I need to be active, moving, and busy, which helps me think clearly and feel happy and energized.
- I feel most excited when I complete new challenges and achieve my goals.
- I feel bored and get stir-crazy when I experience life as stagnant and routine.

Rating: ______

MINDSET 22

- It's my nature to dive into something with a singular focus, complete it, then move on to the next thing, as if going through phases.
- I love to experience the sense of satisfaction that comes from chasing mastery or being good at something.
- I fully immerse myself in my projects and endeavors.
- It drains me when someone interrupts my focus and forces me to digress.
- It drains me when I continue a phase that has come to an end, and I am no longer growing.

Rating: ______

MINDSET 23

- I am motivated to acquire knowledge and share knowledge with others.
- I love sharing information with others and witnessing the moment when someone suddenly sees what they did not previously see.
- I get so mentally absorbed in my work that it's difficult to have to stop what I'm doing.
- I am motivated to follow my urge to explore novel ideas, learn something new, and reveal something previously unknown.
- I don't give up when something doesn't work but instead I try new ideas and get excited about each new test.

Rating: ______

MINDSET 24

- I'm most motivated to positively impact people in meaningful ways.
- I am motivated to be comprehensive and do things well, to ensure people have everything they need (for example, writing a thorough email).
- I love to solve important problems, come up with great solutions, and fix things.
- I hate being misunderstood.
- It pains me when I'm not having a meaningful impact on anyone or anything.

Rating: ______

MINDSET 25

- I'm most motivated when I'm doing something worthwhile, in other words, spending my time doing something that is a good use of my time, energy, or intellect.
- I am motivated to save people time, energy, money, pain, angst, or frustration.
- I hate wasting time (for example, having to remind people to do something they should have already done).
- I seek personal growth and deal with what's not working in my life on an ongoing basis.
- I love finding a sale or getting a deal.

Rating: ______

STEP 5

NARROW DOWN MINDSETS AND TROUBLESHOOTING

Now, you can narrow down your list of 25 Mindsets to three or fewer that could be your mindset by seeing which mindsets rate the highest from your assessments. Using your tally sheet, total your scores from the two assessments and circle the total. For example, if you had rated Mindset 22 a 3 on the Principle and Trigger Assessment and a 4 on the Passion and Void Assessment, you would circle a 7 in the total column.

Once you have narrowed down your list, circle the highest-rated mindsets on your tally sheet and proceed to the Mindset Assessment Key to reveal the mindset names. Then, move on to Part 3 to read the corresponding mindset chapters to land on the one mindset that speaks to you the most.

Use the following tips to help find your mindset:

- If you feel strongly that you have found your mindset, go ahead and read the chapter to further validate that it is the mindset with which you align.

- Do not automatically rule out a mindset because it didn't garner the highest score. For example, if you have one mindset totaling 10 and two mindsets totaling 9, do not confirm your mindset until you read all three mindset chapters and feel one is the most spot on.

- If, after totaling the two assessments, you discover you have rated many mindsets very high, revisit the assessments to narrow the mindsets to three or fewer. See what feels most true for you and differentiate your ratings accordingly.

- As you read multiple mindset chapters, it's normal for you to see aspects of yourself in various mindsets. Mindsets aren't different species, like oranges and orangutans. Mindsets share traits, just as different varieties of apples share characteristics. You will identify your mindset through triangulation—finding the one mindset that accurately characterizes your principle, passion, and purpose.

- If you rated a specific mindset higher than others but find it doesn't feel quite right after reading the mindset chapter, trust that feeling. It should not feel forced. Go back and review other mindsets you rated high. When you find your mindset, it should feel almost laughable and leave you thinking, *Yep, that is me, all right!*

- If you're unsure of your mindset, reflect on your innermost desire for yourself by finishing this sentence: "I just want to…" For example, I just want to be safe, I just want to enjoy life, I just want to feel secure, I just want to be happy. Go within and listen to what is true for you. This feeling should coincide with the purpose statement at the end of the mindset chapter, though the specific verbiage may vary, and can help you determine which mindset you align with.

- If you feel stuck and struggle to narrow down the list, read all 25 Mindset chapters. Read with a sense of curiosity, and don't worry about identifying your mindset. That said, when you get to your mindset chapter, you will likely know it. If not, it's perfectly fine to proceed to Part 4, even if you're not 100 percent certain of your mindset.

- If you land on two or more mindsets, push yourself to feel into the various facets of each mindset to discover the underlying truth of what triggers, motivates, and demotivates you. Your goal is to land on one mindset most true for you.

MINDSET ASSESSMENT KEY

And finally (cue the drum roll...), the mindset unveiling. Use the key below to determine the mindset names, then proceed to Part 3 where you will learn about mindset sub-categories and read about the mindsets you have identified through the assessment process.

MINDSET ASSESSMENT KEY

- **Mindset 1**: The Envisioner
- **Mindset 2**: The Inquisitor
- **Mindset 3**: The Balancer
- **Mindset 4**: The Progressor
- **Mindset 5**: The Intuitor
- **Mindset 6**: The Perceiver
- **Mindset 7**: The Cultivator
- **Mindset 8**: The Harmonizer

- **Mindset 9**: The Authenticator
- **Mindset 10**: The Sensor
- **Mindset 11**: The Captivator
- **Mindset 12**: The Integrator
- **Mindset 13**: The Supporter
- **Mindset 14**: The Pathfinder
- **Mindset 15**: The Stabilizer
- **Mindset 16**: The Producer
- **Mindset 17**: The Connector
- **Mindset 18**: The Protector
- **Mindset 19**: The Risktaker
- **Mindset 20**: The Achiever
- **Mindset 21**: The Accomplisher
- **Mindset 22**: The Adviser
- **Mindset 23**: The Optimizer
- **Mindset 24**: The Observer
- **Mindset 25**: The Synthesizer

PART 3

UNDERSTANDING THE 25 MINDSETS

"I'm not strange, weird, off, nor crazy, my reality is just different from yours."

—LEWIS CARROLL, *ALICE IN WONDERLAND*

INTRODUCING THE 25 MINDSETS

"We are all important parts of a much larger system, pieces of the universe's puzzle that would not be complete without us."

—RUSSELL ERIC DOBDA

While every mindset is distinct, there are some mindsets more like you, and other mindsets that are quite different.

You likely know people who are a lot like you. They "get" you. It's easy. You're on the same page. Meanwhile, there are others—possibly your siblings—who couldn't be more different from you. One of you is a social butterfly; the other is an introvert. One climbs the ladder of success; the other is a free spirit. One is habitually late; the other is always five minutes early. The two of you, of course, have different mindsets.

The Mindset Wheel portrays all 25 Mindsets, with similar mindsets grouped next to each other. Neighboring mindsets share similarities in how they approach life, while mindsets on opposite ends of the wheel show more differences. That said, we are not merely a gradual variation of others. And just because one mindset sits directly across from another doesn't mean the two are complete opposites.

For example, the Risktaker and Captivator mindsets are positioned across from one another, yet both are transparent and tell it like it is. Protectors are born leaders, while Supporters typically steer clear of management roles, yet both stick with what's been tried and tested. Then, there's the Integrator and Balancer who should, arguably, oscillate in the center of the wheel because Integrators make things whole (when aligned with their passion) and Balancers need to keep everything in balance (when aligned with their principle).

The Mindset Wheel showcases all 25 Mindsets and emphasizes how *every mindset* is integral to the whole.

If you discovered your mindset by completing the assessments in Part 2 of the book (as opposed to online), you will find that the mindset ordering in the assessment corresponds with the mindset ordering on the Mindset Wheel. Mindset 1 corresponds with the Envisioner, Mindset 2 with the Inquisitor, and then continues clockwise until ending with Mindset 25, the Synthesizer. You will probably find the mindsets you rated highest are clumped together on the Mindset Wheel.

Although the Mindset Wheel clusters mindsets into five subgroups, it's important to remember that each mindset still upholds a specific principle, passion, and purpose—which is what makes it unique and special.

Yet, as mentioned, specific mindsets share commonalities. Here's an overview of the five subgroups.

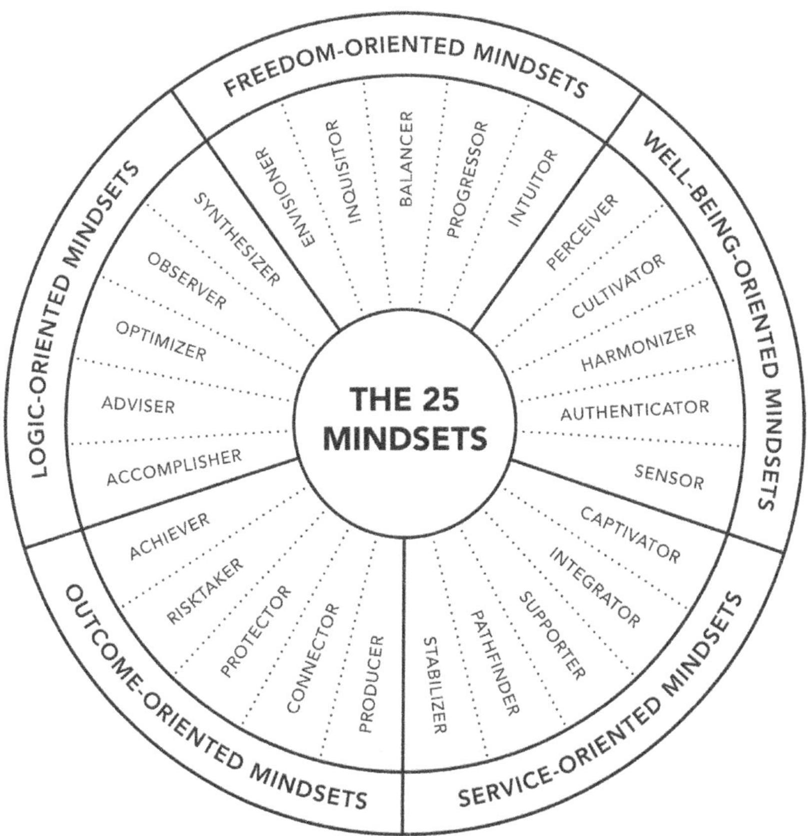

FREEDOM-ORIENTED

- **Mindsets**: Envisioner, Inquisitor, Balancer, Progressor, Intuitor
- **Common Traits**: Sensible (strong common sense), autonomous, independent, big thinking, insightful, intuitive, spiritual, innovative, imaginative, visual, free-spirited, self-directed, idealistic, curious, and wanting to do things differently. They can also be stubborn (not wanting to be

told what to do or how to do something), easily bored, focused on many things, or disliking of authority.

WELL-BEING-ORIENTED

- **Mindsets**: Perceiver, Cultivator, Harmonizer, Authenticator, Sensor
- **Common Traits**: Empathic, caring, sensitive to others' feelings, heartfelt, intuitive, benevolent, supportive, nurturing, encouraging, attentive, good listeners, warm, family-oriented, artistic, appreciative of nature and beauty, and seeking closeness and connection. They can also be emotional sponges, apt to take on others' emotions, prone to worry, feeling different or misunderstood, conflict avoidant, or peacekeepers (at their own expense).

SERVICE-ORIENTED

- **Mindsets**: Captivator, Integrator, Supporter, Pathfinder, Stabilizer
- **Common Traits**: Helpful, dependable, reliable, practical, strong, resilient, supportive, responsive to others' needs, team-oriented, family-oriented, considerate of the whole and future generations, strong ability to see and fill gaps, loyal, generous, and giving. They can also be resentful, giving to others at the cost of themselves, apt to protect themselves with a hard exterior, or prone to feeling underappreciated or taken advantage of.

OUTCOME-ORIENTED

- **Mindsets**: Producer, Connector, Protector, Risktaker, Achiever
- **Common Traits**: Results-oriented, success-driven, fast-paced, tenacious, hard-driving, strong-willed, direct, physical, competent, confident, competitive, decisive, willing to lead and take charge, action-oriented, and protective of their own. They can also be intense, controlling, intimidating, forceful, insensitive, harsh, or impatient.

LOGIC-ORIENTED

- **Mindsets**: Accomplisher, Adviser, Optimizer, Observer, Synthesizer
- **Common Traits**: Conscientious, objective, observant, organized, focused, thoughtful, understanding, analytical, hardworking, thorough, compassionate, diplomatic, quality-oriented, investigative, meaning-seeking, information gathering, and problem-solving. They can also be self-contained, reserved, overthinking, perfectionistic, aloof, unemotional, or unexpressive.

If you relate to traits in more than one group, that's perfectly normal. Keep in mind, this is a generalization. Refer to a particular mindset chapter for a more thorough summary of the polarities residing in that mindset. Just as a cheetah is fast, not slow, and a giraffe is tall, not short, understanding the polarities that exist within you is the key to understanding yourself.

In the remainder of Part 3, the mindsets are listed in alphabetical order for ease of reference. Remember, you need not read all twenty-five mindset chapters. Your objective, for now, is to identify and better understand *your* mindset.

If identifying your mindset proves difficult or you find yourself getting frustrated, know that it's okay to jump ahead to Part 4, even if you don't know your mindset yet. Whether you identify your mindset in minutes or hours, you can be assured that your mindset is perfectly orchestrated and essential—and is exactly whom you are meant to be.

THE ACCOMPLISHER

"Every job is a self-portrait of the person who did it. Autograph your work with excellence."

—TED KEY

Everything Accomplishers do reflects who they are, so they give it their all. Words like *mediocre* and *average* have no place in their vocabulary when *great* and *exceptional* are within their grasp. Accomplishers take pride in what they do. They aim high, then give 100 percent, not one iota less.

When you walk into an Accomplisher's home, you're likely to see the epitome of organized life—uncluttered countertops, an organized pantry, and shoes neatly arranged. "Everything in its place" is part of their philosophy and aesthetic. After all, there's no reason a kitchen, bedroom, or closet can't also be visually appealing. You're unlikely to see them toss dirty clothes on the floor or leave cupboard doors open. Instead, you're likely to find a spotless car, pressed shirts, and the whitest whites.

It's rare to find an Accomplisher who doesn't keep a to-do list. A checkmark signifies a completed goal, big or small, and thus feels worthy of celebration. They need to be active, so they're likely to seek adventure, be outdoors, or engage in physical activities. Whatever they're doing, they love a new challenge and the opportunity to reach new heights or to raise the bar. With a goal in mind, they vigorously work until they've achieved it. Once accomplished, they may think, *Okay, I've done that. Now what?* which primes them for their next challenge and opportunity to better themselves, others, or a situation.

THE ACCOMPLISHER PRINCIPLE AND TRIGGER

Thorough ←——→ *Unthorough*

PRINCIPLE: THOROUGH

Accomplishers work hard, give 100 percent, and take pride in all they do. Accomplishers:

- Take care to do things well.
- Willingly put in the effort and dedication required to achieve excellence.
- Apply themselves conscientiously and complete tasks to the best of their ability.
- Like things organized, uncluttered, minimalistic, neat, and tidy (and consequently are clean, healthy, and sanitary).
- Methodically have a place for everything and everything in its place.

- Take care to present themselves favorably, wanting to be worthy of people's respect.
- Care about quality, details, presentation, placement, visual appeal, and how things look.
- Strive for excellence in all areas, including relationships.
- Believe if you can do better, you should do better.
- See the pursuit of perfection as valuable, even if it's not attainable.
- Are self-motivated, high-energy, hardworking, and disciplined.
- Think ahead, think things through, and often have a backup plan for their backup plan.
- Fulfill their commitments, meet deadlines, and take care to do things right the first time.
- Hold high standards of quality and high personal standards.
- Go above and beyond and exceed expectations, when possible.

TRIGGER: UNTHOROUGH

Accomplishers feel triggered when people:

- Are sloppy, messy, disorganized, apathetic, complacent, lazy, or careless.
- Have a poor work ethic and give only minimal effort.
- Make a mess but don't clean it up (for example, they leave dirty clothes on the floor).
- Don't bother to do things to the best of their ability (i.e., they half-ass it).
- Lack tact or broadcast their flaws, as if intentionally trying to make themselves look bad.

- Procrastinate, miss deadlines, cut corners, or perform below their potential.
- Can do better but don't try to do better.
- Are satisfied with mediocrity or good enough.
- Repeatedly lose, forget, or misplace things (for example, they regularly lose their keys).
- Carelessly ruin things or don't seem to value quality.
- Blame others for their mistakes rather than take accountability and learn from their mistakes.
- Lack self-discipline, self-awareness, or self-respect (for example, they don't bother to comb their hair before going out in public).
- Know better work exists, but they have no drive to pursue it.
- Do the minimal, or less than the minimal, expected of them.
- Diminish quality or lower the standards.

THE ACCOMPLISHER PASSION AND VOID

New Challenges ⟷ *Lack of New Challenges*

PASSION: COMPLETING NEW CHALLENGES AND ACHIEVING THEIR GOALS

Accomplishers are motivated to:

- Make lists and check things off their to-do list (and they may add things just to check them off their list).
- Fully commit to a task, goal, or challenge—either all in or all out—and then finish what they start.

- Seek activities and careers with variety and challenge.
- Play, have fun, seek adventure, enjoy the outdoors, and engage in physical activities and athletics.
- Be active, moving, and busy, which helps them think most clearly, feel happy, and feel energized.
- Compete against themselves and strive to improve, advance, or outdo themselves.
- Achieve their goals, get to the next level, move beyond their previous capabilities, or help others do the same.
- Make things better than they were before they entered the picture (for example, by energizing an audience or leaving a vacation rental cleaner than it was when they arrived).
- Tackle a task from start to finish, ideally, focusing on completing one goal at a time.
- Think creatively, come up with new solutions, and promptly undertake exciting projects that challenge their problem-solving abilities.
- See evidence that they have done a great job, nailed it, or knocked it out of the park.
- Do hard things or do things that others perceive as difficult.
- Pursue a new, unique, or personally meaningful challenge, meet it, and then find the next challenge.
- Move their place of residence or change up their environment.
- Raise the bar, elevate standards, improve quality, and reach new heights.

When Accomplishers align with their passion, they shift:
a new task or challenge
to a challenge they have completed.

VOID: NOT COMPLETING NEW CHALLENGES

Accomplishers feel drained when they:

- Feel bored, stir crazy, or experience life as stagnant and routine.
- Don't get everything checked off their to-do list or don't accomplish as much as they wanted to complete in the day.
- Fail to finish what they start.
- Sit at a desk all day, stay indoors, or otherwise lack mental or physical activity, variety, and excitement in life.
- Don't feel they are performing at their potential but are stuck in the grind doing unchallenging, repetitive, or redundant tasks.
- Are pulled in too many directions causing things to slip through the cracks or not be done to their standards.
- Don't have a clear goal or the necessary information required to be successful.
- See things regress to a lower quality or standard.
- Feel down because they haven't worked out in a long time.
- Complete the same challenge again and again, rather than pursuing a new challenge.
- Maintain a rank, standing, or seat at the top when there's nothing new or exciting to achieve.
- Fail to achieve their goal, are outdone, or fall short of their high self-expectations.
- Don't know whether they did a good job due to a lack of feedback, affirmation, or ambiguity.
- Neglect their personal needs by pushing themselves too hard in their effort to do it all—and do it all exceptionally well (i.e., burning the candle at both ends).
- Reach a plateau and no longer feel there is an opportunity for growth.

THE ACCOMPLISHER PURPOSE AND HURT

Achieve Full Potential ⟷ *Perform Below Potential*

If you are an Accomplisher, this is how the various facets of your mindset come together:

TRIGGER—VOID—HURT

If people don't take pride in what they do but are sloppy, messy, or unthorough (trigger), and if I don't pursue new challenges or don't complete my goals (void), then we will perform below our potential and the standards of people, society, and situations will be lowered (hurt).

PRINCIPLE—PASSION—PURPOSE

If people take pride in what they do and do things thoroughly and completely (principle), and if I pursue new challenges and complete my goals (passion), then we can reach our fullest potential and accomplish all we are capable of accomplishing (purpose).

PURPOSE STATEMENT

My purpose is to complete new challenges and accomplish my goals so that we can reach our fullest potential.

THE ACHIEVER

"Being wealthy is a state of mind. It has nothing to do with possessions, and everything to do with well-being and security."

—GRANT SABATIER

Achiever mindsets believe in a simple philosophy: to do your job well. Teams and businesses are made up of multiple roles, and the overall success depends upon each person fulfilling their designated responsibilities. Achievers expect themselves and others to be accountable and to execute their responsibilities. After all, when everyone does their job, families, teams, and businesses thrive.

Accountability is top priority, so Achievers often feel most comfortable when they're in control, which can include calling the shots or managing a situation to prevent anyone from being upset. They balance their focus and drive with fun and creativity, which are integral parts of the Achievers' makeup. No matter how difficult or routine a task is, they'll figure out a way to make it enjoyable. Relationships are essential to their sense of well-being, while financial security affords them the freedom to live the life they want.

Achievers are passionate about what they do and like to see a similar spark in others. Passion adds an aliveness to everything they undertake, while challenges often motivate them to succeed at difficult or seemingly impossible tasks. When Achievers combine their strong will, strategic nature, intense focus, and determination, they have a winning combination, enabling them to accomplish whatever they set out to achieve.

ACHIEVER PRINCIPLE AND TRIGGER

Accountable ←——————→ *Unaccountable*

PRINCIPLE: ACCOUNTABLE

Achievers take accountability by doing what they say they will do and doing their job well. Achievers:

- Accept ownership and take full responsibility for outcomes.
- Can be counted on to keep their word and do what they say they will do.
- Recognize that everyone has a job to do—and they expect everyone to do their job.
- Welcome leading or being in charge.

- Perform in their role to ensure they meet or exceed expectations, whether those expectations are explicit or implied.
- Take initiative, competently execute plans, responsibly delegate, and make sure projects get done.
- Take pride in their work and uphold high personal standards.
- Articulate themselves clearly and precisely.
- Prefer things to be black and white so people will accept an outcome, even if it's not the outcome for which they hoped.
- Take their responsibilities seriously and reliably see jobs through.
- Are strong-minded, hardworking, practical, and committed to doing things well.
- Take in a lot of information, then simplify and organize it so it's easy to understand before taking action.
- Diligently complete or oversee the completion of tasks if they have agreed to do something.
- Hold themselves accountable and take personal responsibility for others (for example, as a business owner, to ensure employees are happy and able to pay their bills).
- Are fiercely protective of their own.

TRIGGER: UNACCOUNTABLE

Achievers feel triggered when people:

- Are unaccountable or can't be counted on to do what they are expected to do.

- Don't do what they are told to do or what others are relying on them to do.
- Know what is expected of them but fail to meet those expectations.
- Deviate from the plan or don't keep their word (for example, they accept a job but don't show up for work, or they agree to make a fork but instead make a spoon).
- Don't follow through on their commitments.
- Don't have high work standards or don't put in the same level of effort as their peers.
- Are unproductive, give minimal effort, or don't care that their work is low quality.
- Fail to follow simple orders or directions.
- Need to be micromanaged because they lack personal accountability.
- Don't follow the rules or the same playbook as everyone else.
- Fail to execute, fail to get their tasks done, or don't get the right things done.
- Can't be trusted to speak honestly but instead say what they think others want to hear (i.e., they prioritize feelings over facts).
- Criticize people behind their backs instead of giving them constructive feedback that could help them improve.
- Can't do their job, even when they've been shown what to do several times.
- Carelessly delegate, failing to see things through.
- Threaten them or their own.

ACHIEVER PASSION AND VOID

Accomplishing ←——→ *Failing*

PASSION: ACCOMPLISHING CHALLENGES THEY'RE PASSIONATE ABOUT

Achievers are motivated to:

- Rise to the challenge and succeed at difficult or seemingly impossible tasks.
- Pursue work and challenges they are passionate about.
- Challenge and test themselves (for example, by winning a competition, accomplishing a new skill, or starting a business).
- Wholeheartedly devote themselves to their endeavor and fuel their achievements with intense focus, determination, and desire.
- Get clear about what they want to accomplish and how they're going to do it, and then charge after it with a single-minded focus.
- Decide what they want, strategize their actions, and then accomplish whatever they set their mind to.
- Bring energy and aliveness to everything they undertake and use their good sense of humor and gregarious nature to make things light and enjoyable.
- Capture others' attention, ignite others' passion, get people on board, and win others over.
- Set financial goals, create wealth, and be financially secure and independent.

- Take time alone to focus on bettering themselves and take actions to invest in their personal development (for example, by reading, exercising, or working with a mentor).
- Enrich others' lives through service, mentoring, coaching, or job creation so others may build wealth and have the freedom to live the life they want.
- Prioritize people and spend quality time with others, recognizing their relationships are paramount to their happiness and well-being.
- Balance saving with spending by living within their means while also doing the things they love.
- Be intentional with their time and use it wisely so they may get the most value from every interaction and experience.
- Invest in people and champion others in ways that will help them be successful and realize their potential.

When Achievers align with their passion, they shift: a challenge they are passionate about achieving *to* having achieved what they set out to achieve.

VOID: FAILING TO ACCOMPLISH THEIR OBJECTIVE

Achievers feel drained when they:

- Don't follow through on goals they set for themselves.
- Fail to achieve what they set out to achieve.
- Pursue a challenge they aren't passionate about or do not believe in.

- Don't have a challenge they are actively pursuing and feel bored.
- Find it takes longer than expected to achieve their objective or have obstacles get in the way of accomplishing their challenge.
- Fall short of their high standards.
- Can't get people on board with them, can't get people to see their point of view, or fail to successfully win others over.
- See injustices around them or in the world that unfairly hold people back and keep them from living the life they want and deserve.
- Lack financial security, stress about making ends meet, or can't seem to get ahead.
- Spend their time doing things that are not the most valuable use of their time while neglecting higher-priority tasks.
- Waste time on things that don't support their overall objective (for example, micromanaging people who don't do their job).
- Don't have introverted time for themselves to learn, process, develop, deliberate, or decompress.
- See the people they care about feeling unhappy or discontent.
- Feel at fault for a failure, which may include feeling they have failed themselves or failed someone else.
- Are surrounded by people who lack passion and are satisfied with mediocrity.

ACHIEVER PURPOSE AND HURT

Independently Secure ⟷ *Not Independently Secure*

If you are an Achiever, this is how the various facets of your mindset come together:

TRIGGER—VOID—HURT

If people are unaccountable and don't do what is expected of them (trigger), and if I fail to accomplish what I set out to achieve (void), then we will lack security, contentment, and will not be free to live the life we truly want (hurt).

PRINCIPLE—PASSION—PURPOSE

If people are accountable and do what is expected of them (principle), and if I achieve what I set out to achieve (passion), then we can have wealth that affords us the freedom to live the life we want (purpose).

PURPOSE STATEMENT

My purpose is to achieve what I set out to achieve so that we can have wealth that affords us the freedom to live the life we want.

THE ADVISER

"I can give you a six-word formula for success: 'Think things through—then follow through.'"

—EDDIE RICKENBACKER

It's not unusual to catch Advisers with a wistful, contemplative look in their eyes; they're likely contemplating their next challenge or thinking through their current project. Advisers look before they leap, carefully considering each step and how it fits into the full picture. Whereas some people dive right into projects, Advisers gather all the necessary tools, study the directions, and formulate a plan before embarking on a new challenge.

To think that Advisers merely play it safe, however, would be a mistake. Advisers aren't meant to sit on the sidelines of life. Characterized by extremes, they are known for completely immersing themselves in an activity or project. Once they've completed their challenge or get what they need from an experience, they transfer their energy onto something else, as if going through phases, which may last days or years.

As Advisers chase their next challenge, they're likely to explore unrelated facets of reality (for example, relationships, philosophy, travel, business, psychology, and athletics). They prefer to focus on one thing at a time, experiencing each one fully, while interruptions and distractions tend to drain them. When Advisers balance their strong mental focus with their strong intuition, their success in any endeavor is virtually assured.

ADVISER PRINCIPLE AND TRIGGER

Diligent ←——————→ *Negligent*

PRINCIPLE: DILIGENT

Advisers diligently think things through from beginning to end. Advisers:

- Give things prior thought and consideration to ensure successful outcomes.
- Consider the significance of their actions and bring an intense sense of responsibility to all they do.
- Need to understand where they are going before they begin.
- Logically think through each step in a process so they can feel confident in their decisions and have faith that things will work out.
- Easily grasp the big picture and connect the dots to determine what needs to be done.
- Are intellectually curious, logical, decisive, independent, self-sufficient, and determined.

- Feel comfortable in the world of concepts and ideas and can be trusted to competently see projects through.
- Know the value of doing things right and ask, "What are the risks, and how can I mitigate these risks?"
- Look before they leap and safeguard future outcomes by assessing their environment and preventing hazards around them.
- Take calculated risks after carefully evaluating consequences and rewards.
- Weigh a multitude of factors before deciding what to take on and what not to take on (for example, considering: would it be interesting, would I learn, would I succeed?).
- Are mindful of uncertainties and factor the unknowns into their decisions.
- Look at the directions, while others frequently bypass them, so they can visualize outcomes and address uncertainty upfront.
- Feel comfortable challenging ideas, issues, and opinions while offering compellingly persuasive arguments.
- Expect themselves to be informed and therefore need to understand the nature and function of things.

TRIGGER: NEGLIGENT

Advisers feel triggered when people:

- Are irresponsible and don't think things through.
- Are shortsighted and don't think about the consequences of their impulsive actions or careless decisions (i.e., foolhardy).

- Hold extreme opinions and one-sided views they claim are "right" yet refuse to understand alternative viewpoints.
- See potential hazards but don't do anything (i.e., they are lazy in their thinking or actions).
- Claim to be an informed expert, then steer people wrong (for example, a salesperson negligently makes a product recommendation that doesn't meet the need).
- Make mistakes, then proceed to blame others rather than take accountability for their mistakes and learn from them.
- Leave things to chance rather than taking proper care to do things well and do things right.
- Injure themselves or others or cause things to go wrong out of negligence (for example, reckless drivers or unprepared hikers).
- Make poor judgments when they should have known better.
- Have inflated confidence in themselves and take extreme risks that could result in severe consequences or mistakes that could have been avoided.
- Don't factor in potential consequences or uncertainties but, rather, ignorantly assume everything will be fine.
- Tell half-truths or exaggerate in professional settings, causing people to make poor decisions because they relied upon faulty information.
- Assert opinions as facts but haven't bothered to do their homework or look at the bigger picture.
- Make excuses when things don't work out when it's clear that they just didn't think things through.
- Lack forethought and instead make reckless decisions that result in unfavorable outcomes.

ADVISER PASSION AND VOID

Overcoming Challenges ⟷ *Not Being Challenged*

PASSION: MASTERING DIFFICULT THINGS

Advisers are motivated to:

- Take on and overcome new challenges and experiences.
- Dive into a project or experience with a singular focus, complete it, then move on to the next thing with the same intensity, as if going through phases.
- Pursue challenges that are interesting and hard, then tenaciously persist until they have completed what they set out to do.
- Experience the sense of satisfaction that comes from chasing mastery and being good at something.
- Fully immerse themselves in a project or endeavor (sometimes to the point of becoming a crusader).
- Become creatively absorbed with their challenge and get lost in the "flow" of what they are doing.
- Delve into the nitty-gritty and focus on perfecting the technicalities (for example, the technicalities of football, finance, voting, coding, etc.).
- See evidence that they have faced uncertainty, done hard things, overcome obstacles, and positioned themselves for success.
- Overcome the moments of uncertainty and get to the place where they are in the home stretch, where success is a foregone conclusion.

- Meet the desired outcome while also exceeding their personal expectations (for example, by getting things done faster or doing better than expected).
- Focus intensely on their pursuit in a compartmentalized fashion, preferring to continue with one task until it's finished.
- Help others to attain their goals or achieve mastery in some area (for example, math, dancing, software, public speaking).
- Follow their heart's desire, welcome change, experience the extremes, and move through phases encompassing all facets of life, experiencing each one fully.
- Capture every ounce of value an experience may hold for them and make it part of them, recognizing self-integration as key to their fulfillment.
- Honor the mystery of life and remain open to opportunities that present themselves.

When Advisers align with their passion, they shift:
an opportunity to pursue a challenge
to having overcome or mastered a challenge.

VOID: NOT BEING CHALLENGED

Advisers feel drained when they:

- Continue a phase that has come to an end and, thus, are no longer growing.
- Continue to do what they've already done rather than pursue a new challenge.

- Get worse at something or physically regress.
- Sit on the sidelines of life, regret not doing something, or don't have a challenge they are chasing.
- Must shift their focus when actively working on a project or churning something in their mind.
- Are derailed when focused on a project and are forced to digress (for example, they are interrupted, have a computer issue, or must go to a meeting).
- Don't get what they wanted from an experience or are unable to learn and grow from a failure.
- Are not growing or not helping anyone else grow.
- Must focus on learning something that doesn't capture their interest while missing out on an opportunity to learn about something they're drawn to do.
- Work on initiatives where they don't believe it will lead to a safe or successful outcome.
- Feel bored or feel they are wasting the limited amount of time they have.
- Can't solve a problem (commonly the result of trying to logically force a solution rather than posing a question, letting it be, and then allowing the answer to come when they return to it).
- Live their life trying to meet others' expectations rather than chasing their own dreams.
- Try to fit molds or rely on conventional standards rather than honoring their internal guidance.
- Deny new challenges that life presents them and miss out on new experiences.

ADVISER PURPOSE AND HURT

Positioned for Success ←——————→ *Not Positioned for Success*

If you are an Adviser, this is how the various facets of your mindset come together:

TRIGGER—VOID—HURT

If people are negligent, careless, and don't think things through (trigger), and if I don't challenge myself or do hard things (void), then we will experience unwanted stress (hurt).

PRINCIPLE—PASSION—PURPOSE

If people give things prior thought and consideration and think things through (principle), and if I immerse myself in a challenge and continue to master difficult things (passion), then we can be comfortable and positioned for success (purpose).

PURPOSE STATEMENT

My purpose is to immerse myself in challenges and continue to master difficult things so that we can be comfortable and positioned for success.

THE AUTHENTICATOR

"The best and most beautiful things in the world cannot be seen or even touched. They must be felt with the heart."

—HELEN KELLER

Think of a song whose lyrics or melody pierced your soul and moved you emotionally. It's quite possible this song was written or performed by an Authenticator. Authenticators love words that resonate deeply, though they are also motivated to enliven others through endless other mediums, such as landscaping, cooking, interior design, or even practicing law. By enhancing someone's physical or emotional environment, Authenticators positively affect how people feel.

Family and friends are of the utmost importance to Authenticators. That said, it's quality, not quantity, that matters to them most in relationships. They enjoy spending time with people they trust where they're free to let their guard down and express their authentic selves. For this reason, Authenticators are generally selective in whom they let into their lives. Unless they feel comfortable, they're likely to remain guarded in large groups or around strangers.

Truth, justice, and authenticity are imperative to Authenticators. To foster authenticity, they nurture others by creating safe spaces where people can have fun and enjoy being themselves. Having a safe environment allows them to be spontaneous, playful, and creative. Creativity is a receptive state, which requires letting go of the mind and tapping into their creative source. When aligned with essence, Authenticators bring light to dark and pleasure to displeasure, and they create a world where people feel authentic and alive.

AUTHENTICATOR PRINCIPLE AND TRIGGER

Well-Intentioned ⟵⟶ *Ill-Intentioned*

PRINCIPLE: WELL-INTENTIONED

Authenticators are empathic beings who have good hearts and good intentions. Authenticators:

- Are sensitive to other people's feelings and emotional needs and expect others to do the same.
- Make mental notes of people's likes and dislikes, then take care to not cause distress.

- Are empathic, emotionally tuned in to others, and able to feel others' moods and emotions.
- Tend to have small circles so they don't wind up taking on too many people's emotions.
- Feel how others feel, recognizing people and animals as sentient beings who experience pleasure and pain.
- Keep their word and act with people's best interests in mind.
- Make a conscious effort to be a good person and carefully consider their impact on other people and their emotions.
- Know that the intentions behind our actions matter (for example, it matters if someone offers a heartfelt apology for the right reasons or if they are apologizing to get something from someone).
- Use their strong internal instincts to recognize and respond to people's needs (for example, knowing if someone is hurting).
- Are genuine in their intentions and congruent in their heart, words, and actions.
- Are considerate of people's moods, feelings, needs, and wants.
- Stand for truth and goodness and seek justice where people have been wronged.
- Are friendly, approachable, honest, and expect honesty in others.
- Are highly protective of their own, the innocent, and the vulnerable.
- Value truth, integrity, justice, safety, security, and authenticity.

TRIGGER: ILL-INTENTIONED

Authenticators feel triggered when people:

- Manipulate or lie to get people to do what they want them to do.
- Gaslight, exploit, deceive, harm, betray, or prey on others.
- Twist people's words or spin conversations to confuse, deflect, distract, and ultimately project their wrongdoing onto others.
- Turn on their charm to coerce or get their way or pretend to be someone they're not.
- Appear pleasant in their interactions but are cunning in their intentions.
- Take advantage of others to get their own needs met or take credit for other people's work.
- Feed their ego or an addiction to power at the expense of others.
- Project their negativity or bad moods on others and intentionally or unintentionally bring others down.
- Say one thing and then do something else (for example, they say honesty is important to them and then lie, or they make a promise but don't keep it).
- Continue to do something they have been told irritates someone else (for example, leaving globs of toothpaste in the sink).
- Lack empathy for others and consequently cause others pain, discomfort, and suffering.
- Are malicious, calculating, have ulterior motives, or thrive on exerting power and control over others.

- Get away with injustices, such as immorally hurting or wronging others.
- Intentionally inflict pain onto others and cause people to suffer (i.e., psychopathic versus empathic).
- Don't speak the truth and don't act with integrity.

AUTHENTICATOR PASSION AND VOID

Enlivening ⟷ *Not Enlivened*

PASSION: ENLIVENING AND CONNECTING WITH OTHERS

Authenticators are motivated to:

- Be a conduit to connect people to their emotions.
- Spend time with genuine people they know and trust.
- Ignite authenticity in themselves, others, businesses, or in the world.
- Be in safe company, where people are free to be their true and authentic selves.
- Find the perfect word or phrase to stir one's emotions or touch someone's soul.
- Be selective with their time and enjoy time alone to relax, unwind, and be at home.
- Be an advocate for truth and justice.
- Connect with people on an emotional level, serving as a bridge between people's hearts and minds.

- Open hearts so people can let down their walls and feel a message or compassion for the world around them.
- Touch people's emotions through words, art, beauty, music, nature, creativity, connections, experiences, and settings.
- See the physical results of their efforts and influence their own or others' happiness, joy, contentment, or delight.
- Put their own playful or humorous twist on things (which may be dry, edgy, amusingly dark, or sarcastic).
- Positively impact their own and others' emotions by recognizing and appreciating the beauty all around them and recognizing how beauty can elicit powerful feelings of aliveness.
- Help others feel alive or inspired.
- Bring amusement to annoyance, pleasure to displeasure, truth to untruths, connection to disconnection, and light to dark.

When Authenticators align with their passion, they shift: an opportunity to elicit feelings of aliveness *to* feeling enlivened or having enlivened others.

VOID: NOT FEELING ENLIVENED AND CONNECTED

Authenticators feel drained when they:

- Must "play-the-part" and present themselves in an inauthentic manner.

- Engage in forced social interactions and small talk.
- Spend time with people they don't trust, enjoy, or know well.
- Don't have any alone time to rest, relax, recharge, and restore—time that allows them to reconnect with their essence.
- Hurt someone when they didn't mean to.
- Find themselves in unpleasant situations (for example, waiting in a long line).
- Work on insignificant tasks that will be overlooked by others.
- Do mundane things absent of creativity, connection, or enjoyment.
- Relive past hurts, mistakes, or painful memories.
- Do things that feel superficial and inauthentic (for example, selling something they don't believe is right for the customer).
- Are physically or emotionally exhausted, stressed, or have too much on their mind (and consequently will seek out "no-brainer" jobs or alone time to decompress).
- Feel they are simply going through the motions rather than feeling the depth of their emotions.
- Work in stiff, rigid, disrespectful, heartless, or stress-ridden environments that focus on metrics while the human element is neglected.
- Feel emotionally disconnected from the world and people in it.
- Feel taken for granted, unappreciated, invisible, or ignored.

AUTHENTICATOR PURPOSE AND HURT

Be Authentic ⟵⟶ *Be Guarded*

If you are an Authenticator, this is how the various facets of your mindset come together:

TRIGGER—VOID—HURT

If people are ill-intentioned, manipulative, or insensitive (trigger), and if I don't help people feel enlivened and connected to life (void), then we will not feel safe to let our guard down and express our authentic selves (hurt).

PRINCIPLE—PASSION—PURPOSE

If people are tuned into others and act with sincere intentions (principle), and if I do things that allow people to feel alive, appreciated, and connected (passion), then we can feel safe being our authentic selves (purpose).

PURPOSE STATEMENT

My purpose is to help people feel alive and connected so that we can feel safe being our authentic selves.

THE BALANCER

"Life should not be a journey to the grave with the intention of arriving safely in a pretty and well-preserved body, but rather to skid in broadside in a cloud of smoke, thoroughly used up, totally worn out, and loudly proclaiming 'Wow! What a ride!'"

—HUNTER S. THOMPSON

Much like surfers, Balancers constantly move, reposition, and change their stance to keep their balance. The Balancer mindset recognizes balance is a dynamic process. Maintaining it requires reorganizing, rearranging, and readjusting to remain upright and even-keeled. Every new change raises the question, *How will this affect everything else?* As each situation emerges, they manage the logistics and shuffle schedules to satisfy everyone's demands, fit everything in, and get everything done.

In addition to seeking balance within their own lives, Balancers desire balance in relationships. To keep things steady and tension-free, their upbeat personality elevates the spirits of those around them. They have a knack for bringing fun, laughter, and optimism into the tragedies and seriousness of life. Chameleon-like, they meet people where they're at, and their outward views tend to be middle of the road, thus keeping things on the up-and-up. And though people are readily drawn to Balancers' energy, Balancers rarely allow others to get close emotionally until they've proven they can be trusted.

Eager to do it all, Balancers crave the excitement and stimulation of new things streaming into their lives. They enjoy adventure, interacting with different people, and exploring new places. For them, life is an adventure to be fully lived. The reward for fitting everything in and keeping everything in balance is living life to the fullest.

BALANCER PRINCIPLE AND TRIGGER

Dynamic ⟵⟶ *Blindsiding*

PRINCIPLE: DYNAMIC

Balancers dynamically balance life's many demands and expectations, making sure they fit everything in, show up appropriately, and ensure all goes as expected. Balancers:

- Actively manage life's many commitments, expectations, and desires.
- Consider the whole and how one thing will affect everything else.

- Read the room and then act in a manner that is in harmony with the vibe of the environment.
- Tend to be very middle of the road and chameleon-like, able to understand all perspectives and put people at ease.
- Continually reshuffle plans to ensure everything works and gets done.
- Fulfill their obligations and take their commitments seriously.
- Work diligently to keep everything in balance, wanting everything to fit together and be in its proper place, like puzzle pieces, so everything is complete and works.
- Take care to fit everything in so they can keep their commitments—formal or implied—to work, family, friends, themselves, and beyond.
- Are systematic, methodical, and dependent upon everything working together synergistically.
- Are self-motivated, self-directed, and often self-employed.
- Can easily adapt to meet the demands of any audience or situation—being the life of the party, the utmost professional, or a caring friend—to bring about balance.
- Maintain outer balance by ensuring everything works and goes as expected and maintain inner balance by keeping things upbeat and even-keeled.
- Respond appropriately based on the situation and take care to meet people where they're at.
- Make sense of the external cues around them and then bridge the gap to keep things controlled and collected.
- Strive to instill a sense of balance, harmony, stability, predictability, and equilibrium in their life.

TRIGGER: BLINDSIDING

Balancers feel triggered when people:

- Surprise them.
- Don't do what they were expected to do or cause things to not go as expected.
- Spring things on them with little to no notice, making it difficult to fit everything in and make everything work.
- Don't give ample notice but instead blindside them and cause them to have to reshuffle their day.
- Lie or make excuses for being unaccountable.
- Restrict others from living their lives freely and fully.
- Don't do things quite right or as expected, thus causing things to have to be redone.
- Agree to do something, then cancel at the last minute or stand them up (i.e., they flake).
- Can't read the room and consequently create waves and upset the vibe (for example, challenging political beliefs at a family dinner).
- Don't take others into consideration and throw off their outer sense of balance (for example, by showing up late and messing up their plans).
- Don't take others into consideration and throw off their inner sense of balance (for example, by telling lies, acting fake, keeping secrets, or creating drama).
- Throw curveballs that could have been adverted with a little forethought.
- Don't meet their expectations (implied or explicit).
- Don't act as they would expect a friend to behave but instead betray their trust.

- Catch people off guard and don't consider the negative impact of their last-minute demands and curveballs.

BALANCER PASSION AND VOID

Adventure ⟷ *Lack of Adventure*

PASSION: PURSUING NEW EXPERIENCES AND ADVENTURES

Balancers are motivated to:

- Say yes to new challenges, opportunities, adventures, and life (for example, starting a new business, adding a new product line, or going somewhere new).
- Explore new places, travel to unfamiliar locations, or drive down unexplored roads.
- Pursue fresh challenges that allow them to expand their thinking and skillset.
- Socialize and interact with a variety of people.
- Regularly take on new things, do things they're not certain they can do, take qualified risks, and venture into the unknown.
- Help people get the most out of a solution and have a good experience.
- Share new experiences with others and help people live life to the fullest and enjoy life.
- Challenge their artistic, technical, or problem-solving abilities.

- Change things up, such as changing their place of residence.
- Invest in opportunities to learn new things, grow personally, and live authentically.
- Solve problems that help others get the most out of an experience.
- Take chances that will pay off (for example, take a risk on a new business and then see the business succeed).
- Enjoy time outdoors and in nature, enjoying play, recreation, and balancing sports (for example, surfing).
- Use their imagination and explore new ideas, techniques, and solutions.
- Enjoy their freedom and flexibility to live fully and do it all.

When Balancers align with their passion, they shift:
an opportunity to venture into
the unknown and take on a new adventure
to seeing that the adventure was worthwhile.

VOID: NOT HAVING NEW EXPERIENCES COMING INTO THEIR LIVES

Balancers feel drained when they:

- Lack new things coming into their life.
- Lack any sense of adventure in life.
- Work too much and miss out on every other area of life.
- Feel deprived or deficient in some area of life.

- Neglect aspects of life that are important to them.
- Experience life as monotonous, boring, or routine.
- Lack variety, change, and flexibility and instead do the same thing day in and day out.
- Partake in dull tasks, dull activities, dull jobs, dull classes, or dull interactions.
- Spend time with boring people who take life too seriously.
- Take chances that are highly consequential, and the risks can't be managed or controlled.
- See healthy people who are focused on merely surviving rather than focusing on living.
- Are stuck dealing with details (beyond those necessary to provide balance).
- Go deep in one area and consequently miss out on learning or doing other things.
- Work in rigid work environments that restrict their learning, creativity, flexibility, and freedom.
- Feel bored, don't live life to the fullest, or feel they are missing out and unable to do it all.

BALANCER PURPOSE AND HURT

Live Fully ←——→ *Not Live Fully*

If you are a Balancer, this is how the various facets of your mindset come together:

TRIGGER—VOID—HURT

If people do the unexpected and create imbalances (trigger), and if I don't have new things coming into my life but do the same boring things or go deep in only one area (void), then we won't live our life to the fullest (hurt).

PRINCIPLE—PASSION—PURPOSE

If people are dynamic and respond appropriately to external cues and demands (principle), and if I pursue new challenges, learning, adventures, and experiences (passion), then we will be free to experience it all and live life to the fullest (purpose).

PURPOSE STATEMENT

My purpose is to pursue new experiences, challenges, learning, and adventures so that we can live life to the fullest.

THE CAPTIVATOR

"Love yourself, whatever makes you different, and use it to make you stand out."

—ROSS MATHEWS

There's rarely a dull moment with a Captivator. Known for bringing joy into their environment, Captivators have a knack for using humor and laughter to transform the most uncomfortable situations. When things get too serious in life, you can count on them to lighten stressful circumstances and make life fun. They may be the life of the party or a coworker who always makes you smile.

Captivators don't apologize for who they are, nor should they. They are generally comfortable in their skin and wish for others to feel the same. Known for "telling it like it is," there's a tendency to occasionally open-mouth-insert-foot. With pure intentions, the last thing they want to do is offend anyone. Instead, they just expect people, including themselves, to be clear, direct, and straightforward. After all, they can't adequately help someone if they don't understand their needs and expectations.

Captivators genuinely care for people and are at their best when they're working with others. Their altruistic nature motivates them to help people and be there for those who need a helping hand. When people are going through a difficult time, Captivators want to show their support and find ways to bring joy into their life. Highly sociable, caring, considerate, and compassionate, they tend to maintain a certain childlike quality, bringing happiness and joy into a world that desperately needs it.

CAPTIVATOR PRINCIPLE AND TRIGGER

Clear  *Unclear*

PRINCIPLE: CLEAR

Captivators are straightforward, clear, and direct and wish for people to be free to be who they are. Captivators:

- Express themselves freely and honestly.
- Are verbally uninhibited, say what they mean, and say what needs to be said.
- Freely communicate their thoughts, feelings, opinions, needs, and expectations and want others to feel comfortable doing the same.
- Are naturally frank and forthcoming, direct and to the point, and speak in a straightforward manner.

- Want people to feel free to be who they are and to feel comfortable saying what's on their mind or in their heart (for example, if you don't understand something, just say so).
- Talk as a way of clarifying their thoughts, often editing and refining as they speak or using body language to make themselves clear.
- Clearly state their expectations, often making things black and white so others know exactly what is expected and can achieve the desired outcome.
- Treat others with kindness, compassion, and decency and wouldn't want to do anything to intentionally hurt someone.
- Want others to communicate openly and want others to let them know if they inadvertently upset someone so they can address it and, ideally, fix it.
- Express themselves in a carefree manner with childlike innocence.
- Have pure intentions with no ulterior agenda.
- Fulfill their obligations, meet expectations, and reliably do what they say they will do and want others to do the same.
- Are results-oriented and can easily lead, take charge, and step into leadership positions.
- Want people to be able to trust them and feel safe opening up to them, and to know they will not be judged.
- Are excellent team players who accept people for who they are.

TRIGGER: UNCLEAR

Captivators feel triggered when people:

- Won't just spit it out and say what they need to say.
- Beat around the bush or are indirect because they are afraid of hurting someone's feelings.
- Talk around things without making their point, leaving much room for confusion and ambiguity.
- Are vague and fail to clearly articulate their expectations and consequently set up others for failure.
- Know what is expected of them but don't do it.
- Are afraid to share their opinion even when they've been asked to share.
- Won't express who they are for fear of offending someone.
- Hold things inside rather than just saying what they want to say.
- Are overly concerned with others' reactions to everything they say and do.
- Don't feel secure enough to present themselves truthfully and transparently.
- Say they'll do something and don't follow through with it or don't communicate when something changes.
- Allow their insecurities to prevent them from asking for what they need or saying what's on their mind.
- Provide a lot of filler and go on and on about details that take away from what they are trying to say, which makes them difficult to understand.
- Contradict themselves, misconstrue messages, lead people astray, or say what they think people want to hear.

- Have an ulterior motive, hidden agenda, or betray people's trust.

CAPTIVATOR PASSION AND VOID

Spreading Joy ⟷ *Lacking Joy*

PASSION: BRINGING JOY TO OTHERS

Captivators are motivated to:

- Transmit joy to others and into their surroundings.
- Create stress-free environments where people can enjoy themselves.
- Use humor and laughter to lighten stressful and uncomfortable situations.
- Bring energy, enthusiasm, positivity, and aliveness to whatever they undertake.
- Spend quality time socializing with people they enjoy or doing things that bring them joy (for example, playing games, telling stories, making things, or going to Disneyland).
- Express their genuine concern for others and altruistically act on behalf of others.
- See the best in others and give people who could use a helping hand the support they need.
- Inspire people, uplift people, offer moral support, and show people they believe in them.

- Help people by building them up or giving them a chance to prove themselves so they can build themselves back up.
- Share their enthusiasm, boost morale, keep others motivated, and activate others' energy.
- Do things for others that will be appreciated or bring someone joy (for example, helping someone or giving people personalized gifts).
- Ease others' stress, pain, or burden and brighten their situation.
- Make the invisible feel seen, the neglected feel cared for, the sad feel happy, and be a voice for the voiceless.
- Maintain a healthy work-life balance—work hard, play hard—so they can enjoy every day.
- Enjoy themselves, enjoy other people, enjoy activities, and enjoy their love of life.

When Captivators align with their passion, they shift:
an opportunity to bring joy to others
to having brought joy to others.

VOID: NOT BRINGING JOY INTO THE WORLD

Captivators feel drained when they:

- Take life too seriously and experience life as all work and no fun.
- Do something that causes someone to be disappointed or displeased.

- Do things that are unpleasant, boring, and unenjoyable.
- Inadvertently hurt others as a result of being misunderstood.
- Are not given a chance to explain themselves when something does not go as desired.
- Witness others' hardships or basic needs not being met and see that others don't have anyone to care for them or turn to for support.
- Work in unsupportive, unenjoyable environments.
- Are expected to do work that is not clearly defined and consequently do not feel they are positioned for success.
- Have so much expected of them that they can't both meet people's expectations and have time to enjoy their life.
- Work in environments that focus on profit while neglecting the people they serve.
- Spend time with people who are insensitive, uncaring, negative, or untrustworthy.
- Need to ask people to do things they know they won't enjoy or don't want to do.
- Do nice things for others when their efforts are not acknowledged or appreciated.
- See people or animals in a bad situation, but they aren't able to help them (for example, seeing a child begging for money or finding a stranded dog).
- Feel lonely, isolated, abandoned, or separated from the people they care about.

CAPTIVATOR PURPOSE AND HURT

Have Support ⟷ *Go It Alone*

If you are a Captivator, this is how the various facets of your mindset come together:

TRIGGER—VOID—HURT

If people don't clearly express themselves but are indirect or vague (trigger), and if I don't help people and do things that bring joy to others (void), then we will not have the support we need and will have trouble in life (hurt).

PRINCIPLE—PASSION—PURPOSE

If people express themselves clearly, directly, and freely (principle), and if I help people and do things that bring joy to others (passion), then we will have the support we need to thrive in life (purpose).

PURPOSE STATEMENT

My purpose is to help others and do things that bring joy into the world so that we have the support we need to thrive in life.

THE CONNECTOR

"A river cuts through rock, not because of its power, but because of its persistence."

—JIM WATKINS

Just like a river, which doesn't stop for a boulder or a fallen tree but rather finds its path, Connectors need to keep moving forward. They look for the most direct path so they can accomplish things expeditiously. If the direct path is blocked, they'll find their way through, around, or over an obstacle. Connectors don't need to fix every problem they encounter; they just need to make sure it doesn't hinder them on their journey to achieve their desired outcome.

With their need to move forward, Connectors have little patience for those who cause setbacks or keep things from going as well as they could. When situations are at a standstill, it's easy for them to come in and verbally take over, acting as the force that gets things moving. Connectors are excellent communicators known for their determination in accomplishing what they set out to do.

Connectors thrive on interacting with others, listening to interesting people, and connecting people according to their needs, desires, or interests. They're highly motivated to learn what other people know and feel equally motivated to bring information to those who need it. Naturally curious, social, and outgoing, they're in their element when circulating a crowd and derive much of their knowledge and stimulation from interacting with others. Since they listen to a variety of perspectives, Connectors frequently represent the unified voice of many. By being well-informed, Connectors use their elevated perspective to ensure favorable outcomes.

CONNECTOR PRINCIPLE AND TRIGGER

Persistent ←——————→ *Inhibiting*

PRINCIPLE: PERSISTENT

Connectors are persistent with a need to keep things moving forward. Connectors:

- Tenaciously persist until they achieve their desired outcome.
- Act with a sense of urgency.
- Are frequently the force that gets things moving and keeps things moving forward.
- Ask, "How do I get past this or around this?"
- Relentlessly find their way over, around, or through obstacles.
- Make decisions efficiently and confidently, and then course correct as needed.

- Don't need to fix every problem; they just can't let it prevent them from moving forward.
- Are decisive, efficient, fast-paced, direct, intense, action-oriented, and continually on the go.
- Avoid foreseeable setbacks.
- Pursue practical actions that can move plans forward.
- Anticipate obstacles and prepare accordingly, and then adapt to the rest.
- Take care to do things the right way when it positions them for future success and efficiency (for example, placing pens in the proper pocket so they are easily accessible when needed).
- Look for and find the fastest and smoothest way to achieve their outcome.
- Are determined to successfully complete the mission.
- Want to keep things simple and flowing like a well-oiled machine.

TRIGGER: INHIBITING

Connectors feel triggered when people:

- Are unprepared and cause setbacks.
- Seek perfection and resist taking action, thus keeping things at a standstill.
- Are indecisive and need every last detail buttoned up before they can take any action.
- Fail to do things properly, thus adding cycles and causing delays.
- Break the rules and unfairly get ahead.
- Take unqualified risks or are reckless (i.e., foolhardy).

- Tell them what to do (rather than asking them to do something).
- Take advantage of them or inconvenience them.
- Create obstacles that hinder forward momentum.
- Have meeting after meeting without moving anything forward.
- Pursue impractical solutions or over-engineer things.
- Interrupt their flow or progress, causing things to not go as well as they could have.
- Lack any sense of urgency.
- Get in the way or slow them down.
- Make poor decisions that result in an unfavorable experience or a poor outcome.

CONNECTOR PASSION AND VOID

Connecting ←——→ *Disconnected*

PASSION: CONNECTING PEOPLE AND INFORMATION

Connectors are motivated to:

- Listen to interesting people and stories and are eager to glean useful, entertaining, or intriguing information.
- Connect people according to their needs, ideas, desires, or interests.
- Share experiences with others and introduce people to experiences they haven't had.

- Be in the know and learn what other people know, finding they are most effective when they have a good overview of a lot of things.
- Add value to others by utilizing their abundant connections.
- Engage in interactive dialogue, casual banter, and good conversation where the volley is good.
- Ask questions, uncover new insights, and learn from people, books, travel, and nature—all welcomed sources of interesting information.
- Converse, socialize, interact, or circulate a crowd, collecting knowledge from one person and delivering it to another to unite people through information and ideas.
- Connect things on all levels, incorporating the insights of many.
- Gain an elevated perspective, which captures the inputs and viewpoints of many.
- Be well-informed and well-connected, and use this elevated outlook to ensure all ends well.
- Be heard and represent the unified voice of many.
- Make highly informed decisions and recommendations that leverage vast perspectives.
- Communicate their insights and recommended actions.
- Form relationships quickly, cultivate them over time, and hold on to them indefinitely.

When Connectors align with their passion, they shift: an opportunity to connect interesting people, information, and experiences *to* having connected interesting people, information, and experiences.

VOID: BEING DISCONNECTED FROM PEOPLE AND INFORMATION

Connectors feel drained when they:

- Engage in one-way communication (for example, talking *at* people or being talked *at*, rather than engaging in a dialogue).
- Have valuable insight to share but don't have a say, a voice, or a seat at the table.
- Have valuable information that is relevant to others but are not allowed to share it.
- Feel cornered or trapped in an uninteresting conversation and are stuck listening to boring stories.
- Listen to people share excessive detail beyond what is necessary to understand and explain the concept or story to someone else.
- Don't have anyone to talk to or are disconnected from intriguing people.
- Miss out on potentially interesting information.
- Aren't in the know, don't know what is going on, or have people withhold valuable information from them.
- Have tried every possible option and don't feel they can achieve a favorable outcome.
- Aren't listened to, aren't heard out, or don't get a chance to explain themselves and tell their side of the story.
- Don't have a say in matters that directly affect them, or someone else tries to control their actions or experience.
- Attend unimportant or dull meetings or presentations.
- Have exciting intel, but someone steals their thunder.
- Don't have anything interesting or valuable to share.
- Are uninterested, unconnected, or uninformed.

CONNECTOR PURPOSE AND HURT

Have a Good Outcome ←——→ *Have a Bad Outcome*

If you are a Connector, this is how the various facets of your mindset come together:

TRIGGER—VOID—HURT

If people cause setbacks or keep things at a standstill (trigger), and if I do not connect people and information (void), then we will have a bad experience, or the outcome will be less than ideal (hurt).

PRINCIPLE—PASSION—PURPOSE

If people persist and keep things moving forward (principle), and if I make connections, gather insights from various sources, and present a unified voice of many (passion), then we will have a good experience and a favorable outcome (purpose).

PURPOSE STATEMENT

My purpose is to make connections and connect people and information so that we have good experiences and favorable outcomes.

THE CULTIVATOR

"The most precious gift you can give someone is the gift of your time and attention."

—NICKY GUMBEL

Cultivators have a unique ability to make people feel at home around them. Distinguished by an approachability that is hard to define but easy to recognize, people are often drawn to them. Their demeanor is friendly and kind. They express genuine interest in whomever they are talking to, which leaves people feeling seen and heard. Being so receptive to others, people feel unguarded and welcomed in their presence—so much so that perfect strangers occasionally spill their guts to them.

Cultivators are typically more approachable than approaching and usually let others initiate relationships. Because of their sensitivity to others' needs, it's easy for them to direct the conversation or activity. They like to get along with everyone, and they relate well to those around them. It's important for them to maintain stability in their relationships and steer clear of relationship strain.

Cultivators most enjoy spending quality time with the people close to them or focusing their attention on activities they love. They genuinely care about others and derive satisfaction in simply being there for others and offering their assistance. For Cultivators, home, family, and relationships are of the utmost importance, so they're often the glue that creates cohesiveness and stability in groups. They enjoy bringing people together and cherish feeling close and connected. Sensitive and caring, they are often models of success in both personal and business relationships.

CULTIVATOR PRINCIPLE AND TRIGGER

Kind ←——→ *Hurtful*

PRINCIPLE: KIND

Cultivators are personable and kind and want others to be too. Cultivators:

- Show kindness to others and treat people like they are a friend.
- Project sensitivity, sincerity, and warmth and genuinely care about others and their feelings.
- Take care to be a good, honest, loyal person with an intention to do good, or at least do no harm.
- Are attentive listeners who can easily direct conversations and activities with sensitivity.
- Cultivate their relationships and foster connection and belonging within groups.

- Feel more than others and are empathic, emotionally tuned in, and subject to taking on others' feelings.
- Have a calming presence about them and are able to effortlessly make others feel safe, seen, heard, and appreciated.
- Are capable, conscientious, and persistent and can be trusted to responsibly follow through on their commitments and do their job well.
- Are competitive within themselves, wanting to do their best and make sure people are happy.
- Are good team players and frequently function best as part of a team.
- Have an intensity for being nice, caring, nurturing, and accommodating.
- Are uniquely approachable, receptive, and nonintimidating and often find people are drawn toward them.
- Are easy to talk to and in touch with their own emotions, which makes it easy for others to connect with their own emotions in their presence.
- Feel things deeply, lead with their heart, and rely on their emotions and intuition to help guide them.
- Relate well to those around them and like to get along with everyone.

TRIGGER: HURTFUL

Cultivators feel triggered when people:

- Are disrespectful of others and treat others poorly.
- Are condescending and put other people down or make others feel bad.

- Make sarcastic comments that are more hostile than witty.
- Don't listen or pay attention when having a conversation with someone.
- Make someone else's life miserable and become the source of another's pain (for example, bullying, picking on someone, or preying on vulnerable people).
- Disrespect or disregard others (for example, disrespecting someone because of their gender, age, job title, or other arbitrary differences).
- Think they are better or more important than others.
- Act as though other people's opinions or time doesn't have value.
- Lack kindness and general consideration for others and instead have cold, icky personalities.
- Are disruptive and stir up interpersonal conflict, create discord, or cause people to not get along.
- Make callous comments to other people in person or on social media.
- Lack discretion and tact and instead say things that are mean, rude, or hurtful (i.e., insensitive jerks).
- Point out the flaws in others and have a knack for seeing everything wrong but don't give attention to what is right.
- Are not inclusive of others (for example, a meeting where two people are engaged in a conversation but don't engage the rest of the group).
- Do not assume positive intent but instead show a lack of compassion and sensitivity in dealing with other people (for example, parents who scream at their children and only give them attention when they do something wrong).

CULTIVATOR PASSION AND VOID

Provide Stability ←——→ *Lack Stability*

PASSION: BRINGING STABILITY TO THEIR RELATIONSHIPS AND SURROUNDINGS

Cultivators are motivated to:

- Spend quality time with friends, family, and the people close to them.
- Foster stability and cohesiveness in teams, groups, and families.
- Prioritize a sense of community and togetherness and want to get to know the people in their life.
- Work on teams with other hardworking individuals who succeed and get along.
- Be attentive to the needs of others and go out of their way to offer assistance and help kind people.
- Bring stability to teams, groups, and organizations by setting the beat or tone of their environment, which others tend to unconsciously follow.
- Engage in activities that ground them and give them a sense of stability in life (for example, listening to or playing music, designing computer graphics, meditating, or exercising).
- Fix things that will ensure the safety and stability of their home or go out of their way to do things that will provide a good experience for family and friends.
- Carefully plan activities (such as vacations, meetings, or events) to ensure all goes smoothly and people are happy or receive what they need.

- Synthesize various elements and simplify the complex to make things easier for people, save people time, enable collaboration, or provide a foundation to support others' success.
- Break down projects or processes and build them back in ways that will provide the greatest security, structure, and stability.
- Take pride in their work by focusing on quality and giving attention to the details so they can ensure the safety, efficacy, and long-term value of their work.
- Bring people together in ways that feel natural and make people happy (for example, hosting a barbecue or a picnic).
- Give people attention, receive it, and enjoy the company of others.
- Cherish the moments when people are together, everyone gets along, interactions are easy, and all feels right in the world.

When Cultivators align with their passion, they shift:
an opportunity to bring stability to
a relationship or situation
to having brought stability to a
relationship or situation.

VOID: LACKING STABILITY

Cultivators feel drained when they:

- Lack a sense of stability in life (for example, a lack of stability in their relationships or at work).
- Work in environments where people don't care about or get along with each other.

- Feel disconnected or distanced from people or find that people they care about don't prioritize making time for them.
- Feel unsure of their effectiveness or don't feel proficient at what they do.
- Have carefully planned an activity and it doesn't go as planned (for example, a meeting that goes off track because people showed up unprepared).
- Have externally imposed change forced on them when they believe the change will not be beneficial but, rather, will be disruptive and cause problems.
- Need to do things that could be hurtful or detrimental to their relationships (for example, delivering harsh feedback or firing someone).
- Experience relationship strain or watch once strong relationships weaken.
- Don't feel they are valued or cared about and instead feel ignored, forgotten, excluded, or avoided.
- Work in highly political or cut-throat environments, which sacrifice people for profit.
- Work endlessly to provide a sense of stability to others but don't experience it themselves.
- Are restricted or unable to pursue the activities they enjoy (for example, due to an injury).
- Lack peace of mind and instead feel overwhelmed with too much on their plate and not enough time to get it all done.
- Try to help someone learn how to do something, but the person argues or doesn't listen and resists learning the skills necessary to do things right.
- Are unable to fix things, including relationship issues or business challenges.

CULTIVATOR PURPOSE AND HURT

Peace of Mind ⟷ *Lack of Inner Peace*

If you are a Cultivator, this is how the various facets of your mindset come together:

TRIGGER—VOID—HURT

If people are hurtful, unfriendly, or unkind (trigger), and if I don't provide stability for myself, my family, my company, and beyond (void), then we will not experience contentment and inner peace, but, rather, will worry and experience stress (hurt).

PRINCIPLE—PASSION—PURPOSE

If people are friendly and treat others with kindness (principle), and if I bring stability to my relationships and surroundings (passion), then we can feel content and experience peace of mind (purpose).

PURPOSE STATEMENT

My purpose is to bring stability to my relationships and surroundings so that we can feel content and experience inner peace.

THE ENVISIONER

"Everything that is real was imagined first."

—MARGERY WILLIAMS, *THE VELVETEEN RABBIT*

Some people see a bump in the road and think, *Someone should fix that!* Others see the bump in the road and take the initiative to address the issue. Envisioners see opportunities to make improvements. They don't merely view things as they are but, rather, envision how things could be, come up with solutions quickly, and then take action to make things better.

Driven by strong common sense, Envisioners can't help but notice senselessness around them. Feeling the urge to say something when they observe such absurdities, yet not wanting to make matters worse off, they often have a dry sense of humor or a bit of an edge. They're not trying to make people laugh as much as they're trying to make a point. Using their wit, they can masterfully express their sentiments without making the situation worse (and without getting caught).

Optimistic and highly visual in nature, Envisioners are problem solvers who are known for bringing their visions to life. They are motivated to execute good ideas, see progress, and make a difference. They must be progressing *something*—an idea, a project, a solution. Their inner drive to bring ideas to life inspires them to advance projects and implement solutions. Envisioners experience a high the moment they realize their vision.

ENVISIONER PRINCIPLE AND TRIGGER

Improving ←——→ *Nonprogressive*

PRINCIPLE: IMPROVING

Envisioners are solution-oriented and see opportunities to make improvements and make things better. Envisioners:

- Are highly visual in nature, seeing solutions and opportunities in their mind.
- Are solution-oriented and see opportunities to make improvements.
- Are quick to solve problems and find that solutions come quickly to them.
- Envision better ways of doing things.
- See good in even the bleakest of situations, optimistically believing things can be improved.
- Notice issues that go unnoticed by others.

- Use their strong intuition and common sense to pursue practical, down-to-earth solutions.
- Ask, "Is there a better way?"
- Take initiative to make improvements and make situations better (where there's a will there's a way).
- Follow the rules but question rules or practices that don't make sense.
- Consider how their actions affect others and take care not to say something that could make someone's situation worse.
- Can figure out how to repair, solve, fix, streamline, optimize, or build just about anything.
- Keep sight of the big picture as well as how the details connect to create a whole system.
- Are likely to utilize visuals, tools, or a whiteboard to articulate ideas and concepts.
- Often have a dry sense of humor, needing to call out absurdities while making sure their sentiments do not make matters worse.

TRIGGER: NONPROGRESSIVE

Envisioners feel triggered when people:

- Lack common sense or can't see obvious things that need to be done.
- Belittle others, speak down to others, or do something that makes someone else's situation worse.
- Justify problems and refuse to consider ideas that could make things better.

- Resist necessary change or defend the status quo because "it's always been done that way."
- Uphold archaic business practices, follow nonsensical protocols, or do things that make no sense because "the policy says so."
- Claim to be an expert in areas they know nothing about.
- Ask for advice, then refuse to do anything to improve their situation.
- Have a glass-half-empty attitude and continually complain about their situation but won't do anything to make it better.
- Can't see the solution and ask the Envisioner to repeat themselves even when something has been thoroughly explained to them.
- Focus on the gap and the problem rather than seeing the opportunity and the good.
- Make policies that make no sense and don't affect them personally yet require others to follow them despite not understanding their role.
- Give up their identity or sacrifice who they are for someone else.
- Judge others who don't live life by their standards (for example, naively believing they're better than someone because they have more money even though they're dissatisfied and unfulfilled).
- Talk to them like they are stupid or treat them like they are dumb (i.e., mansplaining).
- Worship problems and ignore action.

ENVISIONER PASSION AND VOID

Bring Visions to Life ←——→ *Not Bring Visions to Life*

PASSION: BRINGING THEIR IDEAS AND VISIONS TO LIFE

Envisioners are motivated to:

- Execute their visions and see the fruits of their labor.
- Advance good ideas, creative projects, and valuable solutions.
- Make a difference in people's lives and in the world.
- Make and see progress on something—an idea, a project, or a solution.
- Help people solve problems, overcome challenges, or make their ideas a reality.
- Visually observe their progress and see everything come together.
- Visualize what they want to manifest and then set out to make it happen.
- See their solutions having the desired effect, such as making a friend or client happy.
- Use their creativity to think differently and rethink how to do things, finding ways to do things better than they have been done before.
- Work independently behind the scenes on worthwhile initiatives, doing whatever it takes to realize their vision.
- Fix or build things (for example, a business, a piece of furniture, or a process).

- Do things that make them happy, such as spending time with friends, planning a vacation, being in nature, or doing something creative (and may find they enjoy working with their hands).
- Do things that add value and positively enrich their own or others' lives through experiences, relationships, and optimizations.
- Connect people with others who have insight that could help them and make someone's life better in some way.
- Learn by doing and figuring things out on their own, when possible (as opposed to reading the directions).

When Envisioners align with their passion, they shift:
an idea or a vision
to a reality.

VOID: NOT BRINGING THEIR IDEAS AND VISIONS TO LIFE

Envisioners feel drained when they:

- Are not making progress or advancing anything.
- See things regress to a worse state or do something that makes someone's situation worse.
- Implement ideas they don't believe in or are restricted from implementing good ideas.
- Do things inefficiently when they know there's a better way but are unable to make changes.

- Don't feel they are making a positive difference.
- Participate in ineffective, inefficient meetings that fail to move anything forward.
- Deal with bureaucracy, constant churn, or the grind, or are stuck going through the motions doing busy work that doesn't progress anything or add value to anyone.
- Focus their attention across too many things or are spread too thin, thus not sufficiently progressing any one thing.
- Pursue something strictly for financial gain and do not add value to anyone or anything (for example, selling a product that won't address the client's need).
- Lack the freedom to do what they see needs to be done.
- Are micromanaged, told how they must do something, or are not free to just do their own thing.
- Are subject to boring systemic learning, told every move, or forced to follow directions without knowing why they're doing something.
- Have things not go as they had envisioned (for example, a family vacation doesn't go as they had hoped).
- See a problem and want to make it better but are unable to realize their vision.
- Conclude that no matter what they do, they cannot overcome an obstacle or make it better.

ENVISIONER PURPOSE AND HURT

Live a Fulfilling Life ⟷ *Lack of Satisfaction*

If you are an Envisioner, this is how the various facets of your mindset come together:

TRIGGER—VOID—HURT

If people resist progress and improvement (trigger), and if I do not bring my ideas and visions to life (void), then our lives will not be rich and fulfilling (hurt).

PRINCIPLE—PASSION—PURPOSE

If people take initiative to make improvements, make progress, and make things better (principle), and if I bring my ideas and visions to life (passion), then we can experience life as rich and fulfilling (purpose).

PURPOSE STATEMENT

My purpose is to bring my ideas and visions to life so that we can live rich and fulfilling lives.

THE HARMONIZER

"This world belongs to all of us, and all people should be able to live in respect and harmony."

—MICHELLE YEOH

Harmonizers are respectful and accepting of others' differences. Just as people are diverse, there is diversity all around us. Tropical rainforests, for example, are home to millions of different plants, trees, insects, birds, reptiles, and other animals. Within this complex and beautiful ecosystem, the varied organisms live in harmony and thrive among vast diversity. Like the rainforest ecosystem, Harmonizers believe we can be different but still support one another and coexist in peace.

Because harmony is so important to their sense of well-being, Harmonizers want others to feel comfortable. They strive to maintain harmony in their relationships and surroundings and are susceptible to taking on the role of a peacekeeper where there is disharmony. Conflict feels unbearable, so even minor misunderstandings are likely to disrupt their sleep until the problem is resolved.

Harmonizers are known for being a positive influence in the lives of others by bringing a smile to someone's face and making the world a brighter place. They are inspired to see good, do good, be good, and do things that make themselves and others feel good. They carry optimism, encouragement, and kindness throughout their sphere of influence. In doing so, Harmonizers bring peace to others and peace on earth.

HARMONIZER PRINCIPLE AND TRIGGER

Tolerant ←——————→ *Intolerant*

PRINCIPLE: TOLERANT

Harmonizers are tolerant of people different from themselves—they know we can have different needs and still support each other and live in harmony. Harmonizers:

- Work diligently to maintain social, emotional, and environmental harmony.
- Genuinely respect others, despite any differences.
- Are easygoing, personable, open-minded, inclusive, understanding, and tolerant of other beliefs and opinions.
- Value kindness, tranquility, loyalty, family, friends, relationships, and home, and aim to keep their lives calm, peaceful, and drama-free.

- Have strong social skills, a good sense of humor, and get along well with others.
- Seek respect for others, from others, and for themselves.
- Have a strong ability to read people and notice the slightest bit of disharmony, even amidst much harmony.
- Are highly perceptive of, and attentive to, the needs and feelings of others.
- Like clear expectations so everyone can do their part, which keeps their life clean, orderly, and balanced.
- Are good listeners who give people their full attention.
- Effectively and reliably fulfill their commitments.
- Are social, yet also highly task-oriented, self-motivated, and responsible.
- Follow through when they commit to a project, making it their focus and getting it done well with the utmost efficiency.
- Uphold their commitments to others and get projects done efficiently.
- Bring a calming presence to their relationships and surroundings.

TRIGGER: INTOLERANT

Harmonizers feel triggered when people:

- Are intolerant of people different from themselves.
- Present a dominating, my-way-or-the-highway attitude.
- Are biased, racist, prejudiced, discriminating, or unwilling to understand others.
- Disrespect or undermine them (for example, by rolling their eyes).

- Disrespect other people, animals, or the environment.
- Bully, treat others unkindly, or lack compassion and concern for others.
- Invalidate others' feelings or don't consider others' viewpoints.
- Talk over others or don't pay attention to what someone is saying (i.e., they don't listen).
- Lie about things big or small.
- Work against others rather than with them (for example, attacking, accusing, assuming, or blaming).
- Disregard established plans or rules, so things don't go as intended or they take longer than expected.
- Don't do their part or don't do what is expected of them.
- Make waves and instigate conflict.
- Push people's buttons.
- Unnecessarily upset the peace.

HARMONIZER PASSION AND VOID

Positively Influencing ⟵⟶ *Negatively Influencing*

PASSION: BEING A GOOD AND POSITIVE INFLUENCE IN THE WORLD

Harmonizers are motivated to:

- Be a positive influence and make a positive impact in others' lives.
- See good, do good, inspire good, and make others feel good.

- Bring joy and delight to their customers, family, friends, and others.
- Act on their humanitarian impulses (for example, volunteer to coach a youth baseball team or volunteer at the food bank).
- Do things that have a positive impact on themselves, others, nature, or the environment.
- Connect and stay connected with family and friends.
- Help others, work hard, and go the extra mile to ensure others are pleased and feel good.
- Express their gratitude and focus on the good in life.
- Give voice to those unable to speak for themselves: the young, elderly, disabled, animals, nature, or the environment.
- Find greater meaning in life, which may lead them to immerse themselves in an impactful, meaningful, or artistic project or to study a subject in depth.
- Witness another's satisfaction, progress, insight, healing, laughter, or delight.
- Do things that brighten others' days, practice random acts of kindness, or bring peace into others' lives.
- Laugh out loud, have a giggle fit, or laugh so hard they cry.
- Find alternative, more optimistic ways of looking at things when others voice complaints.
- Absorb themselves in the moment and feel at peace with everything around them.

When Harmonizers align with their passion, they shift:
an opportunity to be a positive influence
to having positively influenced someone.

VOID: NEGATIVITY

Harmonizers feel drained when they:

- Spend time around negative people.
- Went through the day and don't feel they've had a positive impact.
- Listen to people complain, gossip, focus on everything wrong, or spend time with people who throw pity parties and can't find anything good in life.
- Witness negativity in the world: unfairness, injustice, violence, or cruelty.
- Observe people mistreating other people, animals, nature, or the environment.
- See overly commercialized holidays have a negative influence on people.
- Do things that could have a negative impact on other people, animals, or the environment.
- Inadvertently hurt someone or cause someone to feel bad and can't fix it.
- Do something that causes conflict, misunderstanding, or upsets the peace.
- Lose sleep due to unresolved conflicts or misunderstandings in their life.
- Do something for themselves when it could have a negative impact on someone else.
- Don't feel they are being a positive influence within their family, work, team, or community.
- Are unsuccessful at making others feel good.
- See suffering around them but can't, or don't, do anything to make it better.
- Aren't contributing to good in some way.

HARMONIZER PURPOSE AND HURT

Feel Peace ⟷ *Lack Peace*

If you are a Harmonizer, this is how the various facets of your mindset come together:

TRIGGER—VOID—HURT

If people are disrespectful or intolerant of people different from them (trigger), and if I focus on the negative and do not have a positive influence on others or in the world (void), then we will experience conflict and lack a sense of peace and harmony (hurt).

PRINCIPLE—PASSION—PURPOSE

If people respect one another and coexist in harmony despite their differences (principle), and if I am a positive influence in people's lives and bring good into the world (passion), then we can experience peace within ourselves and peace on earth (purpose).

PURPOSE STATEMENT

My purpose is to do things that have a positive impact on others so that we can experience peace and harmony.

THE INQUISITOR

"Freedom without responsibility is like weight without gravity in physics—a logical impossibility."

—ROBERT C. SOLOMON

Inquisitors follow a "no-wake zone" approach to life. In boating, no-wake zones require boaters to slow down to a minimal speed so they don't erode the shoreline or endanger others. Once outside the no-wake zone, boaters are free to go fast and have fun. Similarly, Inquisitors assess situations and use common sense to do what is appropriate for the situation so they don't create waves. When driving through a neighborhood with kids at play, it makes sense to drive slowly. Once they're on the highway, they're free to go fast. Inquisitors don't want anything unnecessary holding them back and will restrain themselves if their actions will negatively impact others. To an Inquisitor, the world doesn't need more rules; it just needs people with more sensibility.

Inquisitors' happiness revolves around keeping life light and free flowing. Restrictive rules that limit them or their imagination suck the fun out of things. They'd much rather think outside of the box and pursue something original, like building an ant farm or going to Mars. For them, creative expansion is the name of the game. Regurgitating information that can easily be looked up bores them. They're driven to move beyond current limits and imagine new ways of doing things.

Inquisitors approach life with a childlike sense of wonder, openness, and delight. With many interests, they'll follow their strong sense of curiosity wherever it leads them, so much so, they sometimes feel like a grown-up kid, whatever their age. By constantly learning and being stimulated by fresh ideas, concepts, or technology, Inquisitors bring happiness to others and into the world.

INQUISITOR PRINCIPLE AND TRIGGER

Sensible ⟷ *Nonsensical*

PRINCIPLE: SENSIBLE

Inquisitors use common sense and sound reasoning to keep things feeling free flowing in nature. Inquisitors:

- Assess situations and act appropriately (i.e., if it could harm someone, don't do it; if it doesn't affect anyone else, go for it).
- Need things to make sense and ask "why?" if it doesn't.

- Are naturally responsible and capable, and expect themselves to use good judgment.
- Have a genuine concern for humanity and will go out of their way to help someone.
- Take care not to create waves for others.
- Are tactful, easygoing, and diplomatic with strong verbal and social skills.
- Know poor decisions come with consequences, so they avoid giving people a reason to limit them.
- Take care to be a good person and expect others to do the same (for example, if you break a glass, clean it up so no one gets hurt).
- Are friendly and cheerful, which often conceals their strong will and resilience—traits that are less apparent to others and only surface over time.
- Strive to keep things free flowing in nature, where people are free to think, imagine, dream, and have fun.
- Give people the latitude to do as they wish, assuming their actions don't infringe on others.
- Aren't big on rules overall but are fine with rules provided they make sense.
- Take things in stride and don't typically get upset over circumstances beyond their control.
- Wish to protect the endless possibilities responsible freedom affords them.
- Want people to be happy and free of unnecessary limitations.

TRIGGER: NONSENSICAL

Inquisitors feel triggered when people:

- Lack common sense or don't use their brain.
- Wrongfully limit or restrict people's freedom, ideas, imagination, creativity, fun, or happiness.
- Put artificial limits on others for arbitrary or non-predictive reasons.
- Set rules, restrictions, or limitations that are unnecessary, unwarranted, or don't make sense.
- Are deceitful and create waves for others or compromise someone's happiness for their own benefit.
- Don't take care of things themselves and consequently cause problems for others and negatively impact people's happiness.
- Claim there is only one right way to do something and force people to think small.
- Abuse their power or authority or play favorites.
- Are closed off to new ways of thinking and do things strictly by the book.
- Make across-the-board judgments.
- View others as inferior, less capable, less educated, or less worthy for irrelevant reasons.
- Put rules in place that do serve a purpose but don't enforce them when people don't follow them.
- Limit the Inquisitors' learning or limit their learning to what someone else deems important.
- Harm people or animals.
- Put blanket mandates in place based on things that don't matter (for example, requiring a college degree without considering applicants with exceptional talent).

INQUISITOR PASSION AND VOID

Push the Limits ⟷ *Do Boring Things*

PASSION: SUCCEEDING IN PUSHING THE LIMITS

Inquisitors are motivated to:

- Think outside the box and do cool things.
- Come up with original ideas and imagine new ways of doing things, asking, "How else can something be done?"
- Work hard at a challenge, see the fruits of their labor, and succeed in what they set out to do.
- Constantly learn and be stimulated by original concepts, brilliant ideas, uncommon quality, rare finds, or new technology.
- Think, problem solve, use their brain, figure out how things work, and pursue mental challenges and creative expansion.
- Push the limits, go beyond, defy the ordinary, and do things differently.
- See breakthroughs in technology or innovation where people have pushed the limits and leave them wondering "How is that even possible?"
- Be intrigued, amazed, fascinated, awe-inspired, and in wonder of things that stretch their mental limits.
- Experiment, explore, and learn about cool stuff, and enjoy feeling accomplished when something works (or keep working on it if it fails).

- Approach life with a childlike openness, inquisitiveness, and creativity, and pursue their many interests that pique their curiosity.
- Do things on their own and realize success, despite it being difficult (for example, succeed in achieving a goal, making someone happy, solving a problem, or completing an experiment).
- Make or create things and learn while doing it (and may find themselves in an unrelenting pursuit of something out of the ordinary).
- Socialize, make people happy, keep life interesting and fun, and share their interests, ideas, and discoveries with others.
- See infinite possibilities and ways of doing things.
- Bring joy and happiness into the world and to those they encounter.

When Inquisitors align with their passion, they shift:
an opportunity to push the limits
to having succeeded in pushing the limits.

VOID: DOING BORING, UNINTERESTING, OR ORDINARY THINGS

Inquisitors feel drained when they:

- Do pointless tasks, mundane work, or boring assignments.
- Are expected to be a regurgitator of information instead of an innovator (and consequently may be perceived as bright, yet find traditional school settings insufferable).

- Are restricted from using their imagination to do things in new or creative ways.
- Must do something in a prescribed fashion with no room to push the limits or think differently.
- Do things that are uninteresting, unchallenging, and unenjoyable, and are instead forced to think small and remain in the tight confines of uninspired rigidity.
- Feel someone they care about has lost faith in them.
- Do what's already been done, in the way it's always done, or do the same thing as everyone else.
- Are forced to do something or expected to complete non-urgent, boring tasks.
- Fall behind, then run the risk of having people upset with them.
- Can't explore new ways of doing things but must do things in an exacting way.
- Must memorize mundane facts they could easily look up.
- Are not successful in what they set out to do.
- Work on unexciting, unoriginal, outdated products or technology.
- Have to pick up others' slack and consequently must divert their attention away from advancing their own initiative or must compromise their fun.
- Sense that people are unhappy.
- Hang out with people who are boring and take life too seriously.

INQUISITOR PURPOSE AND HURT

Feel Happy ←——→ *Feel Unhappy*

If you are an Inquisitor, this is how the various facets of your mindset come together:

TRIGGER—VOID—HURT

If people lack common sense and put unnecessary rules and restrictions in place (trigger), and if I don't push the limits but do things that are boring, uninteresting, and ordinary (void), then we take the fun out of life and we will feel unhappy (hurt).

PRINCIPLE—PASSION—PURPOSE

If people use common sense and act appropriately for the situation (principle), and if I strive to push the limits and I succeed in what I set out to do (passion), then we can enjoy life and be happy (purpose).

PURPOSE STATEMENT

My purpose is to think outside of the box and succeed in pushing the limits so that we can enjoy life and be happy.

THE INTEGRATOR

"That which is not good for the beehive cannot be good for the bees."

—MARCUS AURELIUS

In the emergency room, triage nurses must quickly assess a patient's illness or injury and prioritize their care based on the seriousness of their condition. It's not first come, first served, but, rather, they provide assistance where it is needed most. Integrators approach life in a similar way. If someone is in need, they're likely to drop everything and help. Along with aiding others, they're also motivated to prioritize the many other areas of their life that are worthy of their attention, including friends, family, work, recreation, learning, and relaxation.

With a "triage" approach and mentality, Integrators are a rare breed who thrive under pressure. Whereas others may crumble under intense stress, Integrators are calm, focused, decisive, and productive. They're at their best when they are needed and have the skillset required to meet the need. With their attention drawn to the areas that are most urgent or exciting, Integrators are frequently pulled in many different directions. It's not uncommon for them to evolve into a jack of all trades, where they can use their vast knowledge and skills to fill gaps and contribute to the lives of others.

For Integrators, common decency is a basic life philosophy. Integrators seem to intuitively recognize that we are all part of a greater whole, which depends on everyone doing their part. Conversely, when people don't do their part, somebody else feels the burden. Integrators don't look for a single individual to carry the weight of the team; instead, they recognize everyone has strengths and is meant to pull their weight. The reward when we all contribute—when we all do our part—is that everyone can feel good and enjoy life.

INTEGRATOR PRINCIPLE AND TRIGGER

Decent ←——→ *Indecent*

PRINCIPLE: DECENT

Integrators demonstrate common decency by doing their part and being a contributing member of the team or society. Integrators:

- Expect everyone to carry their weight rather than having one person carry the team.

- Recognize we don't have to be all things to all people, but we each need to do our part to contribute to a healthy whole.
- Expect people to maintain minimum standards of common human decency.
- Are good listeners who respond objectively, without judgment, making people feel comfortable, understood, and at ease.
- Believe principles trump personal gain and simply want people to "be good humans."
- Respect social rules, etiquette, and norms, recognizing there is a right and a wrong way to behave.
- Listen to and apply constructive feedback, which makes them good and adaptable learners.
- Are personally responsible and self-sufficient.
- Are strong collaborators who are easygoing, enthusiastic, fun, nice, and work well with others.
- Are strong communicators who want to know what is expected of them and ensure others know what's expected of them too.
- Have a knack for bridging communications and being a "translator" of sorts by communicating information across disparate audiences to make things understandable.
- Are very accepting of people, provided they aren't hindering others.
- Readily adapt to change (more so than the average person) and take things in stride.
- See the good in people, recognizing individual strengths.
- Value integrity, fairness, honesty, and appreciation.

TRIGGER: INDECENT

Integrators feel triggered when people:

- Hinder others because they didn't do their part.
- Lack common human decency and, therefore, hinder the common good.
- Lack personal accountability and impede others by doing less than their fair share.
- Put more work on others because they didn't do their part.
- Are rude, arrogant, disrespectful, hypocritical, interrupting, unfriendly, cold, or make other people feel unimportant.
- Don't follow a basic code of conduct that everyone is expected to follow but, rather, act as if the rules don't apply to them.
- Don't communicate their expectations and instead act as though people are mind-readers, then get mad when people don't meet their objectives.
- Blindside them with negative feedback (for example, a manager waiting until a performance review to tell them about a problem).
- Repeat the same mistake again and again and don't learn from it.
- Don't contribute or are lazy, and are consequently drains on other people, teams, or society (for example, a roommate who doesn't help clean).
- Do things that are blatantly wrong or unprincipled (for example, lying, stealing, or not tipping well for good service).
- Are not team players and instead disrespect the people around them or do things at the expense of others.

- Are ungrateful for others' hard work when it benefits the collective.
- Don't do their part in a group project, then make others pick up their slack or cause the entire team to look bad or get a bad grade.
- Fail to do what is right for their age or ability and know better but just don't care.

INTEGRATOR PASSION AND VOID

High Priority or Interest ←——————→ *Low Priority or Interest*

PASSION: GIVING ATTENTION TO THINGS THAT MATTER MOST

Integrators are motivated to:

- Say yes to things that matter most and no to things that don't.
- Be a calming force in intense situations and be there for people when they need someone most.
- Do something of consequence by serving people in a way that makes a difference in their lives.
- Step up and step into action in moments of crisis when they have the training or capabilities to help.
- Prioritize family and friends, have a good time, hang out, stay up late to talk, laugh, make memories, and share experiences with people they enjoy spending time with.
- Help where they can help, add value, offer encouragement, lift people's spirits, and drop everything to help a friend in need (and are likely the one their friends call).

- Follow their excitement and enthusiasm wherever it leads them, and thus learn many things and tend to be quick learners.
- Have a variety of experiences, be pulled in many different directions, and develop a variety of skills, often resulting in them becoming a versatile jack of all trades and master of many.
- Explore a wide range of interests, which are likely to include adventurous activities where they can go fast, take chances, and enjoy moments of high intensity when they feel ultra-focused and calm.
- Introduce others to nontraditional ideas, exciting discoveries, or new ways of doing things that could make someone's life easier or better.
- Work in environments where there is external stimulation and then rise to the occasion and respond to urgent matters, finding they thrive under the pressure of a deadline, stress, or time constraints.
- Do what others can't or won't do (for example, working in high-stress situations).
- Enjoy their flexibility and downtime, which allows them to prioritize areas of their life that have been neglected or need their attention (for example, relaxation, adventure, family, or friends).
- Travel to a new place or enjoy a day at home where they have total freedom to choose how they're going to spend their entire day.
- Connect the dots, find the gaps, assess what is needed, and integrate disconnected or overlooked elements to make things whole and help others succeed (for example, by

building an integrated team that leverages the strength of each individual).
- Honor the natural ebbs and flows by "triaging" or prioritizing urgent matters, as well as creating space to prioritize the people, projects, and activities that are most important in life.

When Integrators align with their passion, they shift:
a priority that needs their help or attention
to a priority or need that has
received help or attention.

VOID: GIVING ATTENTION TO BORING OR INCONSEQUENTIAL TASKS

Integrators feel drained when they:

- Have to do things that are routine, repetitive, mundane, monotonous, or uninteresting.
- Work on boring projects, do the same thing day in and day out, or aren't excited about what they are doing.
- Feel like they are merely going through the motions but are not enjoying life.
- Don't feel their contributions are valued or appreciated.
- Work for a bad boss or a micromanager.
- Are thrown into situations and expected to do something when they don't feel they have the necessary capabilities required to be successful or don't have clear expectations of what success looks like.

- Don't have control over their schedule or freedom in how they go about their day (for example, being shackled to a desk working in a rigid nine-to-five environment).
- Overcommit themselves, because they were eager to help, and then find they don't have the flexibility to do the things they want to do.
- See people struggling or having a tough time and they aren't able to help them.
- Can't enjoy their flexibility and downtime because they are pulled back into work (i.e., no separation of work and leisure).
- Need to do something after the momentum has dissipated (or was never there, to begin with).
- Must do non-urgent, boring tasks "right now" for people who think their needs are more important than anything else.
- Don't feel they are doing things that are of consequence to anyone or anything.
- Do tasks they dread doing or do things they don't deem as important as other things in their life.
- Work in teams that make things far more complicated than they need to be.

INTEGRATOR PURPOSE AND HURT

Enjoy Life ⟵⟶ *Not Enjoy Life*

If you are an Integrator, this is how the various facets of your mindset come together:

TRIGGER—VOID—HURT

If people don't do their part but, rather, put the burden on others (trigger), and if I spend my time working on boring or inconsequential tasks (void), then we won't be free to enjoy life (hurt).

PRINCIPLE—PASSION—PURPOSE

If everyone does their part and contributes to the whole (principle), and if I prioritize my commitments and give my attention to the things that matter most (passion), then we will feel good and can enjoy life (purpose).

PURPOSE STATEMENT

My purpose is to give my attention to the things that matter most so that we can enjoy life.

THE INTUITOR

"Trust your Inner Guidance to reveal to you whatever it is you need to know."

—LOUISE HAY

Intuitors can uniquely see the underlying truth of a situation. With an extraordinarily strong intuition, Intuitors "know things" in a way that baffles others. Their intuitive discernment helps them recognize if the information being presented to them is truthful or merely a lie pedaled as truth. While these insights are obvious to them, Intuitors are used to being challenged by people who live by a seeing-is-believing mentality. Consequently, they often feel misunderstood when others don't understand their reality.

Intuitors are free-spirited and choose to follow their inner knowing, not the crowd. With a strong need to follow their inner guidance, Intuitors often avoid working in conventional hierarchical structures, which limit their freedom. It's draining for them to follow orders that go against their inner sense of knowing, whereas working for themselves allows them to focus on a task and let their inner knowing guide them. They readily perceive things unapparent to others, and since they're susceptible to a constant barrage of internal ideas and information, talking helps them process information and remember their abundant insights.

Intuitors are happiest when they go within, connect with source, and follow their inner guidance wherever it leads them. They honor their path and are motivated to help others do the same. Self-motivated and constantly striving to do greater and greater things in life, they often pursue their desires to support, advise, counsel, coach, heal, read, or guide others. In doing so, they fulfill their inner need to help themselves and others realize their potential.

INTUITOR PRINCIPLE AND TRIGGER

Insightful ←——→ *Blinded*

PRINCIPLE: INSIGHTFUL

Intuitors are extraordinarily intuitive and insightful, thus they can see into the truth of things. Intuitors:

- Can see the underlying truth of a situation.
- Have exceptionally strong intuitive prowess.
- Use their insights to avoid what needs to be avoided and get themselves into a good situation.
- Get a gut feel for things, which may be subtle or strong, and trust their inner sense of knowing.

- Can discern truth from illusion.
- Have a knack for seeing through lies, deception, and propaganda (and are often baffled how others don't see through the lies that are so obvious to them).
- Reveal truths unapparent to others, as if lifting the veil.
- Talk as a way of collecting and focusing their thoughts.
- Possess a strong ability to comprehend abstract concepts, ideas, and possibilities.
- Receive unconventional insights without judgment, often on the leading edge of new thought or psychology.
- Need to verbalize or write down their abundant ideas and insights or risk losing them.
- Know things in a way that baffles or doesn't make sense to others (and doesn't always make sense to the Intuitor, either).
- Can see the bigger picture and feel into situations, yet often feel misunderstood when others cannot see or understand the Intuitors' reality.
- Find the answers they seek within themselves.
- Are bright, quick-witted, discerning, idealistic, independent-thinking, strong-willed, high-energy, and free-spirited.

TRIGGER: BLINDED

Intuitors feel triggered when people:

- Challenge their intuitive insights and demand the Intuitor back up all statements with facts, evidence, and proof.
- Must see something to believe a thought or idea is real and not imagined.

- Respond to intuitive insights in a condescending fashion or act as if they are better than others.
- Don't use discernment but, rather, believe anything they are told if it comes from a person of authority or someone with credentials.
- Can't recognize the difference between a fact and a manmade belief and accept both as fact.
- Are tuned into the noise or group dogma while tuning out their inner voice.
- Won't believe the Intuitor or listen to them because they don't have facts to prove what they are saying (for example, not believing they shouldn't hire someone that the Intuitor knows has ill intentions).
- Blindly believe the lies being fed to them and can't see through the bull.
- Intentionally spew lies, propaganda, or ignorantly repeat lies they've been told.
- Listen to crazy information, allow themselves to be brainwashed, and can't see the deeper truth beyond what they read and hear.
- Belittle intuition if they don't trust their own intuition, implying their narrow method of understanding the world is superior.
- Reject the Intuitor's ideas and refuse to consider concepts that don't fit the reality they've bought into.
- Dismiss the Intuitor's insights and then get burned (for example, disregard a warning that a coworker is not trustworthy and then get taken advantage of).
- Are negative or drag themselves and others down instead of bettering themselves.
- Repeatedly go down the wrong path, make choices detrimental to themselves, or waste their potential.

INTUITOR PASSION AND VOID

Follow Inner Knowing ⟷ *Deny Inner Knowing*

PASSION: FOLLOWING THEIR INNER KNOWING

Intuitors are motivated to:

- Follow their inner knowing wherever it takes them (for example, creative pursuits, daring adventures, interesting classes, or meaningful interactions).
- Live freely in the moment, doing what they want, when they want, how they want, and with whom they want.
- Achieve their potential and help others see and unleash their infinite potential.
- Enjoy their freedoms of thought, action, ideas, insights, and choices.
- Relate to nature and take in and enjoy the sunshine, beauty, plants, animals, the wild, and the small joys of life.
- Allow inventions and ideas to come to them and enjoy the moments when a new idea crystalizes.
- Advise, counsel, coach, heal, read, or guide others, and help people find and pursue their path in life.
- Support others in moving toward a better, more truthful direction so they can honor their purpose.
- Help people break free from the bonds that hold them back from achieving their potential.
- Connect with their spiritual center and enjoy facing uncertainty (for example, by walking in the dark,

bringing an idea into reality, or traveling without an itinerary).
- Seek quiet, peaceful environments where they can meditate, go within, express gratitude, or appreciate the beauty that surrounds them.
- Connect to something greater than themselves, connect with abundant source, or connect to the spiritual world of oneness.
- Pursue work that is personally meaningful, which allows them to work for themselves, be in charge, or be in control of their part.
- Work in nonrestrictive environments where they can let life flow and trust the process.
- Dream big, help humanity, and make the world a better place.

When Intuitors align with their passion, they shift: an opportunity to follow their inner knowing *to* having followed their inner knowing.

VOID: DENYING THEIR INNER KNOWING

Intuitors feel drained when they:

- Take orders from controlling people or are expected to submit to others' directives.
- Waste energy gathering evidence to prove what they already know.
- Work in conventional hierarchical structures that limit their connection and freedom.

- Are obligated to do something a certain way or on someone else's terms and timelines.
- Do something that runs contrary to what they are internally led to do.
- Have people telling them what to do or think, expecting they will passively take orders.
- Deny their nature and instead try to fit a mold, do things in a conventional fashion, or be who others want them to be.
- See people living in fear, limiting themselves, or not honoring their gifts.
- Feel misunderstood for who they are and feel no one gets them.
- Can't turn their mind off and find that their thoughts get in the way of their connection.
- Do something they perceive could have a negative ripple effect in the world.
- Work in environments that are noisy, restricting, stressful, or rigid.
- Lack a sense of inner direction or lack the clarity they are seeking.
- Spend time with people attached to their victimhood who refuse to move onto a better path.
- Quit before they complete their mission, fail to accomplish what they set out to achieve, or feel they are falling short of their potential.

INTUITOR PURPOSE AND HURT

Realize Potential ←——→ *Not Realize Potential*

If you are an Intuitor, this is how the various facets of your mindset come together:

TRIGGER—VOID—HURT

If people lack insight and don't see into the truth of things but rely solely on what they see and hear (trigger), and if I follow others rather than following what I am internally led to do (void), then we will not realize our potential or be the best we can be (hurt).

PRINCIPLE—PASSION—PURPOSE

If people are insightful and see into the truth of situations and people (principle), and if I follow my inner knowing (passion), then we can realize our potential and see our greatness (purpose).

PURPOSE STATEMENT

My purpose is to follow my inner knowing so that we can realize our potential.

THE OBSERVER

"The quest for meaning is the key to mental health and human flourishing."

—VIKTOR E. FRANKL

Observers care deeply about other people and how decisions impact them, so they work diligently to ensure they don't negatively impact anyone downstream. They gather information, listen to varied perspectives, and objectively weigh all data available to them. Being objective allows them to take their own emotions and biases out of a decision so they can do what is right for others who may be impacted. Unsurprisingly, Observers generally come across to others as level-headed.

Along with being thoughtful of the impact of their decisions, Observers are motivated to do things that positively impact others. To make sure people have everything they need, Observers are thorough and comprehensive. You can expect they've run every scenario through their mind and covered all the bases to be certain their work is complete. They loathe being misunderstood, so their communications are detailed and well thought out.

Observers' sense of self-worth comes from doing something meaningful. For them, everything has a purpose. They want their actions to mean something or to positively impact someone. For this reason, it's not enough for Observers to merely know something; it's important to apply it in a way that provides a beneficial impact. It's common for them to be constantly problem-solving in their head, and they may struggle to turn off their brain. By doing things well and making a meaningful impact, Observers ensure others have what they need to thrive.

OBSERVER PRINCIPLE AND TRIGGER

Thoughtful ←——————→ *Rash*

PRINCIPLE: THOUGHTFUL

Observers take care to make wise and thoughtful decisions. Observers:

- Are responsible decision-makers who consider the downstream impact of their decisions and actions.
- Possess highly developed powers of observation, noticing details others miss.
- Possess a superior ability to gather, collect, and analyze information.
- Process from a detached, unbiased, unemotional, and logical perspective.

- Care a great deal about others and take them into account, putting in the extra effort to ensure they consider varied viewpoints and do what's right.
- Do their due diligence so they can make informed decisions that will positively impact others.
- Want complete information and the whole story, but once the facts are in, they want to make a decision rather than sit on the fence.
- Are highly observant and thoughtful of the world around them.
- Obtain information and conscientiously apply it so they can positively impact themselves or others (for example, choosing to not eat fast food after learning about negative impacts on health).
- Listen intently and are actively engaged, even if they are not speaking.
- Take in and utilize all information and perspectives available to them and ask, "What did they mean by that?"
- Tend to be even-keeled, proper, tactful, and seldom give way to anger, though they can be intense and will vigorously defend a strongly held position.
- Give things forethought and planning, carefully deliberating over problems before arriving at a decision.
- Play out various scenarios in their mind, thinking about every angle to see how things might unfold in the future.
- Freely take in new information without judging or censoring it and are willing to make changes to ensure the best outcome.

TRIGGER: RASH

Observers feel triggered when people:

- Make rash decisions that could have a negative downstream impact.
- Bulldoze others and run people over to get their way.
- Don't care enough to do their due diligence or do things well, even when their choices and actions affect other people.
- Jump to conclusions and make uninformed, irrational, emotionally driven decisions.
- Don't do what's right and instead do what's good for themselves.
- Care about their own self-serving biases and don't seem to care about others.
- Hurt others because they didn't bother to be thorough and diligent.
- Miss obvious details resulting in foolish mistakes.
- Refuse insights because they believe they already know everything.
- Cannot be reasoned with and are instead dogmatic and refuse to consider perspectives that challenge their fixed opinions.
- Shut out information, feedback, and perspectives that could be valuable.
- Won't change their direction, even when it's the right thing to ensure the best outcome.
- Talk over others, talk "at" others, put words in people's mouths, or won't give people a chance to share their perspective.
- Rush important decisions, despite a lack of information or the possibility of making a poor choice that negatively impacts others.

- Delay decisions when they have all the necessary information and authority.

OBSERVER PASSION AND VOID

Meaningful Impact ←——————→ *Lack Impact*

PASSION: BEING EFFECTIVE IN HAVING A MEANINGFUL IMPACT

Observers are motivated to:

- Be effective in achieving their objective, making things better, or having a meaningful impact on someone or something.
- Identify and solve meaningful problems, come up with great solutions, fix things, organize things, or bring order to chaos.
- Do things exceptionally well and in doing so, make something better for someone else or positively impact others.
- Do things thoroughly and completely to ensure people have everything they need (for example, writing an email that is as complete as possible).
- Prioritize people and relationships and their impact on others.
- Do things with a purpose (i.e., if I do "this," then I can positively impact "that").
- Work independently behind the scenes to make things easier, better, efficient, or enjoyable.
- Ask, "How can we do things better?" and then give attention to details that can improve circumstances for others.

- Self-reflect and continually work on improving themselves and making themselves better.
- Make things understandable and thoroughly explain things so that people will "get it."
- Make comprehensive processes, protocols, and frameworks that have factored in all the details and provide people with everything they need.
- Make it easy for people to learn things, be prepared, make good decisions, and do things well.
- Strive for an ideal, recognizing there is an ideal of what something could be, and try to figure out how to achieve that desired outcome (for example, ideal health).
- Engage in worthwhile pursuits that can improve people's lives or impact others in a meaningful way.
- See evidence they are having a positive or meaningful impact on themselves or others (for example, they progressed in a sport, or someone feels happy because of their actions).

When Observers align with their passion, they shift: an opportunity to make a meaningful impact *to* having made a meaningful impact.

VOID: NOT HAVING A MEANINGFUL IMPACT

Observers feel drained when they:

- Don't feel they are being effective or having a meaningful impact on anyone or anything.
- Are misunderstood (and therefore cannot be effective).

- Work on tasks or projects that are ambiguous, vague, ill-defined, or lack a clear objective.
- Can't have the desired impact because they don't know what they're trying to achieve, so they waste time spinning their wheels.
- Aren't successful in getting their point across, or people don't understand them.
- Spend time doing repetitive tasks or busy work that doesn't make anything better.
- Inadvertently hurt someone (for example, giving well-intentioned feedback to help someone improve, but seeing the recipient perceive it as hurtful instead of helpful).
- See people settle rather than strive for an ideal that is within their reach.
- Don't have what's required to solve a problem, be effective, or make a meaningful impact.
- Aren't fixing, problem-solving, improving, or making anything better.
- Feel impeded from doing anything meaningful or productive (for example, a guidance counselor who is assigned to work with far too many students).
- Are given incomplete information, which requires them to fill in the holes themselves to have everything they need.
- Work with people who don't see the value in a complete protocol or thorough deliverable, despite people not having what they need to be successful.
- Have a great solution, but people aren't willing to listen, so they can't make an impact.
- See a problem that is hurting people, but they can't do anything about it.

OBSERVER PURPOSE AND HURT

Have What You Need ←——→ *Needs Are Not Met*

If you are an Observer, this is how the various facets of your mindset come together:

TRIGGER—VOID—HURT

If people make poor decisions and don't consider the impact of their actions (trigger), and if I don't do things that have a meaningful impact (void), then we won't get our needs met, and we will be hurt (hurt).

PRINCIPLE—PASSION—PURPOSE

If people use information wisely and consider the downstream impact of their decisions (principle), and if I am effective in making a positive and meaningful impact (passion), then we will have what we need to flourish in life (purpose).

PURPOSE STATEMENT

My purpose is to have a meaningful and positive impact so that we will have what we need to flourish in life.

THE OPTIMIZER

"An investment in knowledge always pays the best interest."

—BENJAMIN FRANKLIN

Optimizers are often known for their strong, active minds. With an inquiring nature, they pursue interests and careers that allow them to put their knowledge into action. They are intellectually oriented and want to do things right, so they gather information in detail. While they are especially good at abstract analysis, they're also imaginative and artistic. In a desire to apply their knowledge, Optimizers tend to think in less conventional and more creative ways than most.

For Optimizers, it's extremely important that people be truthful and do what is right, which also means not causing harm. Consequently, they're inscrutably honest, articulate, and conscientious in whatever they undertake. They uphold a standard of moral ethics and expect themselves and others to take accountability for their words and actions. In their need to honor truth, Optimizers can occasionally come across as cold or mentally defiant. While their intention is not to be antagonistic, their tone stems from their genuine concern for others and a desire to protect people from the harms of deception.

Optimizers hold a wide range of interests and enjoy investigating a variety of topics with adept resourcefulness and lively curiosity. They're motivated to make the unknown known, thus are eager to acquire and share knowledge. With their innate perseverance and tenacity, they effectively apply themselves and can resolve the most intricate problems they may encounter. Optimizers often carry a need to find their personal direction and to make an impact on humanity. When armed with a clear direction or novel idea, they pursue their objective with such focus and intensity that progress is all but guaranteed.

OPTIMIZER PRINCIPLE AND TRIGGER

Truthful ⟵⟶ *Untruthful*

PRINCIPLE: TRUTHFUL

Optimizers know the value of doing things right and being truthful, honest, and factual. Optimizers:

- Stand for truth and are likely to challenge or question those who make false claims or say absurd things.
- Recognize there is great power in truth and great danger in deception.

- Do what they say and say what they mean.
- Are honest in their actions and spoken word and expect the same from others.
- Treat people with respect and genuinely care about other people and humanity.
- Are thorough, meticulous, and take care to do things with precision and accuracy.
- Believe language matters, so they are articulate, factual, and technically precise in their speech.
- Consume information and remember details with remarkable precision.
- Gather information, research extensively, and do their homework to avoid mistakes and ensure the quality of their work and word.
- Back up their recommendations and claims with cited resources, data, facts, and evidence.
- Are analytical, objective, and investigative while also being respectful, intuitive, and imaginative.
- Know the value of doing things right and doing the right thing.
- Strive to operate at the highest possible level and apply themselves conscientiously to whatever they undertake.
- Seek absolute truth and believe in speaking, depicting, and relaying what is real and true.
- Strive to be courteous and the kind of person other people want to be around.

TRIGGER: UNTRUTHFUL

Optimizers feel triggered when people:

- Present untruths or make baseless claims that can't be backed up.
- Do or say things that have the potential to cause harm.
- Do whatever they want and don't take accountability for their words, actions, or decisions.
- Lie or deceive with an intent to mislead or hurt another.
- Don't have a standard of ethics but are unethical, evil, cruel, abusive, malevolent, or dangerous, putting others at risk.
- Make assertions that are patently false and have no facts or evidence to support them.
- Regurgitate lies, spread garbage information, make absurd statements, present adulterated information, repeat false dogma, or are purposefully obscure.
- Make mistakes or poor decisions that could cause harm to others.
- Rush decisions without gathering information and instead follow their whims and hunches without considering potential downstream consequences.
- Manipulate data and statistics to tell a story that works in their favor rather than telling the truth.
- Do horrible things if they can get away with it (for example, hurting a segment of the population so they can personally benefit).
- Give people bad information, make things up as they go, or tell someone what to do when they haven't done their homework.
- Change their tune based on whom they are talking to, saying what they think others want to hear rather than speaking the truth.
- Don't care about other people or pretend to care when their actions suggest otherwise (i.e., they're phony).
- Use language to mistreat or mislead people.

OPTIMIZER PASSION AND VOID

Transferring Knowledge ⟷ *Not Transferring Knowledge*

PASSION: TRANSFERRING KNOWLEDGE

Optimizers are motivated to:

- Investigate a variety of topics that appeal to their inquiring nature and active mind.
- Share knowledge with others and witness the moment when the light bulb comes on and someone suddenly connects the dots, seeing what they did not previously see.
- Use their intellect and creativity to come up with novel ideas and solutions.
- Take in large quantities of information and distill it into a tangible form that can be shared with others.
- Follow their urge to acquire knowledge, learn something new, and reveal what was previously unknown.
- Transfer knowledge, whether they are acquiring knowledge themselves (for example, through tinkering, experimenting, researching, or observing) or sharing knowledge with others (for example, through teaching, podcasting, writing, or lecturing).
- Come up with and test new ideas or ways of doing something, learn from attempts that don't work, and remain committed to their pursuit.
- Not give up when something doesn't work but instead persist, try new ideas, and get excited about each new test.

- Explore novel ideas and learn through their experiences.
- Tune into the needs of those around them and provide information and solutions that are beneficial to others.
- Discover the optimal way to do something through research, interviews, or experimentation (for example, the best way to solve a problem or learn a skill).
- Do hard things, figure out what others cannot, reveal truths, right wrongs, and put their knowledge and skills to good use.
- Add knowledge or make contributions to other people or in their field (for example, in science, medicine, law, poker, comedy, journalism, music, film, etc.).
- Do great things, leave their mark on the world, delight others, or use their gifts to make a difference to humankind however they can.
- Find their direction and then move forward in that direction, making progress toward their goal.

When Optimizers align with their passion, they shift:
an opportunity to learn or
share knowledge presently unknown
to having transferred knowledge
that was previously unknown.

VOID: NOT TRANSFERRING KNOWLEDGE

Optimizers feel drained when they:

- Work hard at something but don't feel like they're making any forward progress.

- Are restricted from sharing knowledge that would be beneficial to others (or hurtful if not shared).
- Lose rank or standing, flounder in their position, move in the wrong direction, or feel stuck.
- Are interrupted when focused on their pursuit and must stop what they are doing.
- Do the same thing over and over when it won't move anything forward (for example, cleaning something when you know it's going to just get dirty again).
- Continually churn information in their brain without applying or testing their ideas.
- Don't have a clear sense of where they're going, what they're trying to achieve, or what the "right" direction for them is.
- Share monumental information with people who fail to see its significance or are unwilling to stretch their mental capabilities.
- Engage with individuals or audiences that don't want to listen to them or don't understand, trust, or believe them.
- Have to figure out what to make for dinner at the end of a mentally exhausting day.
- Regurgitate the same information or innovations rather than learning or discovering novel information or creative solutions.
- Do something they feel would cause them to appear stupid or could hurt innocent people.
- Feel trapped in a situation that feels unrecoverable or hopeless.
- Do something that could have unfavorable consequences or leave a negative mark on their own or someone else's life.
- Don't feel their above-and-beyond efforts are valued.

OPTIMIZER PURPOSE AND HURT

Move Forward ←——→ *Move Back*

If you are an Optimizer, this is how the various facets of your mindset come together:

TRIGGER—VOID—HURT

If people do or say things that have the potential to cause harm to others (trigger), and if I don't explore novel ideas or acquire and share knowledge (void), then we will move in an unfavorable direction (hurt).

PRINCIPLE—PASSION—PURPOSE

If people are truthful and take accountability for their words, actions, and decisions (principle), and if I explore novel ideas and acquire and share knowledge (passion), then we can move forward in a worthwhile direction (purpose).

PURPOSE STATEMENT

My purpose is to explore novel ideas and acquire and share knowledge so that we can move forward in a worthwhile direction.

THE PATHFINDER

"Give a man a fish, and you feed him for a day. Teach a man to fish, and you feed him for a lifetime."

—CHINESE PROVERB

Dogs earn their distinction as man's best friend due to their unselfish and loyal nature. People, in contrast, will too often vie to get ahead at the cost of others. Pathfinders would much prefer to follow the example of our furry friends and act in ways that benefit others. More giving than taking, they are known for being there through thick and thin. They help because it is the right thing to do, not because they are angling to get something out of it for themselves.

Pathfinders approach the world with a "we" versus "me" attitude. For them, it's about the family, team, or community. You can always count on them to carry out their duties and obligations, as they would never want to make things more difficult for someone else. And while they contribute a lot, they're extraordinarily humble. They don't like to toot their own horn; they prefer their actions to speak for themselves—to be known by their fruits. Some people proclaim how wonderful they are, despite their words not being backed by action. Pathfinders, in contrast, demonstrate who they are through their actions, without needing to tell people about it.

While Pathfinders are kind and considerate, they are also tough and resilient. Their independent nature stems from their inner motivation to be self-sufficient, self-reliable, and self-competent. They not only master these abilities themselves but also share their knowledge and skills to strengthen others. By passing on knowledge from one person—and generation—to the next, Pathfinders unify life.

PATHFINDER PRINCIPLE AND TRIGGER

Beneficial ←——————→ *Mistreating*

PRINCIPLE: BENEFICIAL

Pathfinders are generous and considerate, and act in ways that are beneficial to others. Pathfinders:

- Are exceptionally reliable, dependable, and loyal.
- Responsibly do their part, carry their weight, and uphold their commitments.
- Show respect, compassion, and kindness toward others.
- Bring a "we" versus "me" mentality to their work and interactions.

- Give generously of their time, effort, and resources, helping others if it is beneficial to the recipient or group.
- Do for others, without an expectation of getting something in return or worrying about whether someone deserves it.
- Contribute to the welfare of others in practical ways, helping when it's the right thing to do.
- Are known for being there through thick and thin, willing to help and make life less difficult for someone else.
- Selflessly put the needs of others ahead of their interests and wish for others to act similarly (and consequently may just find they like dogs more than people).
- Show compassion and sensitivity to those who may be going through a difficult time.
- Give people the benefit of the doubt, recognizing we don't know the full picture of what's going on in someone's life.
- Give credit where credit is due and celebrate the team before themselves.
- Consider how their actions affect others and act with others' interests in mind.
- Work as a team and strive to win as a team.
- Are modest and let their actions speak for themselves.

TRIGGER: MISTREATING

Pathfinders feel triggered when people:

- Are self-serving or "me" centric.
- Use or mistreat others to meet their own selfish desires.

- Make themselves look good, even if it comes at others' expense (for example, by taking all the credit for something that was a group effort).
- Use their position of power to take advantage of others.
- Use people or prey on people's kindness and generosity.
- Don't bother to say "thanks" when people go out of their way to help them.
- Don't do their part, or don't proactively ask for help if they need it, and then cause the entire team to fail.
- Expect people to help them but don't offer assistance when others need them.
- Help others only if there is something in it for them.
- Hoard information or resources that would be valuable to others or the team.
- Are belittling, mean, rude, condescending, or otherwise cause people to feel alone and unsupported.
- Get others to take the fall for their mistake.
- Act as if their needs are more important than everyone else's.
- Contribute the least and expect the best or most.
- Discount others' ideas, talk down to people, or talk over people to make sure their voice is heard above everyone else.

PATHFINDER PASSION AND VOID

Self-Sufficient ⟵⟶ *Not Self-Sufficient*

PASSION: STRENGTHENING THEMSELVES AND OTHERS

Pathfinders are motivated to:

- Teach people how to fish—help others develop life skills and be self-sufficient.
- Develop practical skills so they can be self-sufficient and independently competent.
- Strengthen themselves through learning, skill development, physical activity, creative pursuits, or healthy practices.
- Take an active interest in the success of others (for example, a client, student, team, or business).
- Face challenges and demonstrate strength, courage, grit, resilience, toughness of spirit, and strength of character (i.e., being comfortable with being uncomfortable).
- Lay the groundwork, provide a solid foundation, and pave a path to help others turn the corner, grow as a person, or succeed.
- Disseminate information that supports others to become more capable, competent, and confident.
- Patiently support others' development in practical ways, giving people the space to make mistakes and learn in their own way.
- Lead and serve in ways that strengthen their family, team, customers, community, or country.
- Help others learn and grow (taking a noninvasive approach) and enjoy the opportunity to get better along with them.
- Teach, mentor, and plant the seeds to support positive transformation.

- Put things together so they flow, ensuring events or processes are fully functional and firing on all cylinders.
- Cultivate relationships, build community, bring people together, offer encouragement, have fun, and facilitate supportive connections.
- See their children, students, peers, employees, or acquaintances learn, grow, flourish, thrive, or witness their dreams come true.
- Unify life by passing on skills and knowledge that can flow from one generation to the next.

When Pathfinders align with their passion, they shift:
struggling at something or
not yet being self-sufficient
to being independently competent,
self-sufficient, and thriving.

VOID: NOT STRENGTHENING THEMSELVES OR OTHERS

Pathfinders feel drained when they:

- Hand someone a fish without teaching them how to fish—give people the answer while knowing the recipient didn't learn anything and will need to consult others for the answer in the future.
- Support others but don't see evidence they are making any progress.
- Teach, help, or support people who refuse to learn.

- Work in unsupportive environments, where people don't contribute to one another's success.
- See people lay down in defeat, even when given encouragement and support.
- Implement inadequate solutions that could create future problems for others.
- Are doing useless busy work, following illogical or inefficient processes, or not contributing to something meaningful.
- Are expected to do something that goes against what they believe is the right thing to do (for example, selling a product to a customer when they don't believe it will be beneficial).
- Help someone who takes their assistance for granted.
- Fail themselves or feel they have failed someone else.
- Can't do something on their own or are unable to master a skill.
- Watch people claim to "help" by pointing out someone's flaws and ultimately do more harm than good.
- Are sick, injured, or otherwise not self-sufficient.
- Focus all their energy on others while doing nothing to strengthen or support themselves.
- Recognize that the people who need help are not willing to help themselves.

PATHFINDER PURPOSE AND HURT

Feel Supported ⟷ *Feel Unsupported*

If you are a Pathfinder, this is how the various facets of your mindset come together:

TRIGGER—VOID—HURT

If people mistreat others so they can serve their selfish desires (trigger), and if I don't do things that strengthen myself or others (void), then we will not feel supported but, rather, will feel alone or hurt (hurt).

PRINCIPLE—PASSION—PURPOSE

If people are generous, giving, and act in ways that benefit others (principle), and if I do things to strengthen myself and the people around me (passion), then we will feel supported and know we are not alone (purpose).

PURPOSE STATEMENT

My purpose is to do things to strengthen myself and the people around me so that we can feel supported.

THE PERCEIVER

"People don't want to be talked out of their feelings. People want to be heard, seen, felt, and understood."

—RACHEL SAMSON

Perceivers are highly attuned to other people and their feelings, so much so that it often seems as if they have a radar that extends much further than others. Highly intuitive and discerning, they use their feelings to understand and connect with others, life, and the world around them. They care deeply about relationships and others' existence, so it's important to them that people feel seen, heard, understood, and appreciated. Consequently, they're good listeners who are attentive to others.

Perceivers balance their emotional acuity with their strong intellect. They are lifelong learners (and teachers) whose interests tend to be a bit ahead of the curve. Expansion—intellectually, spiritually, or emotionally—is essential in their lives, and pursuing their curiosities allows them to expand their horizons. They're stimulated by personal growth and need variety and change to gain new life experiences. Since expansion is essential in their lives, feelings of being restricted or held back become strong motivations for change.

As free-spirits, Perceivers are typically a bit unconventional in their thinking and are rarely bound by tradition. Altruistic, imaginative, and idealistic, they're apt to daydream about what they'd like to have happen or about various "what-ifs" that could lead to a more-ideal world. With high standards and a strong desire to do things right, Perceivers are extremely capable and generally achieve whatever they set out to accomplish.

PERCEIVER PRINCIPLE AND TRIGGER

Caring  *Oblivious*

PRINCIPLE: CARING

Perceivers genuinely care about people and how others feel. Perceivers:

- Are highly attuned to others' feelings and care deeply about others' existence.
- Show care and concern for all life: people, animals, plants, birds, fish, etc.
- Have strong subtle awareness and feel things, including others' feelings of which others are unaware.
- Use their feelings as a tool to connect with and understand others and life around them (i.e., as if telepathic).
- Sense incongruence in others, such as knowing there is more to the story than what is said.
- Make win-win choices that consider everyone involved.

- Maintain peaceful environments, being mindful of their effect on others and their surroundings.
- Tune into and connect with others.
- Listen attentively and give caring attention so people feel acknowledged.
- Are uniquely able to connect with the essence of life and others.
- Consider the needs of all, not some, and serve overlooked or underserved demographics.
- Foster environments where people feel seen, heard, felt, and appreciated.
- Hold high standards and self-expectations, with a need to do things right.
- Are respectful, thoughtful, compassionate, intuitive, altruistic, sensitive, and vigilant.
- Value relationships, harmony, listening, home, peace, and genuine connections with others.

TRIGGER: OBLIVIOUS

Perceivers feel triggered when people:

- Lack any awareness or concern for others.
- Don't care about how others feel.
- Lack care and compassion for other people and life in general.
- Are oblivious to others and their needs.
- Treat living things like they don't matter.
- Think small and don't consider others (for example, someone who takes two pieces of cake which causes others to go without).
- Only care about their success and are oblivious to others.

- Don't seem to notice or care about their adverse impact on others or their surroundings (for example, leaving a shopping cart in the middle of a parking lot).
- Are disconnected from life and other people.
- Are out of touch with the people around them and what they are feeling.
- Don't stand up for someone who is being unfairly criticized.
- Disrespect performers by being loud and inattentive.
- Have no awareness of how they are intruding on others' space (for example, by wearing heavy cologne or playing loud music).
- Are cruel, heartless, inhumane, hurtful, callous, condescending, selfish, or disrespectful.
- Take advantage of others or do whatever is good for them, even if it hurts someone else.

PERCEIVER PASSION AND VOID

Expanding Horizons ←——→ *Not Expanding*

PASSION: EXPANDING HORIZONS

Perceivers are motivated to:

- Be lifelong learners and learn about many things.
- Teach and share their knowledge and expansive wisdom with others.
- Be curious and ask the questions no one is asking or no one has answered, including big, existential life questions.
- Learn from others who are ahead-of-the-curve and

ahead-of-their-time, gathering everything they can on a new subject until they fully understand it.

- Expand horizons, their own and others, by elevating people's perspectives and expanding awareness.
- Be of service to others and have a positive impact on the lives of others.
- Learn from their life experiences, recognizing personal challenges as an opportunity to expand and grow.
- Witness moments of enlightenment when the light bulb goes off in someone's mind and they suddenly see what they did not previously see.
- Bring beauty, delight, and understanding into the world.
- Follow their artistic and creative instincts and come up with novel ways of doing things.
- Create warm environments conducive to learning, connecting, and conversing.
- Act on their humanitarian instincts and follow their free-spirited, idealistic inspirations.
- Explore unconventional ideas and solutions that address unmet needs or discover ways to serve overlooked populations.
- Help people experience insight, freedom, or relief by broadening their minds, expanding their thinking, or shifting their perspective.
- Satiate their thirst for knowledge by venturing out into the world, applying their learning in their own life, and returning with greater insight and knowledge.

When Perceivers align with their passion, they shift:
an opportunity to expand
their own or another's awareness
to having expanded their own or another's awareness.

VOID: NOT LEARNING, GROWING, OR EXPANDING

Perceivers feel drained when they:

- Do mundane, repetitive, or monotonous tasks.
- Are stuck doing conventional, boring jobs or tasks.
- Are serving populations that are already overserved.
- Do unoriginal things that benefit the masses while others' needs go neglected.
- Do what everyone else is doing, or do the same thing they've been doing, and are no longer growing.
- Follow the crowd while ignoring their innermost inspirations.
- Do things that feel frivolous and don't serve anyone.
- Work in restrictive environments that limit creativity, innovation, and unconventional thinking.
- Spend time with people who are small-minded and refuse to expand their thinking (for example, people with a victim mentality who believe there is no point in trying to make a change).
- Are unable to get through to people.
- Do something that doesn't make any difference, leaving them to wonder, *What's the point?*
- Feel trapped in the uninformed darkness of ignorance.
- Feel restricted by present-day realities or doubt their capacity as one person to make a difference in a big-world problem.
- Are bogged down in hierarchical administrative requirements.
- Repeat the past by doing what they've already done.

PERCEIVER PURPOSE AND HURT

Feel Valued ⟷ *Not Feel Valued*

If you are a Perceiver, this is how the various facets of your mindset come together:

TRIGGER—VOID—HURT

If people are oblivious to others and don't care about others' feelings (trigger), and if I rely on conventional wisdom and don't expand my own or others' thinking (void), then we will not feel seen, understood, or valued, and we will not feel like we matter (hurt).

PRINCIPLE—PASSION—PURPOSE

If people are attentive and tuned into others and care about how others feel (principle), and if I expand my horizons and help others do the same (passion), then we will feel seen, understood, valued, and know that we matter (purpose).

PURPOSE STATEMENT

My purpose is to expand my horizons and help others do the same so that we feel seen and understood and know that we matter.

THE PRODUCER

"Fail to plan, plan to fail."

—WINSTON CHURCHILL

Producers keep their eyes on the prize while, at the same time, clearing a path to achieve their goal. Whether running errands, going on a vacation, or leading a project of major proportion, Producers connect the big picture and the details to ensure all runs smoothly. Armed with a plan, Producers maintain sight of their end goal and don't stop until they get there.

Producers' tenacious spirit occasionally comes across to others as being confrontational. Though they are friendly and social, their intensity is motivated by their need to button up the details, get results, and get things done. Harmony is essential to Producers, yet harmony, for them, depends upon everything running smoothly. Conflict is agonizing and can be averted when things get done right. They'd prefer everyone work together and get along, so they're apt to redirect contentious conversations to something less controversial, such as refocusing on the overarching objective.

Producers feel most motivated when they are making a significant impact or adding value to others. Consequently, they thrive on helping others, especially those they respect and enjoy. With their natural ability to plan, organize, and execute, Producers excel in managing large projects or running events. With a strong mental focus, they are good at figuring things out and resolving challenging tasks, especially when others view the task as impossible, or next to it. By being an asset to others, Producers help people experience a sense of security in knowing that things will work out.

PRODUCER PRINCIPLE AND TRIGGER

PRINCIPLE: EFFECTIVE

Producers are tenacious doers who get results and get things done. Producers:

- Map out their plan and then clear the path to effectively accomplish their objectives.
- Successfully carry out projects and plans.
- Tend to be extraordinarily responsive, replying promptly to texts and emails to give people the information they need.
- Keep the big picture in mind and then dig into the details required to achieve the desired outcome.
- Want to know that the details have been accounted for so they can feel confident that a solid plan is in place and things work out.

- Organize plans, remove barriers, and lay out the steps needed to get from "here" to "there."
- Demonstrate tenacity by sticking with projects until they achieve the desired result.
- Focus on getting the right things done and getting things done right so things work out.
- Tend to ask a lot of questions so they can remove ambiguity and ensure they have the necessary information to develop and execute an effective plan.
- Err on the side of overcommunication, with a desire to create clarity and make things understandable at all levels.
- Excel at managing large projects, running events, and simplifying communications to unite everyone in working together harmoniously.
- Are friendly and seek harmony yet may come across as intense or intimidating in their need to obtain information and get things done.
- Act resourcefully and figure out how to get things accomplished (for example, finding their way around the red tape that gets in the way of selling the largest deal in the company's history).
- Like to finish projects ahead of a deadline when working on initiatives that involve others so they can feel secure in knowing all will run smoothly.
- Start with the end in mind and maintain a clear vision of what success looks like.

TRIGGER: INEFFECTIVE

Producers feel triggered when people:

- Under-communicate or fail to share information or plans necessary to get things done.
- Are not responsive or don't provide requested information when time is of the essence or when the information is necessary to move things forward.
- Think they're right but they're wrong.
- Don't communicate (for example, they don't let someone know when they don't do what they said they would do).
- Don't think they'll hit their target, so they just set their goal lower rather than making a plan to meet the original goal.
- Fail to communicate problems or issues that need to be aired so they can be addressed and instead claim all is well when it is not.
- Are not focused on the outcome and instead lose sight of what's most important, and spend time working on unessential tasks that don't move the needle any closer to the desired result.
- Only focus on their little sliver of responsibility and don't connect the dots to work toward achieving the overarching objective (i.e., they can't see the forest through the trees).
- Don't carry their weight and count on others to pick up their slack.
- Waste people's time or cause others to be unproductive (for example, they don't do what they should have already done, so people need to micromanage them).
- Are in a leadership role but fail to clearly articulate the objective or keep moving the target.
- Focus on activities or metrics that don't get results.
- Don't get results because they're too busy building processes

or attending training rather than doing their job (i.e., they don't focus on the right things).

- Act in counterproductive ways that negatively impact outcomes (for example, they complain rather than work toward a solution).
- Don't get their part done and consequently place outcomes at risk or cause things to not run smoothly.

PRODUCER PASSION AND VOID

Adding Value ←——————→ *Not Adding Value*

PASSION: ADDING VALUE AND HAVING AN IMPACT

Producers are motivated to:

- Be an invaluable asset to people and projects.
- Take on big assignments or projects that add value to others.
- Recognize areas that are complicated or frustrating for others and then find ways to make them simple and painless.
- Tailor communications to make things understandable and well-received by diverse audiences.
- Take the steps necessary to ensure things run smoothly and go as planned.
- Earn people's trust through consistent delivery.
- Make themselves useful, achieve their goals, and deliver measurable and impactful results.

- Take on large-scale or daunting projects that others view as being unattainable.
- Work on teams that accomplish a lot, produce results, and get along.
- Socialize, spend time with friends, share stories, and enjoy moments of harmony where everyone gets along.
- See that guidance they've shared or solutions they've put in place are still useful and valued years after their involvement.
- Be recognized as the lynchpin of success or earn positive feedback from people they respect.
- Help others solve problems, improve communications, generate revenue, remove obstacles, simplify processes, or fill a need.
- Multiply their impact at scale by adding value across multiple people or multiple businesses.
- See evidence that their efforts are impactful and appreciated by others.

When Producers align with their passion, they shift: an opportunity to add value or make an impact *to* having added value or made an impact.

VOID: NOT ADDING VALUE OR HAVING AN IMPACT

Producers feel drained when they:

- Feel underutilized as a resource.
- Feel irrelevant or don't feel like they add significant value (for example, to a project or a conversation).

- Help rude, unappreciative people who don't value their efforts.
- Don't feel they have had the desired impact (for example, they fail or fall short of the goal).
- Waste their time doing things that do not provide any value to others (for example, participating in poorly managed meetings with undefined objectives).
- Have availability and see someone who needs help but is unwilling to ask for it or accept it.
- Are asked to do something without a clearly defined outcome.
- Are told what to do and how they must do something, step by step.
- Aren't personally successful, or their team is not successful.
- Feel unappreciated, unvalued, taken advantage of, or taken for granted.
- Experience conflict and disharmony with people they respect.
- Get dragged into projects that don't have any perceived value, have too many uncontrollable variables, or are destined for failure.
- Don't feel secure in their role, relationship, or situation but are instead on shaky ground (for example, professionally, socially, or financially).
- Don't feel confident things will work out, and instead fear things will fall apart.
- Do things no one values or appreciates.

PRODUCER PURPOSE AND HURT

Feel Secure ⟷ *Lack Security*

If you are a Producer, this is how the various facets of your mindset come together:

TRIGGER—VOID—HURT

If people compromise outcomes or get in the way of results (trigger), and if I don't add value or have an impact on people and projects (void), then we won't feel secure but will experience conflict, chaos, and disharmony (hurt).

PRINCIPLE—PASSION—PURPOSE

If people are effective in working toward and achieving results (principle), and if I do things that add value and have an impact on people and projects (passion), then we will experience harmony and can feel secure in knowing that things will work out (purpose).

PURPOSE STATEMENT

My purpose is to be impactful and add value to others so that we can feel secure in knowing that things will work out.

THE PROGRESSOR

"Think for yourself, or others will think for you without thinking of you."

—HENRY DAVID THOREAU

Progressors ask the tough questions rather than blindly following the majority or trusting something simply because an authority said so. Take cigarettes: Before cigarettes were known for causing cancer, they were touted as benign. Messages like, "More doctors smoke Camels than any other cigarette" circulated in magazines. The public widely accepted these claims—that is, until someone questioned them. Progressors don't rely on anyone to tell them what to think, and they don't believe everything they hear, even if it's the popular opinion. If something doesn't feel right, they become curious, ask questions, and reach their own conclusions.

Progressors are kind and friendly but are certainly not pushovers. Only one person oversees a Progressor's life: the Progressor.

With their own sense of direction, they're strong-willed and stand up for what they believe. They challenge groupthink and persuade others to see what's been overlooked. They don't challenge ideas to be difficult; they challenge because they care and don't want people to be duped.

Progressors see the world in a million shades of gray. There's not one right way to act, one right thing to believe, or one right path to follow. If someone wishes to engage in debauchery or live in a van, so be it, provided it doesn't harm others. They're inspired to do things differently from the usual life experience, and in doing so, they pave the way for others to do what they love and be their genuine selves.

PROGRESSOR PRINCIPLE AND TRIGGER

Self-Directed ⟵⟶ *Conforming*

PRINCIPLE: SELF-DIRECTED

Progressors are self-directed, make their own decisions, and think for themselves. Progressors:

- Think critically and question things that don't feel right.
- Welcome alternative viewpoints and ways of thinking but form their own opinions.
- Are friendly and caring while also being bold and strong-willed.
- Are not led by the masses or easily influenced by what others think but are autonomous.

- Are tolerant of diverse perspectives or life choices, provided they don't negatively impact or harm anyone else.
- Are very curious and want to learn from others and make sense of a nonsensical world.
- Maintain their own sense of direction and need the freedom to live their life in their way and want others to have the freedom to do the same.
- Tend to be philosophical in nature, open to exploring various beliefs, opinions, and ideologies, including the unorthodox and unconventional.
- Don't feel the need to buy into popular narratives but, rather, honor their personal beliefs, even if it means going against the grain (therefore, they often find themselves on the side of the minority).
- Recognize the importance of people having different perspectives and standing up for what they believe in.
- Challenge other people, groupthink, authority, and the status quo in their attempt to open people's minds.
- Can be influential and persuasive in their attempts to change someone's mind or expand someone's way of thinking.
- Need to live their life in their way rather than living life according to what someone else says they should do.
- Do not see the world as black and white but, rather, in a million shades of gray.
- Recognize that they think differently about things than most other people.

TRIGGER: CONFORMING

Progressors feel triggered when people:

- Tell them what to do.
- Won't think critically for themselves and instead surrender their thinking to others.
- Jump on the bandwagon and get excited or upset about whatever is popular at the moment, without forming their own conclusions.
- Blindly follow orders and believe everything they are told without asking questions or thinking things through for themselves (i.e., sheep).
- Do something because it's expected of them, not because they believe in it (for example, voting for a certain political party because their friends vote that way).
- Cannot back up their opinions and beliefs with any valid justification beyond believing it because others said so.
- Trust authority without questioning anything, or let other people control their decisions, opinions, and life direction.
- Lack curiosity and refuse to consider alternative viewpoints or ways of thinking.
- Paint a fake image of themselves—as opposed to a genuine one—to control others' perception of them.
- Act as if they know what is best for others and discourage people from thinking for themselves.
- Claim to have all the answers or imply only one right perspective exists.
- Make decisions for others and expect people to blindly follow orders.
- Come across as arrogant, particularly when they don't have the expertise to back it up and are being fake.
- Hurt, harm, or take advantage of the innocent and vulnerable.
- Are controlling, manipulative, indoctrinating, authoritative, or hungry for power.

PROGRESSOR PASSION AND VOID

Moving Beyond ←——→ *Being Restricted*

PASSION: MOVING BEYOND THE USUAL LIFE EXPERIENCE

Progressors are motivated to:

- Move beyond the narrow confines of the usual life experience.
- Do things differently or contrary to what is typical, normal, usual, orthodox, or expected.
- Explore new ideas or ways of doing something, go down a variety of different paths (even if only in their mind), and enjoy the freedom to dream.
- Pursue unique activities and experiences, which vary from the typical experience.
- Discover eclectic music, out-of-the-ordinary activities, and creative solutions.
- Cultivate their relationships, socialize, interact, converse, and share experiences with others.
- Engage with people and act in the moment to positively impact how someone feels, help people feel seen, or make someone's day better.
- Work in service-oriented vocations where they can support others and establish emotional connections.
- Defy the odds, achieve the unexpected, be a rebel, prove people wrong, and do what people say cannot be done.

- Express themselves in practical, yet creative, ways (for example, through teaching, cooking, socializing, or healing).
- Stand up for the underdog, raise awareness around unknown viewpoints, or fight for a worthy cause.
- Seek out and find the outliers—the "wow" experience—which could be a spectacular dining experience, a pristine ski run, or the perfect moment.
- Explore their capabilities, figure things out on their own, and methodically master their craft in their way (for example, photography, fly fishing, dancing, or golfing).
- Do what is personally fulfilling to them and encourage others to do the same.
- Participate in experiences that palpably elevate their emotions (for example, enjoying extraordinary musicians, speakers, performers, or athletics).

When Progressors align with their passion, they shift:
an opportunity to move
beyond the usual life experience
to having moved beyond the usual life experience.

VOID: LIVING WITHIN NARROW CONFINES

Progressors feel drained when they:

- Feel trapped in the narrow confines of society or the status quo.
- Are restricted from doing anything original, different, or innovative and instead must maintain the usual, ordinary, and mediocre.

- Have their voice and expression stifled by other people or implied societal standards.
- Compromise their personal fulfillment by doing what everyone else is doing instead of doing what they love.
- Are dismissed when they merely mentally entertain or verbally express a potentially unconventional idea.
- Witness once spectacular experiences be bastardized, standardized, and commercialized.
- Don't feel free to be who they are but, rather, feel they need to act in an ingenuine way (for example, diluting themselves to meet professional expectations).
- Aren't living in congruence with who they are or compromising their dreams to pacify someone else's expectations.
- Are not genuine and instead do something that goes against their beliefs (for example, selling a product they don't believe will help someone).
- Inadvertently hurt or disappoint someone they care about.
- Watch people be duped while being unable to talk sense into them or help them.
- See individual freedoms limited, resulting in people sacrificing their fulfillment for someone else's selfish gain.
- Witness people's freedoms being restricted for nonsensical reasons.
- See innocent people caught in bad circumstances (for example, people who are victims of natural disasters).
- Spend time with people who are superficial or fake.

PROGRESSOR PURPOSE AND HURT

Be Genuine ←——→ *Not Genuine*

If you are a Progressor, this is how the various facets of your mindset come together:

TRIGGER—VOID—HURT

If people aren't self-directed but instead blindly follow others (trigger), and if I accept nonsensical limitations and do what is usual, standard, and expected (void), then we won't be free to be our genuine selves (hurt).

PRINCIPLE—PASSION—PURPOSE

If people are self-directed, think for themselves, and come to their own conclusions (principle), and if I move beyond the usual life experience and do things differently (passion), then we will be free to be our genuine selves and do what we love (purpose).

PURPOSE STATEMENT

My purpose is to do things differently and move beyond what is usual so that we are free to be our genuine selves.

THE PROTECTOR

"I don't believe in luck, I believe in preparation."

—BOBBY KNIGHT

Just as airplane pilots prepare for circumstances like turbulence to ensure the safety of their passengers, Protectors prepare in advance so they can protect themselves and others in the face of uncertainty. Turbulence in flights, as in life, is to be expected. Preparation gives Protectors an edge so they can safely and competently navigate an uncertain future.

Protectors are born leaders who are quick to jump in and take charge. They've done their homework up front, so they tend to trust themselves more than others. Their commanding approach may come across as intimidating to others when really, they just need to ensure a positive outcome. Protectors recognize that someone needs to be responsible in unpredictable situations, and frequently, it is them.

Having readied themselves in advance, Protectors are motivated to face unknown situations where success is dependent upon their ability to overcome the challenge. Challenges that contain an element of risk to them are most exciting, which could involve presenting to a large group or heading out on an expedition (where you can be sure they'll have the appropriate equipment, gear, and emergency kit). As their name suggests, Protectors' strong sense of responsibility ensures they, and others, remain safe and protected.

PROTECTOR PRINCIPLE AND TRIGGER

Prepared ⟷ *Unprepared*

PRINCIPLE: PREPARED

Protectors prepare for things in advance so when situations arise, they are equipped to deal with them. Protectors:

- Equip themselves with the necessary knowledge and tools so they're ready for what comes next.
- Do their homework, anticipate challenges, and give tasks thought ahead of time.
- Prioritize risk management by preparing themselves for the risks ahead of them.
- Are highly protective of their own.
- Remain cautious, alert, and attentive to their surroundings.
- Do what they need to do, including looking out for others, before doing what they want to do.
- See risk as inevitable, so they do what they can to make sure that when they encounter risk, they are ready for it.

- Come prepared with the appropriate equipment, gear, and an emergency kit.
- Embrace proven tactics, dependable tools, and tried-and-true techniques.
- Equip themselves and others with information that can help protect people.
- Recognize someone needs to be responsible in unpredictable situations, and frequently, it is them.
- Trust themselves to be in charge and competently lead others.
- Act with a sense of urgency and take quick, decisive action.
- Stand their ground and are not easily influenced by others.
- Bring structure, organization, rigor, stability, and predictability to their environment.

TRIGGER: UNPREPARED

Protectors feel triggered when people:

- Are unprepared for the task at hand or unequipped for the challenge ahead.
- Show up ill-prepared and put others at risk of danger, loss, injury, or embarrassment.
- Put themselves or others in harm's way.
- Don't dress appropriately for adverse conditions.
- Unfairly hurt or add risk to someone else (for example, inappropriate aggression on the playing field).
- Assume a position that requires responsibility but don't act responsibly (for example, drinking alcohol and then driving with a bunch of people in their car).

- Don't act with urgency when something needs to get done.
- Don't do what they are told to do when it's for their protection.
- Ignore well-intended (and potentially lifesaving) advice.
- Attempt to lead others when they're not qualified.
- Act foolishly or carelessly, thus creating risk for others (for example, reckless or inattentive drivers).
- Use unreliable or untested tactics, which could fail.
- Fail to take proper precautions.
- Force ill-advised change onto others without seeing the shortcomings of such a change.
- Attempt to take advantage of them or their own.

PROTECTOR PASSION AND VOID

Demonstrating Competence ⟵⟶ *Lacking Competence*

PASSION: DEVELOPING AND DEMONSTRATING COMPETENCE

Protectors are motivated to:

- Take on and conquer personally meaningful challenges that have an element of risk (for example, speaking in front of a large audience).
- Persevere when the going gets tough and then experience the satisfaction that comes from proving they could do something, despite uncertainty.

- Place themselves in unknown situations where there is no user manual or guarantee of success—as if a warrior going into battle—and then win, succeed, overcome, or triumph.
- Take calculated risks and put their capabilities to the test.
- Engage in physical, athletic, adventurous, or unique pursuits that challenge them (for example, rock climbing, hiking, traveling to Antarctica).
- Take on big challenges of their choosing and persevere until they achieve victory or prove themselves competent.
- Make bold assertions and then back them up with action.
- Set goals and then learn and do everything necessary to achieve their goals.
- Tenaciously follow through on their personal goals.
- Help others build competence, protect themselves, or mitigate risk (for example, mitigate physical risk, financial risk, or overcome limiting beliefs).
- Use the skills they have acquired to save themselves and others from grief, pain, or risk.
- Choose to put themselves in consequential situations where there are no guarantees and then demonstrate competence (for example, as an airline pilot).
- Walk into situations where there are unknown variables at play and then take action to bring about stability.
- Surprise themselves by doing what they weren't certain they could do.
- Protect their own and their community.

When Protectors align with their passion, they shift: an unknown, unpredictable, or uncertain challenge *to* demonstrating competence.

VOID: NOT DEMONSTRATING COMPETENCE

Protectors feel drained when they:

- Can't keep up and feel like they are behind the eight ball.
- Don't feel competent in what they are doing.
- Fail to conquer their challenge or fall short of their goal.
- Don't succeed in what they set out to do.
- Make a mistake, which causes things to spiral out of control.
- Don't feel they can develop the skills necessary to thrive in an area that matters to them.
- Participate in others' pastimes that require no skill, strategy, or opportunity to demonstrate competence (for example, playing the card game Go Fish).
- Working in risk-averse environments where people merely wish to maintain the status quo.
- Create physical, financial, or emotional risk for someone (for example, buying an unsafe car for their newly licensed teenager).
- Feel strongly that someone they care about is in a vulnerable position and is unprepared for the risk at hand, should something go wrong.
- Are at a disadvantage or are not at the top of their game.
- See people at risk and not know it yet are unable to do anything to help.
- Know that people don't have the information or tools they need to overcome the challenges facing them.
- Don't have a challenge they are pursuing and instead are stuck doing boring, repetitive, unchallenging work.
- Feel average, inferior, or subpar at something.

PROTECTOR PURPOSE AND HURT

Be Protected ←——————→ *Be Vulnerable*

If you are a Protector, this is how the various facets of your mindset come together:

TRIGGER—VOID—HURT

If people are unprepared and don't ready themselves in advance (trigger), and if I don't develop competence by conquering difficult challenges (void), then we will be vulnerable in the face of risk and uncertainty (hurt).

PRINCIPLE—PASSION—PURPOSE

If people are prepared and ready themselves in advance (principle), and if I develop and demonstrate competence by conquering personally meaningful challenges (passion), then we will be protected in the face of uncertainty and risk (purpose).

PURPOSE STATEMENT

My purpose is to develop competence by conquering challenges so that we will be protected in the face of uncertainty and risk.

THE RISKTAKER

> **"Success tends to bless those who are most committed to giving it the most attention."**
>
> **—GRANT CARDONE**

Risktakers know success doesn't magically happen on its own. It demands hard work, competence, and bold action. Whatever they pursue, they're willing to work hard, learn, and do whatever it takes to get the job done. Hungry to make an impact and realize success, Risktakers know anything is possible if they believe it's possible, and they're willing to work at it.

As their name suggests, Risktakers are motivated to take risks that pay off. They're eager to think big, swing for the fences, venture into the unknown, or do things in a way never done before. Direct and verbally uninhibited, they're apt to address the elephant in the room, saying what others are too scared to say. For Risktakers, truth and transparency are essential cornerstones of success.

Career success is often crucial to their sense of well-being, so Risktakers do well in their chosen line of work. They thrive on excitement and success and excel in fast-paced environments. As natural leaders, they can easily control and guide a crowd. With a commanding presence and physical comfort in the world, they make themselves heard, and people listen. Risktakers are known for being hard-driving, competitive, and success-oriented, yet it's when they help others realize success that they feel most successful.

RISKTAKER PRINCIPLE AND TRIGGER

Competent ←——→ *Incompetent*

PRINCIPLE: COMPETENT

Risktakers are in it to win it and will do whatever it takes to develop competence and succeed. Risktakers:

- Are success-oriented and aspire to do well in their field or chosen line of work.
- Wear many hats and do whatever it takes to get the job done and succeed.
- Are articulate, blunt, direct, and verbally uninhibited.
- Are willing to get in, work hard, and get their hands dirty.
- Are self-made through hard work and persistence.
- Process quickly, see the big picture, and pursue practical, down-to-earth tactics and solutions.
- Zero in on what they want and put the work in to develop their skills, achieve their goals, and get results.
- Are strong performers who are willing to learn as much as they can and put in the time and energy that's required to excel.

- Welcome competition and put their capabilities to the test.
- Like to be in total control of a task or situation so they can influence the outcome.
- Aspire to be the best at what they do and be a top performer among their peers.
- Want the brutal facts so they can take the appropriate actions to bring about a successful outcome.
- Are quick to get to the heart of a matter and expose flaws in another's argument.
- Put the work in to be a valuable team player and contribute to the success of the team, seeing failure as a reminder to work harder.
- Are strong, physical, resilient, independent, hard-driving, hustling, high-energy, and action-oriented.

TRIGGER: INCOMPETENT

Risktakers feel triggered when people:

- Aren't willing to learn, try, or put the necessary work in to excel at something.
- Don't care about winning and would rather ride on the coattails of others' hard work and hope to receive some credit.
- Participate in a project so they can tell their boss they are involved but aren't willing to work hard.
- Are obsessed with "staying in their lane" and aren't willing to do anything outside their job description (for example, they only help sell a product if they're a salesperson).
- Point out what's wrong but don't bring any ideas to the table on how to improve it.

- Are poor performers who are not good at what they do.
- Think success is a matter of luck, not a result of hard work, so they don't put in the necessary work required to succeed.
- Blame their poor performance on others or complain they aren't more successful yet don't work hard to learn and improve (for example, complain they didn't get enough training).
- Mess up the play, compromise success, or cause the team to lose.
- Aren't good at their job or can't get the job done because they haven't bothered to develop the skills and qualifications necessary to do the job well.
- Can't handle the truth or are dishonest, unrealistic, impractical, ignorant, vague, or secretive—all of which can compromise success.
- Lack authenticity by saying one thing and then doing something else (for example, a leader says it's ok to fail, then punishes someone who took a risk and failed).
- Waste time on things that don't matter and are consequently ineffective and irrelevant.
- Ask the same questions over and over and won't step out on their own.
- Put the success of the team in jeopardy.

RISKTAKER PASSION AND VOID

Taking Worthwhile Risks ←——→ *Not Taking Risks*

PASSION: TAKING RISKS THAT PAY OFF

Risktakers are motivated to:

- Take bold action.
- Win, succeed, and help others to do the same.
- Put things together in a way that's never been done before.
- Take on challenges that provide an opportunity to make a notable impact.
- Face ambiguity, uncertainty, and venture into unknown territory with a willingness to dive into new projects, even if they're not sure how to do something.
- Prove people wrong, do what people say cannot be done, and use the naysayer's negativity to fuel their success.
- Lead from the front, demonstrate courage, and be the first to act when action is warranted.
- Speak up in audiences, address the elephant in the room, rip off the Band-Aid, and say what others are too scared to say.
- Be disruptive, be transformative, try something different, and upset the status quo.
- Swing for the fences and boldly go where no one has gone before.
- Work in fast-paced environments where they can get in, hit hard, get it done, and get out.
- Make the shot, take the chance, think big, dream big, take a risk, and go for it.
- Pursue activities that are stimulating or produce an adrenaline rush (for example, athletics, contact sports, sales).
- Pour their heart and energy into initiatives to ensure their successful realization.
- Transform bold ideas into a tangible form, which can be seen, felt, or experienced, or take actions that result in radical transformation.

When Risktakers align with their passion, they shift:
an opportunity to take a risk
to having taken a risk that has paid off.

VOID: MAINTAINING THE STATUS QUO

Risktakers feel drained when they:

- Play it too safe and don't take big enough risks.
- Aren't taking any chances but are preserving the status quo.
- Work in slow-paced environments.
- Experience life as routine, predictable, and stagnant.
- Work on initiatives that won't allow them to make a substantial impact on anything or anyone.
- Spend time dealing with over-engineered processes that don't drive success and slow them down.
- Aren't in the game but instead are sitting on the sidelines of life.
- Lose, miss the target, or feel they've let people or the team down.
- Don't win or do not hit their goals or objectives.
- Work for risk-averse companies or managers.
- Are physically hurt, worn down, or having an "off" day.
- Feel restless, bored, impatient, or unable to escape the tedious doldrums (for example, being stuck working on a dull project).
- See people lay down in defeat or let failure keep them down.
- Can't delegate mundane details or tasks but, rather, are stuck doing them themselves.
- Don't take risks and, as a result, don't reap the rewards.

RISKTAKER PURPOSE AND HURT

Succeed ←——————→ *Not Succeed*

If you are a Risktaker, this is how the various facets of your mindset come together:

TRIGGER—VOID—HURT

If people are incompetent and won't do what it takes to get the job done (trigger), and if I play it safe, don't take risks, and merely maintain the status quo (void), then we will not succeed (hurt).

PRINCIPLE—PASSION—PURPOSE

If people develop competence and do what it takes to get the job done (principle), and if I take bold action and take risks that pay off (passion), then people, teams, and organizations will be successful (purpose).

PURPOSE STATEMENT

My purpose is to take risks that pay off so that we can succeed.

THE SENSOR

"Strong people don't put others down. They lift them up."

—MICHAEL P. WATSON

Sensors readily offer encouragement in a world where support is so very needed. Their strong nurturing qualities and social skills make them exceptionally adept in working with children, in service professions, or with people in general. It's natural for them to create a warm, nurturing environment where others feel safe and appreciated.

Sensors use their feelings as a way of receiving information. Being sensitive to their surroundings, they easily pick up on subtle energies, ranging from voice inflections to the weather. Through their heightened empathic nature, they tend to take in everything they experience. If they're not careful, witnessing others' emotional suffering will cause their spirits to sink, but this sensitivity also allows them to experience the fullness of life with a lively intensity. As social beings, they enjoy connecting with people, the earth, nature, energy, and animals.

As the name suggests, Sensors like to fully experience their senses. They find satisfaction in simple pleasures, like the taste of foods or the feel of various textures. Highly visual, they may even have a photographic memory. Sensors often get a "feel" for something because they tend to assimilate new information through their feelings. Intuitive, yet grounded, they enjoy revealing aspects of life generally unknown and then sharing their discoveries with others. It is through their supportive nature and keen ability to reveal discoveries that others feel safe in a sometimes harsh world.

SENSOR PRINCIPLE AND TRIGGER

Supportive ←——→ *Unsupportive*

PRINCIPLE: SUPPORTIVE

Sensors create warm, supportive, and nurturing environments where people feel safe, accepted, and cared for. Sensors:

- Are sensitive and responsive to other people and their needs.
- Cheer others on, build people up, make people feel good, and readily offer caring words and support to those who need it.
- Take precautionary steps to ensure people's needs are taken care of.
- Feel and do their best in harmonious environments.
- Care about other people and take care not to hurt people's feelings.

- Foster others' growth, development, and confidence.
- Offer helpful, encouraging, and supportive words to others and share their own experiences so people know they are not alone.
- Typically feel and perceive more than others, which is reflected in a heightened empathic feeling energy.
- Are affected by their environment, including the weather, people's moods, and subtle energies around them.
- Are dependable in whatever they commit to.
- Provide reinforcement, which helps people believe in themselves and gives them the confidence needed to pursue and achieve their dreams.
- Are easy to talk to and provide a safe place for people to be authentic and express their emotions.
- Like having a plan, being prepared, and taking proactive measures where warranted to ensure people's safety.
- Defend, protect, look out for, and take care of their own, whether it's a friend, parent, client, or employee.
- Have an enviable love for life and all its creatures and approach life with a sense of selfless altruism.

TRIGGER: UNSUPPORTIVE

Sensors feel triggered when people:

- Are critical, unsupportive, discouraging, or disapproving.
- Call out flaws and point out every little thing someone does wrong.
- Tear people down or put people down.
- Criticize their children or talk badly about the people closest to them.

- Discourage someone from following their dreams.
- Rear their children by punishing, ridiculing, or reprimanding them.
- Say hurtful things that deflate someone's confidence or joy.
- Make assumptions about people (for example, an assumption that girls are not good at sports) rather than finding out what interests someone.
- Let them down when they were counting on them.
- Are dishonest, untrustworthy, or manipulative.
- Hurt animals or intentionally make someone feel bad.
- Lack sensitivity and warmth and instead are harsh, cold, insensitive, mean, condescending, or standoffish.
- Are unnecessarily hard on others and make them feel bad rather than being supportive and encouraging.
- Put people in danger or don't do what they need to do to ensure their safety.
- Don't look out for their own or are not there for the people in their life who need them.

SENSOR PASSION AND VOID

Making Discoveries ⟷ *Not Discovering*

PASSION: MAKING DISCOVERIES

Sensors are motivated to:

- Use, channel, or engage their senses to receive ideas, information, and insights.

- Discover and reveal aspects of life generally unknown.
- Find satisfaction in revealing natural, simple pleasures around them: the taste of foods, the sound of music, the feel of silk, the smell of spices, and the visual stimulation of bright colors and designs.
- Stretch their "known" reality by experiencing life and expanding their awareness.
- Stick with a challenge until they clear away the fog, put the pieces together, and derive clarity from fragments.
- Continue to reveal new things to themselves (for example, in nature, technology, culture, or psychology).
- Come up with clever ideas, such as discovering a solution to a problem or a new way of doing something.
- Witness joy in others and enjoy the miracles of life (for example, marveling at a child's wonder and curiosity).
- Enjoy adventure, take risks, and have fun, provided they have taken the proper precautions and feel prepared.
- Satiate their intellectual curiosity by reading, figuring things out, or finding out what they did not know previously.
- Use their imagination and enjoy watching their creations unfold (for example, while cooking, painting, or writing).
- Work in service professions where they engage with others and make people happy.
- Enjoy the fullness of life and the world's physicality by engaging all their senses in an experience.
- Socialize, connect, laugh, play, and understand the hearts and minds of others and discover what makes people tick.

When Sensors align with their passion, they shift:
a curiosity to discover what is currently unknown
to having discovered or experienced something new.

VOID: NOT MAKING DISCOVERIES

Sensors feel drained when they:

- Work on projects that lack excitement, creativity, or interaction.
- Feel bored doing overly mundane, mechanical, or conventional work that does not allow them to engage their senses or discover anything new.
- Spend days on end in gloomy weather or surrounded by people in bad moods.
- Feel a loss of control in their life or fear they will lose control.
- Learn through limited senses (for example, memorizing versus visualizing or interacting with something to understand it).
- Implement ideas, plans, or solutions that feel forced.
- Work in a job that has stability and security but is boring.
- Spend time dealing with politics.
- Don't have a meaningful challenge, creative outlet, or opportunity to have fun.
- Spend time in settings that feel unnatural, unwelcoming, uncomfortable, or unsafe.
- Put energy into controlling information rather than receiving or allowing it.
- Anticipate being met with disapproval if they share their awareness with others.
- Retreat into their inner shell and miss out on opportunities to connect with the world around them and make new discoveries.
- Have situations not work out as expected or desired.
- Don't feel supported by their manager, parents, or significant people in their life.

SENSOR PURPOSE AND HURT

Feel Safe ←——————→ *Not Feel Safe*

If you are a Sensor, this is how the various facets of your mindset come together:

TRIGGER—VOID—HURT

If people are insensitive, discouraging, and unsupportive (trigger), and if I don't engage my senses and make discoveries (void), then we will not feel safe (hurt).

PRINCIPLE—PASSION—PURPOSE

If people are supportive, nurturing, and encouraging (principle), and if I engage my senses, glean new awareness, and make discoveries (passion), then we will feel safe (purpose).

PURPOSE STATEMENT

My purpose is to engage all my senses, glean new awareness, and make discoveries so that we can feel safe.

THE STABILIZER

"If you're not early, you're late."

—UNKNOWN (BUT QUITE CERTAINLY A STABILIZER)

Stabilizers recognize the importance of foundational rules, which allow our days to run smoothly. In the science lab, for example, following the rules is imperative: don't sniff the chemicals, do properly dispose of chemicals, don't randomly mix chemicals together, and so on. If people don't follow the rules, things can, quite literally, blow up. Stabilizers understand there are consequences when people don't follow processes, so they take care to do things the right way, not the easy way. Stabilizers respect fundamental guidelines that provide the necessary structure and stability to maintain a sense of order.

With a high regard for structure and consistency, Stabilizers like to have a plan in place and have people follow that plan. When things do *not* go as planned, they're apt to express their frustration or present a hard exterior. Conversely, when Stabilizers positively impact people's lives, they're especially helpful, compassionate, and nurturing. They have a strong desire to help individuals, as well as humanity in general.

Stabilizers possess an intense sense of responsibility and remain loyal indefinitely, especially when they have identified with the group or cause. They commit to their choices with unusual and unwavering resolve and don't typically quit until they finish a job, particularly when it's for someone else. Their high sense of responsibility makes them patient teachers, and the appreciation of their students, patients, or clients makes all their efforts worthwhile. With an aspiration to bring stability into the world and to others, Stabilizers experience stability and balance themselves.

STABILIZER PRINCIPLE AND TRIGGER

Disciplined ←——→ *Undisciplined*

PRINCIPLE: DISCIPLINED

Stabilizers are punctual and disciplined, and they reliably uphold their commitments to others. Stabilizers:

- Stick to their word, honor their commitments, and do what they say they will do.
- Do things the right way, not the easy way.
- Are punctual and expect others to be on time for meetings, appointments, and formal commitments too.
- Uphold established rules, standards, and principles that keep the environment steady, stable, and smooth-running

(for example, respecting traffic signals and road signs that keep people safe).

- Hold firm beliefs of what is appropriate and how something should be done.
- Like to have a plan and follow it.
- Are self-controlled and self-disciplined.
- Do their part to ensure things go predictably as planned.
- Actively pay attention during meetings and discussions.
- Bring rigor, structure, order, and stability to their environment.
- Uphold their principles and beliefs.
- Follow the rules that bring stability to situations and mitigate chaos.
- Know there are consequences if things are not done right.
- Create stability and consistency by ensuring things flow as expected.
- Work behind the scenes to ensure things run smoothly.

TRIGGER: UNDISCIPLINED

Stabilizers feel triggered when people:

- Are late.
- Do what is convenient rather than doing what is right.
- Fail to do what they say they will do when others are counting on them.
- Don't follow the plan, mess up the plan, or needlessly change the plan.
- Ask a question and then don't listen to the answer or attend a meeting but don't pay attention.

- Disregard basic rules, standards, and norms and instead do whatever they want.
- Habitually show up late to meetings or appointments.
- Cause things to not go as expected.
- Are unreliable and don't do their part or show up unprepared and wing it.
- Multitask during meetings and then make speakers repeat already covered information.
- Don't allow others to voice their concerns or ideas.
- Reward people who are rude, rule-breaking, or who set a poor example for others.
- Blindside them and consequently shake their foundation.
- Instigate chaos and cause things to not run smoothly.
- Do not keep their commitments but instead quit.

STABILIZER PASSION AND VOID

Positive Impact ⟷ *No Impact*

PASSION: HAVING A POSITIVE IMPACT ON PEOPLE'S LIVES

Stabilizers are motivated to:

- Do things that make a difference in people's lives.
- Find creative ways to make experiences special, enjoyable, memorable, and impactful.
- Be recognized for a job well done or see evidence that their efforts were impactful and appreciated by others.

- Patiently stick with someone and go the extra mile, doing what is necessary to ensure others are positioned for success.
- Pursue careers that allow them to have a beneficial or significant impact on people's lives.
- Do things that have a positive impact on their well-being by providing a sense of balance, freedom, or stability (for example, through creative, religious, or adventurous pursuits).
- Diagnose and fix problems to ensure the success of an individual, organization, event, or cause.
- Deconstruct issues or objects so they can learn and discover ways to build them back better.
- Identify gaps and opportunities to make programs and processes better and then take the initiative to improve them.
- See opportunities to make an impact in their community and lend a hand where it's needed.
- Work in advance and time things perfectly to deliver the best possible experience (for example, preparing a meal that is ready when guests arrive).
- Volunteer their time for the benefit of others or serve a purposeful cause.
- Invest in people and worthwhile causes where they can make a valuable contribution.
- Make an experience the best it can be (including making bad experiences better).
- Help people and change their lives for the better.

When Stabilizers align with their passion, they shift:
an opportunity to make a positive impact
to having made a positive impact.

VOID: NOT HAVING AN IMPACT

Stabilizers feel drained when they:

- Do things that don't have a meaningful impact on anyone or anything.
- Don't feel like they are making a significant impact in anyone's life.
- Are restricted from using their creativity to make things better.
- Give and give, but their hard work becomes expected rather than appreciated.
- Go out of their way to do something nice for someone, but their efforts go unnoticed or are rejected.
- Are taken for granted or are not appreciated.
- Don't feel valued by the people they serve.
- Have an experience ruined by someone who refuses their gift.
- Continue to do the same thing when they're no longer making a significant impact.
- Direct their energy in the same place rather than shifting to where they can have a greater impact serving different people, projects, or causes.
- Feel like they have let someone down.
- Do something that adversely affects themselves or others.
- Have their life turned upside down by circumstances outside their control.
- Lack stability in life or have things blow up.
- Find that their plans do not go as expected and instead bring chaos and disorder.

STABILIZER PURPOSE AND HURT

Experience Stability ←——→ *Experience Instability*

If you are a Stabilizer, this is how the various facets of your mindset come together:

TRIGGER—VOID—HURT

If people don't follow basic rules and instead do what is convenient rather than doing what is right (trigger), and if I do things that don't have a positive impact and my efforts are not valued (void), then we will not experience a sense of stability (hurt).

PRINCIPLE—PASSION—PURPOSE

If people are disciplined, follow the rules, and do what is right (principle), and if I do things that have a positive impact (passion), then we will have a strong and stable foundation from which we can thrive (purpose).

PURPOSE STATEMENT

My purpose is to have a positive impact on people's lives so that we can have stability in life.

THE SUPPORTER

"The purpose of life is to contribute in some way to making things better."

—ROBERT F. KENNEDY

Supporters aren't ones to seek the limelight. They're happiest working behind the scenes, doing essential jobs that keep a home or business running smoothly and successfully. Leadership roles aren't generally of interest to them because they'd rather play an active role in progressing a project or task. Supporters view every task as containing a goal or a purpose and aspire to do whatever's necessary to move toward that goal, which could be as simple as making dinner or as expansive as helping to build a skyscraper.

Supporters are known for being helpful, hardworking, self-motivated, and dependable. Social harmony is a high priority to Supporters, so they steer clear of negativity and drama. Besides, toxic attitudes work against the attainment of a goal, and they are motivated by progress. In their desire to maintain a peaceful environment, Supporters are apt to give up their personal preferences to ensure others' contentment. They have an easygoing, kind, and altruistic nature.

Much of Supporters' satisfaction comes from making themselves useful to those around them. If they see something needs to be done, they'll step in and do it. Supporters recognize everyone has a part to play—the paramedic, electrician, CEO, stay-at-home mom, and farmer—and every role is valuable and as important as the next. They believe that when everyone contributes, people can experience the rewards of contentment, harmony, and tranquility. By helping and serving others, Supporters are at their best and are definite assets to families, teams, and organizations.

SUPPORTER PRINCIPLE AND TRIGGER

Useful ⟷ *Unhelpful*

PRINCIPLE: USEFUL

Supporters make themselves useful to those around them and contribute when things need to be done. Supporters:

- Jump in and help with whatever is needed.
- Are easygoing, get along well with others, and have seemingly few triggers.
- Are hardworking, accountable, loyal, dependable, reliable, and self-motivated.
- Are kind, friendly, collaborative, accommodating, helpful, generous, and take care to be a good person who treats people well.
- Are excellent team players who contribute to others and the whole.
- Keep things steady, stable, consistent, and peaceful by doing whatever needs to be done.

- Are extraordinarily helpful and willing to help whenever needed.
- See every person and every role as important, equally valuable, and able to accomplish something.
- Are quick to assist and work toward a common end and expect everyone to contribute so everyone can succeed.
- Take action if it will benefit others or if there is a practical reason for doing it.
- Want to relieve angst in people's lives and take care to avoid conflict or strife.
- Want people to feel they are part of something and feel appreciated for their contributions, recognizing a simple "thank you" can go a long way in motivating others.
- Nurture, support, and serve others by taking action.
- Will go out of their way to help others who are willing to work and learn.
- Do their part to be a decent human, treat others well, and contribute to the success of the whole.

TRIGGER: UNHELPFUL

Supporters feel triggered when people:

- Don't contribute when things need to be done.
- Have a job to do but don't do it and instead do nothing when they should be doing something.
- Are lazy, idle, unhelpful, ineffective, or unproductive.
- Negatively impact the success of the team or others by doing nothing.
- Aren't helping or doing anything productive when things need to be done.

- Don't help or do less than what is minimally expected.
- Expect help from others if it benefits them but are not willing to reciprocate and help others (i.e., they take, but don't give).
- Ask people for help but then don't help themselves and instead watch others work.
- Are self-absorbed and don't consider others or the whole.
- Don't bother contributing and are happy to let the workload fall on someone else.
- Don't carry their weight and do less than the minimum expected of them.
- Are pessimistic, disruptive, and make their problem everyone else's problem.
- Hinder more than they help because they bring conflict, negativity, and drama into their surroundings.
- Don't make a worthwhile contribution yet expect a participation ribbon.
- Hinder the success of projects with poor workmanship, poor service, poor work ethic, or a poor attitude.

SUPPORTER PASSION AND VOID

Progressing Tasks ←——→ *Not Progressing Tasks*

PASSION: COMPLETING WORTHWHILE PROJECTS, GOALS, AND TASKS

Supporters are motivated to:

- Make progress toward the overall goal.

- Advance projects, tasks, and initiatives that benefit themselves, others, or a successful outcome.
- Provide value to others by being a doer and getting things done.
- Learn practical skills, take practical action, and fulfill practical needs.
- Exceed expectations by getting projects done faster or better than anticipated.
- Work behind the scenes doing essential jobs that are necessary to keep a home or business running.
- Complete tasks and enjoy the gratification that comes in knowing their efforts were worthwhile or appreciated.
- Help people and be an asset to people and organizations.
- Help to make someone feel better or make a difference in someone's world.
- Develop expertise in their chosen area and continue to grow in their field.
- Work hard and enjoy the sense of accomplishment that results from doing a job well.
- Find the most direct route to complete something, using tried-and-true tactics to ensure things go smoothly and are done right the first time.
- Get work done ahead of schedule, without wasting time, and enjoy the occasional "thanks" for their above-and-beyond efforts.
- Work with others, give credit where credit is due, help others succeed, and succeed as a team.
- Come to the rescue when they have the expertise and can help move things forward.

When Supporters align with their passion, they shift:
an uncompleted project, goal, or task
to a completed project, goal, or task.

VOID: NOT PROGRESSING PROJECTS, GOALS, OR TASKS

Supporters feel drained when they:

- Work on tasks that take longer than they should have taken.
- Don't get as much done in a day as they wanted to.
- Waste time redoing something that wasn't done right the first time.
- Use unproven tactics or tools, only to have them fail.
- Do things that don't benefit somebody or something.
- Inadvertently do something that hinders the overall goal or upsets others.
- Fall behind schedule or have projects move backward.
- Have their day planned out and then be hijacked by unanticipated demands, thus being unable to do what they had planned.
- Get sick or injured and, therefore, are unable to contribute to the success and forward momentum of projects.
- Feel their efforts are expected rather than appreciated (i.e., they're taken for granted).
- Witness others close to them being taken for granted.
- Are expected to learn everything at once rather than being able to learn as they go and integrate each step along the way.
- Do work that is unessential in that it doesn't directly advance a task or project (i.e., middle management).
- Are expected to learn or do something when they don't have a practical reason for learning or doing it.
- Work in environments that are toxic, negative, political, or ripe with conflict and drama.

SUPPORTER PURPOSE AND HURT

Feel Good ←——————→ *Not Feel Good*

If you are a Supporter, this is how the various facets of your mindset come together:

TRIGGER—VOID—HURT

If people don't contribute when there are things to do (trigger), and if I don't complete essential projects and tasks (void), then we will not feel good but will experience tension and discomfort (hurt).

PRINCIPLE—PASSION—PURPOSE

If people are useful and help when there are things to be done (principle), and if I take the necessary steps to complete essential projects, goals, and tasks (passion), then we can feel good (purpose).

PURPOSE STATEMENT

My purpose is to complete essential projects, goals, and tasks so that we can feel good.

THE SYNTHESIZER

"A little consideration, a little thought for others, makes all the difference."

—A. A. MILNE, *WINNIE-THE-POOH*

Synthesizers are deeply aware that their actions affect those around them. With strong compassion and empathy for others, they consider others before they act and think before they speak; in other words, they synthesize the anticipated impact on the whole. Since they take time to see all sides of an issue, they can easily relate to others.

While they're sociable and receptive, there's typically a whole lot more going on with Synthesizers than what they express. Due to their code of privacy and independence, they tend to be more understanding of others than they need to be understood. When they find their ideas are met with confusion or defensiveness, Synthesizers keep to themselves. On the flip side, when people express interest, they may tell long stories, go off on tangents, and lose the point of their story in their wanderings because they're so eager to share insights that could be of value to someone else.

Synthesizers thrive on doing worthwhile things and are often idealistic, yearning to make a contribution to the world. They don't say "yes" to every opportunity presented, but they ask, at least at an unconscious level, "Will it be worthwhile?" They're motivated to improve people's experience, such as saving them time, money, pain, or frustration. When Synthesizers decide to do something, they go to great lengths to fulfill their obligations, persevering long after many others would have given up.

SYNTHESIZER PRINCIPLE AND TRIGGER

Considerate ⟷ *Inconsiderate*

PRINCIPLE: CONSIDERATE

Synthesizers are considerate of how their actions affect other people. Synthesizers:

- Have strong compassion and empathy for others and take care not to hurt, offend, or trigger others.
- Consider other people's perspectives and want to see things from another's point of view.
- Thoughtfully consider other people's experiences and how their words or actions will affect someone else and want others to do the same.
- Are deeply aware that their actions affect more than just themselves.

- Care about what is important to others and want people to feel comfortable being who they are.
- Are hardworking, observant, idealistic, and dedicated to whatever they undertake.
- Will go to great lengths to fulfill their obligations to others.
- Synthesize how various actions would impact others and the whole, asking, "How will this affect others?"
- Care about their effect on others, so they will put ample thought into what they say or will think about how something they said may have affected someone.
- Find themselves playing devil's advocate, not because they want to be adversarial but because they want to ensure all relevant perspectives have been considered.
- Come up with theories and then test them and try to break them so they can eventually refine, validate, or discard those theories.
- Want to understand viewpoints different from their own, so they typically lack fear in exploring ideas or concepts that challenge conventional beliefs.
- Find writing helps them organize their thoughts in a meaningful way.
- Want to understand where someone is coming from; therefore, they can generally relate to all types of people.
- Are able to see what needs to be done, and they take initiative to get it done (i.e., self-motivated).

TRIGGER: INCONSIDERATE

Synthesizers feel triggered when people:

- Speak to others in a demeaning, disparaging, or dehumanizing tone.
- Are not authentic but, rather, present themselves in a fake manner to try to elicit a particular reaction instead of just being who they are.
- Brag and boast while directly or indirectly slighting others.
- Belittle or speak down to others (and Synthesizers feel more triggered when others are belittled than they are when someone belittles them).
- Talk badly about someone who is nearby and could be hurt if they overheard what was said.
- Scoff at people, as if inferring they are inferior, or talk in a tone that implies people are subhuman or less-than.
- Don't make the effort to consider what's important to others or see another's perspective.
- Lack tact and make comments inappropriate for the audience (for example, talking about money and causing others to feel uncomfortable).
- Broadcast personal details that someone else had told them in confidence and should have been kept private.
- Don't complete a task they committed to doing, or they do the task poorly, thus negatively impacting others and wasting people's time.
- Are self-absorbed and can't see beyond themselves.
- Seek validation and act with the intent of getting people to tell them how great they are.
- Are fake, materialistic, or toot their own horn to make sure people know how important they are (i.e., blowhards).
- Cause someone to feel uncomfortable, hurt, or ashamed.
- Present themselves as all-knowing or better than others.

SYNTHESIZER PASSION AND VOID

Worthwhile ←——→ *Not Worthwhile*

PASSION: INVESTING TIME AND EFFORT IN DOING WORTHWHILE THINGS

Synthesizers are motivated to:

- Save people time, energy, money, pain, angst, or frustration.
- Invest time and effort upfront doing things that have the potential to pay off later (for example, helping someone prevent frustration or streamlining processes to save time).
- Prevent suffering and help others in big or small ways.
- Seek personal growth and deal with what's not working in their lives on an ongoing basis.
- Research and study subjects in depth that could be valuable to themselves or others or immerse themselves in one of their various intellectual or spiritual pursuits.
- Solve problems and proactively remove obstacles that hinder others to make others' experience frictionless.
- Remove obstacles for people so they can honor who they are and do what they do best.
- Pursue a goal, such as learning a new skill, and then keep at it until they've mastered it or until they shift their efforts to something they perceive as more worthwhile.
- Research a variety of topics or pursue a variety of interests they believe are worthwhile (for example, researching health topics that can help themselves and others).

- Do work behind the scenes, which will enable other people to have the best experience with the least amount of effort.
- Invest their time, energy, and intellect in doing worthwhile things that could have a net positive gain.
- Be productively engaged in something meaningful or make a significant contribution to the world.
- Find a bargain or sale or get a deal.
- Come up with practical solutions that address problems impacting many.
- See evidence that their efforts were worthwhile and have paid off in some way.

When Synthesizers align with their passion, they shift:
an opportunity to invest their effort
in doing something worthwhile
to seeing that their efforts were worthwhile.

VOID: DOING THINGS THAT ARE A WASTE

Synthesizers feel drained when they:

- Do something for nothing (for example, making a meal no one eats).
- Waste time, energy, resources, or effort (for example, duplicating efforts).
- Do things inefficiently when they, consciously or unconsciously, know there is a better way.
- Don't feel they are doing something worthwhile or don't see their efforts making any real difference in the world.

- Waste time micromanaging or babysitting adults who are incompetent in their role or don't do what they are supposed to do.
- Must backtrack when driving somewhere (for example, someone claims to know how to get somewhere, but they don't).
- Do something they feel could cause a negative future consequence (for example, breaking the law).
- Repeatedly react to fire drills without addressing the root cause of the problems.
- Feel that what they are doing is pointless, unproductive, or not a good use of their time.
- Don't feel they can be themselves around certain people who just want to engage in small talk and aren't open to topics that challenge their way of thinking.
- Spend time with people who force their beliefs on others, don't allow others their voice, or think less of those with dissenting views.
- Have valuable feedback to share with someone to help them or their business but don't share it because it would be met with defensiveness, and thus be a waste of time.
- Listen to people repeat what they already said or listen to videos that are mostly fluff and take forever to get to the point.
- Spend sixty minutes attending a meeting that could have been completed in five minutes.
- Do things that take more effort than the value they get out of it (for example, spending four hours reading a book that was neither entertaining nor educational).

SYNTHESIZER PURPOSE AND HURT

Be Who You Are ⟷ *Be Who You're Not*

If you are a Synthesizer, this is how the various facets of your mindset come together:

TRIGGER—VOID—HURT

If people are belittling and don't consider how their actions affect others (trigger), and if I do things that aren't worth my time, energy, and effort (void), then we will not feel free to be who we are and do what we do best (hurt).

PRINCIPLE—PASSION—PURPOSE

If people are respectful and considerate of how their actions affect others (principle), and if I invest my time and energy in doing worthwhile things that will pay off (passion), then we can be who we are and do what we do best (purpose).

PURPOSE STATEMENT

My purpose is to invest my time and effort in doing worthwhile things so that we can be who we truly are and do what we do best.

PART 4

LIVING IN ALIGNMENT WITH YOUR MINDSET

"Would you tell me, please, which way I ought to go from here?"
"That depends a good deal on where you want to get to."

—LEWIS CARROLL, *ALICE IN WONDERLAND*

BE THYSELF

"Be yourself; everyone else is already taken."

—OSCAR WILDE

It might not surprise you, but I love personality profiles. Around 2010, I even once uttered the words, "I would love to create a personality profile..." and then my voice trailed off, finishing the sentence with, "but people just don't do that."

The first personality test I took was in seventh grade. I was part of a community project in Barnesville, Minnesota, and each participant, young and old, took the Myers Briggs, or MBTI®, assessment. While working at Microsoft, I was part of a team based in Fargo, North Dakota, that completed the DiSC assessment. Years later, I was part of a global team, which met in Seattle to delve into Insights Discovery, which revealed if we were red, blue, yellow, or green. I also had the honor of participating in values-based training, including *Bury My Heart at Conference Room B* with Stan Slap and *Strength Essentials* with Marcus Buckingham. On my own, I explored the 5 Love Languages, Enneagram, and others.

So many of us are seeking to know: *Who am I?*

So *who are you*? Can you answer this question? Is it a question that has an answer? Or is it a riddle, an enigma, a great puzzle?

By discovering your mindset, you untangled your multifaceted nature. By identifying the polarities that exist within you, you're able to make sense of your personal beliefs, preferences, and motivations. You see traits that once seemed random aren't random at all. You now have clarity of your principle, passion, and purpose. The question, *"Who am I?"* could plausibly be answered by specifying your *How, What, and Why*.

Yet, for many, it feels like there's still something missing—something more is desired beyond *knowing yourself*.

That "more" has to do with *finding yourself* and *being yourself*.

Know Yourself
Find Yourself
Be Yourself

Finding yourself has to do with discovering your place in the world and knowing you fit somewhere. Perhaps you feel your gifts aren't valued in our noisy, materialistic, achievement-oriented world, though I can promise you that they are desperately needed. Even if you're going through a rough patch or you feel alone in the world, you matter—because every up and down on your journey matters. Understanding what makes your gifts unique and important, rather than taking your strengths for granted because "it's just who I am," shows how your mindset is essential to the whole, be it a family, group, community, organization, or humanity. You are not separate from others but a part of something greater that includes us all. You are part of an interconnected whole, which is better when you share your principle, passion, and purpose.

Finding yourself is about realizing that the world needs your gifts—the world needs you to be exactly who you are.

Being yourself means aligning with your mindset—your principle, passion, and purpose—and living authentically. My yearning to know *"Who am I?"* has always been rooted in a deeper desire to know *"How do I be who I am?"* When misaligned, we oftentimes get "stuck," and feel miserable in the process. When living in alignment, we feel less friction, more satisfaction, and more alive.

Your opportunity involves putting the awareness you have about yourself into action so that you can align with your mindset and live in an authentic way.

To live in alignment, it's necessary to be clear on what being aligned looks like. To do this, imagine drawing a horizontal line through the middle of the Mindset Framework. Above the line are positive poles: principle, passion, and purpose. Below the line looms trigger, void, and hurt. Above the line, you're aligned; below, you're misaligned.

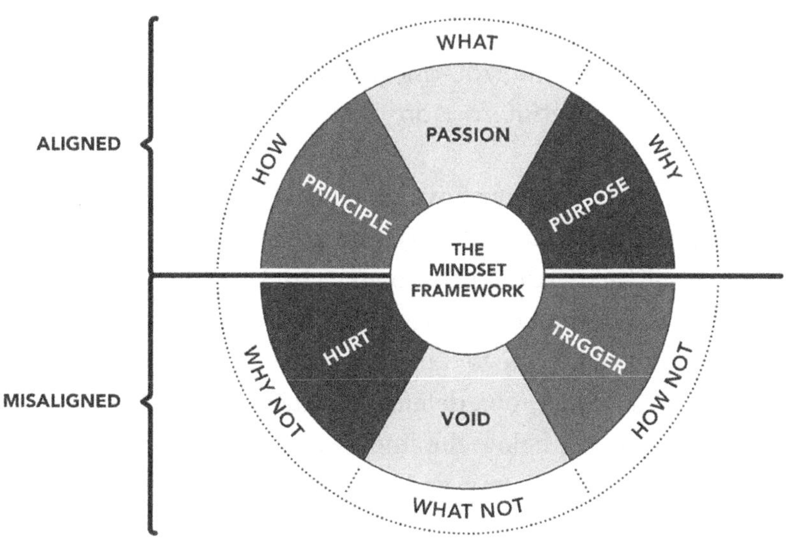

You can think of this line as the line of authenticity or the line of integrity. But for simplicity, let's just call it "the line" because when someone triggers you, they've crossed a line—*this* line. When an activity drains your energy, it drags you below *this* line. When you're aligned with who you are, your sense of ease has everything to do with being above *this* line.

At any given moment, you're either above the line or below it: aligned or misaligned.

Due to the mutually exclusive nature of the polarities, you cannot simultaneously experience both ends of a polarity: you can't be loving what you're doing while also loathing what you're doing. You can experience them consecutively, but not concurrently. You might be having the time of your life, and then someone severely triggers you, and down you go. Once you fall below the line, you can stay there for minutes, hours, or days.

> Mutually exclusive refers to opposing behaviors, actions, or states of being that cannot take place simultaneously. For example, you cannot do what you love and do what you loathe at the same time.

If your goal is to stay above the line, you must learn to avoid the trap of misalignment. If this were innate, we'd all be doing it; when misaligned, we'd quickly bounce back and realign. Because it's not obvious until you recognize it, many of us frequently find ourselves below the line for far too long.

Once misaligned, our defense mechanisms have a cunning way of keeping us below the line. Our reactions aim to protect us, but they can also trap us by relentlessly steering our attention deeper into the problem. When we reprimand someone for triggering us, we focus on our trigger—below the line. If we begrudgingly do a job we loathe, our attention is on our void—below the line. If we're worried about making a fool of ourselves, our attention remains on our insecurity—also below the line. Our instinct to focus our attention on the problem keeps us misaligned. Consequently, realignment doesn't happen as automatically as we might hope.

One of the many powerful words of wisdom I took away from Dr. David Martin after attending his "Fully Live Workshop" in November 2021 was:

"What gets your attention
is not the intention."

Our attention is frequently captured by things that cause misalignment: triggers, resentment, remorse, voids, insecurities, and hurt. They seize our *attention* yet steer us away from our true *intention* of living in alignment.

What we're unconsciously *led to do* and what we *need to do* to get back into alignment are oftentimes at odds with one another.

As it turns out, we've been interpreting the misaligned state all wrong. We can't solve our problems by employing the defense mechanisms that keep us misaligned.

To realign, we can't zero in on "the problem" that's causing the misalignment. Yet, that's what we automatically do, so we stay stuck below the line. It's as though the check engine light comes on in our car, and rather than looking under the hood, we try to fix the dashboard light to get the check engine light to turn off.

There is a way out—or should I say *up*. If we recognize when we are misaligned, we can use this uncomfortable awareness as a reminder to realign.

Your trigger, void, and hurt alert you that you're misaligned. These facets grab your attention as if flashing a yellow light warning you: *you need to refocus your attention above the line.*

Author Garth Stein shares a similar philosophy in *The Art of Racing in the Rain*: "In racing, they say that your car goes where your eyes go. The driver who cannot tear his eyes away from the wall as he spins out of control will meet that wall; the driver who looks down the track as he feels his tires break free will regain control of his vehicle."

Just like racecar drivers, our best strategy for success involves placing our attention on where we want to go: above the line.

That means, when you're triggered, attend to your principle. When burned out, focus on your passion. When consumed by insecurities, align with your purpose. To move into an aligned state, you must shift your attention above the line, and in doing so, you invert the polarity and naturally align.

Alignment is the destination, and your mindset will show you the way. When it comes to overcoming burnout, what works for a Sensor won't work for an Optimizer, an Intuitor, or any other mindset. The concepts are the same, but to align, the specific actions you take must align with *your* mindset, not anyone else's.

The following chapters walk you through the process of getting back above the line when you find yourself below it.

ALIGNING WITH THE MINDSET PRINCIPLES

"Life is the only game in which the object of the game is to learn the rules."

—ASHLEIGH BRILLIANT

Imagine, if you will, four students working summer jobs at the community pool. Jill's job is to ensure pool-goers, many of them children, are safe, which often translates to a strict "no running" policy. Kai's duty is to keep people hydrated. Carlo oversees fun. And Madisson keeps the pool and surrounding area clean.

The students get to work, each narrowly focused on their individual role. Without knowing and respecting each other's duties, chaos ensues. Jill (in charge of safety) becomes furious when Carlo (in charge of fun) gathers up a gaggle of children and races to the diving board. Madisson (in charge of cleanliness) is enraged when

Kai (in charge of hydration) gives bottles of blue Gatorade to toddlers, thus putting a germ-free pool at risk.

As rudimentary as this example seems, it accurately depicts what occurs every day when we go through life unaware of the principles other people uphold. We're each narrowly focused on upholding our own mindset principle, generally unaware as the people around us uphold other principles. We're trying to play the same game, yet we're playing by different rules.

With this perspective, should it come as any surprise that we occasionally find ourselves at odds with others?

Our ignorance of others' principles is the reason for so much angst, conflict, and misunderstanding. Without knowing the playbook, people trigger us, and we trigger them. When unaware that 96 percent of people operate differently from us, the world can, at times, feel like a very lonely and frustrating place. It's easy to think there is something wrong with us—or with everyone else. Neither is true.

When we understand the playbook, things suddenly become easier, just as they would for our pool employees. When each employee understands the others' responsibilities, they no longer step on each other's toes but, rather, support each other. As Carlo honors Jill's role, he encourages kids to have fun without running around the pool. When Kai is mindful of Madisson's role, he is more careful about where and how he keeps the kids hydrated. Similarly, when we recognize that each person upholds one of the 25 Mindset principles, and we understand what those principles mean, we suddenly realize we're all on the same team. We just have different responsibilities.

And we *are* on the same team, even though it might not always feel like it. Every one of us is trying to uphold a moral principle that benefits everyone else. When we keep this in mind, it becomes easier to support each other.

With a basic understanding of the mindset principles, you can take actions to support both yourself and the people in your life so everyone can spend more time above the line. In this section, you will learn:

- How to be triggered less often by the people closest to you.
- How to make sense of others' "unreasonable" demands.
- How to stop the rumination cycle when you are guilty of not upholding your mindset principle.
- How to reveal your blind spot to avoid unknowingly triggering others.

HOW TO BE TRIGGERED LESS OFTEN

"Defensive strategy never has produced ultimate victory."
—DOUGLAS MACARTHUR

How did you learn not to rest your hand on a hot stove? Who taught you to blink when the wind blows dust into your eyes? And how ever did you master the leg kick when the doctor taps your kneecap with a pointy rubber hammer?

You didn't learn these things because they are all involuntary reflexes. They serve you and protect you.

Like it or not, your triggers operate similarly. When someone compromises your mindset principle, your *"Grr!"* reflex automatically kicks in. Just like your physiological reflexes, this psychological reflex serves and protects by safeguarding a virtue of humanity.

Triggers don't come with an off switch. You cannot learn to *not* be triggered. This means that no matter how many times someone tells you, "You're overreacting," "It's not a big deal," "You're too sensitive," "You care too much," or "You shouldn't let it bother you"—you *will* be triggered.

But you can reduce how often you're triggered, which is important, because triggers can hijack your essence, hurling you below the line in an instant.

Once we've been triggered, many of us will try to "teach people a lesson." In the heat of the moment, we zero in on the wrongdoer: *You should not have done that; you should know better; you did a bad thing; you are the problem; you are to blame; you need to change your ways.* Our fight instinct is to point the finger at the other person.

Sometimes, it feels like we're getting through to them, or at least making them aware of their intolerable actions. More often, our reaction puts the offender on the defensive, which creates a whole new series of issues. In our minds, we just want them to understand where we're coming from and uphold the principle that's so very important to us. In their minds, we're pointing out their flaws, trying to change them, telling them what to do, or implying they are stupid or inadequate.

Getting defensive, pointing fingers, or harboring resentment resolves little because the bottom line is this: your attention is below the line. Your focus remains on your trigger and the wrongdoer. Rather than standing *for* something, you stand *against* it, which is a recipe for misalignment.

When you're triggered, emotions run high. An automatic reflex can quickly escalate into an unruly reaction. You need to distinguish between the two—a *reflex* is when your leg kicks; a *reaction* is then grabbing the rubber hammer and whacking your doctor with it. It can be helpful to think of your trigger as a reflex, an unconscious action, or a feeling. The reflex—the "*Grr!*" sensation—can't be controlled. However, how you respond—what you do next—is in your control.

Next time you get triggered, aim to moderate your response and permit yourself to address the trigger later when you're above the line. When you're triggered, you're not thinking clearly. You're in big-dumb-wild-animal mode, apt to do or say something you'll later regret. With a defensive approach, you'll likely put others on the defensive. So in most situations, it's best to hit the pause button, count to five, sip your water, or walk away and choose not to participate.

This is especially important if the person triggering you is a perfect stranger. You can't control the people around you; you can only control your response. So you can get yourself worked up as you try to teach them a lesson they probably won't learn, or you can take a breath. On your exhale, focus on your principle: *I value being "insightful," I value "competence,"* or whatever your principle is. You can moderate your trigger reaction by choosing not to react immediately and instead choosing to realign by focusing on your principle, passion, or purpose.

Once you realign, a more productive use of your energy involves helping the people closest to you understand your principle, which can result in you being triggered less often. If your triggers go unaddressed with family, friends, or coworkers, it will likely harm the relationship, causing you to resent or avoid someone.

To invert the polarity, your focus must be on your principle, not the trigger. Communicating your principle is most effective when you're aligned with it, not when you are triggered.

Once you're back above the line, you can share what's important to you in a way people can truly hear and understand. Above the line, your thoughts are more coherent. You're no longer focused on the trigger or the wrongdoer, so you're not likely to put people on the defensive.

To help others understand the importance of your mindset principle, you could simply ask your spouse, coworker, or friend to read your mindset chapter or tell them about your mindset in your own words. For example, an Integrator, who values common decency, could share something like this: "I don't expect anyone to win the Nobel Prize; I just want people to be decent humans. If we don't all do our part in our families, teams, or communities, then we make it someone else's problem. That's why I get frustrated when people don't do their share—because then it puts the burden on someone else, and I don't think the burden should fall on any one person. If we all do our part, then we can all enjoy life."

When you help others understand your mindset principle, it's important that you take ownership and keep the focus on yourself: This is who *I* am, and this is what's important to *me*. As soon as the script flips and you point out others' wrongdoing, suggesting that *they* are to blame, you're likely to put people on the defensive. Sharing below-the-line sentiments, such as "That's why it irritates me when you're such a jerk" or "Here is a list of things that annoy me about you," is a sure way to guarantee people won't hear you out.

When you align with your principle, there is no blame, no finger-pointing, and no hostility. You're simply sharing why the principle is so important to you and how you feel when someone—anyone—threatens that principle. With this approach, people can listen and take in the information. And because they're able to understand your perspective, they can make small changes to uphold it—not because they're being forced to, but because they care about you.

When people learn about your mindset principle, will they stop triggering you overnight? Probably not. Then again, people can surprise you. Aim for progress, not perfection. Your message might not land immediately, because people perceive the world—and others—through the lens of their own mindset.

This also explains why, after sharing your principle with people, they may respond with "Really? I didn't know that about you." Sometimes this can sting, especially when you discover that someone close to you didn't know something so essential about who you are. But go easy on them. People see things from their own perspective, that is, until you help them see yours.

By using your trigger as a reminder to realign yourself and then share your principle with those closest to you, you stand a chance to be more understood and less triggered.

HOW TO MAKE SENSE OF OTHERS' "UNREASONABLE" DEMANDS

"If one does not understand a person, one tends to regard him as a fool."

—CARL JUNG

When my husband would do the dishes, there always came a moment when he'd start grumbling about some dish that wasn't properly rinsed off. Exasperated, he'd make sure my son and I knew we failed to soak a dish, acting as if a bowl caked with dried oatmeal was akin to a nuclear catastrophe.

After begrudgingly acknowledging our misdeed, I'd go on my merry way, silently thinking he was overly dramatic. *Seriously? He's getting that worked up over having to soak a dish?*

When people get worked up, it provides a strong clue that they are triggered. So often in relationships, we regurgitate the same argument again and again, though it doesn't always look or sound the same. One day, my husband is annoyed I didn't rinse a plate. A week later, he was irritated that I didn't jump in line to get on the airplane the instant our boarding group was called. What appears to be a new dispute is rooted in the same trigger: He doesn't want anyone hindering his forward momentum.

Inevitably, we say or do something "harmless," someone "over-reacts," and it sets off a cantankerous downward spiral. Through the lens of your mindset, it's not that big of a deal, so watching someone react so strongly to something "minor" can leave you shaking your head in judgment or confusion. You can easily defend your position: *It doesn't bother me, so why should it bother them?* From there, it's easy to conclude that *clearly, there's something wrong with them.*

When people uphold a principle different from ours, we often view their heightened reactions as unreasonable, overly sensitive, or self-righteous. Consider that many Balancers would feel uncomfortable if you threw them a surprise party. They carefully orchestrate their days to fit everything in, so something as seemingly benevolent—and loving—as throwing them a surprise party could blindside them. Meanwhile, other mindsets would love such a surprise. What gives?

People react based on their mindset, *not yours.*

Just because you aren't bothered by something doesn't mean someone you care about isn't irked by it. And just as you can't change what triggers you, neither can they. A Harmonizer can't overlook a little white lie. A Stabilizer can't ignore when meeting participants arrive eight minutes late. A Balancer can't help but be frustrated when they must reshuffle their entire day because people don't do what's expected.

When we only see through the lens of our own mindset, it's difficult to rationalize, or even comprehend, others' reactions. Behind all their "unreasonable" reactions, however, is likely a principle someone is not upholding. Underneath it all, the people in your life just want you to uphold their mindset principle.

If you're triggering someone, it's up to *you* to make the small changes to support them. You can't appreciate someone for their principle, passion, and purpose and, at the same time, despise them for their trigger, void, and hurt. They come wrapped in the same package.

My husband became triggered when my son and I failed to rinse a bowl because his principle is being persistent. His need for forward momentum contributes to his strengths in sales, planning vacations, and even pushing me to get my work out into the world. When I understood that he feels as strongly about being persistent as I feel about being considerate, it was easy for me to make slight changes in my behavior to uphold his principle. His expectations of me no longer seemed unreasonable, just different from my own.

To understand the people closest to you, ask them to discover their mindset. Hand them this book. Encourage them to determine their mindset, as opposed to guessing their mindset or telling them who they are. To determine the mindset of children, observe their behavior and ask them what brings about a "*Grr!*" sensation in them.

Once you identify someone's mindset, listen to them, review their mindset chapter, and practice perceiving things through their mindset lens. Let it sink in that how you feel about your principle is how they feel about something different. Supporters feel just as strongly about being useful as Optimizers feel about being truthful. Progressors feel as strongly about thinking for themselves as Sensors feel about being encouraging and supportive.

When you understand other people's principles *relative to your own*, they suddenly make sense. Then, you can more easily uphold what you formerly viewed as irrational expectations. Rather than bitterly upholding their unruly demands, in this new light, you *want* to take steps to uphold their principle because you care about them. You know maintaining their principle is important in keeping them aligned, which makes them much more pleasant to be around and creates overall harmony within the relationship.

If you're feeling adventurous, you can even come up with a "safe word" that those closest to you can say when you trigger them. When they yell "hairball," you'll know your actions have landed them below the line. It sends the message, "I'm triggered," while effectively acknowledging that "We're working on this." A playful word can add levity to an otherwise tense situation—not to mention, it's a good alternative to other words they might want to call you.

And don't worry, learning to uphold others' principles is not a full-time job, and it can actually feel fun, or at least caring. You simply need to do, or not do, certain things you know matter to someone else. You don't need to be hypervigilant or weird about it. In most scenarios, it consists of minor adjustments. For example:

- Instead of calling out the "idiot" next to you, speak in a non-condescending manner so people aren't put on the defensive.
- Instead of leaving your shoes in the middle of the hallway, put them in the closet so people don't trip over them and get hurt.
- Rather than telling a little white lie, tell the truth so people can trust you.
- Instead of telling people how great you are, let your actions speak for themselves so people can come to their own conclusions.
- Rather than waiting for someone to remind you to return the phone charger you borrowed, return it as soon as your phone is charged so you don't add more work for other people.

- Instead of tiptoeing around what you're trying to say, be clear and say what you mean so people can help you.
- Instead of putting a dirty dish in the sink, rinse it and put it in the dishwasher so people aren't inconvenienced by you.

As you uphold someone else's principle, you don't need to deny your own. Some of your defense mechanisms may be challenged (such as lying, exaggerating, conforming, bulldozing, gossiping, or complaining), but it's worth working through them. As you forgo habits that don't serve you or the people around you, you help others live in alignment.

The 25 Mindsets give us a common language that, when used, can help all of us spend more time above the line. With an elevated perspective, we're able to make sense of each other and support one another. Relationships suddenly flow easier and feel more enjoyable, all because we're living above the line.

HOW TO STOP THE RUMINATION CYCLE

"We define ourselves far too often by our past failures.
That's not you. You are this person right now.
You're the person who has learned from those failures."
—JOE ROGAN

My void is doing things that are a waste, which includes wasting time. It drives me bonkers when my email blows up because someone decided to "Reply All" rather than "Reply," when their response is not relevant to "all." To complicate matters, when others try to "help" and then "Reply All" to tell people not to "Reply All," it about pushes me over the edge.

Several years ago, after too many people decided to "Reply All" to an organization-wide email, I emailed a meme to another manager, who I assumed was equally baffled. I sent him an image of an adorable kitten levitating through the green grass, which read, "Every time you hit 'Reply All,' God kills a kitten."

Isn't it interesting how it's only after hitting "Send" you think, "Oops. That was probably inappropriate." And to think I sent this meme to a person of faith who is a consummate professional. Seriously, what was I thinking?

Queue the guilt, regret, and remorse—all because I reacted from my trigger, below the line, rather than aligning with my principle of being considerate.

That's what happens when we're triggered: while being considerate is important to me, I still manage to be inconsiderate, according to my ideals, too often. That's when the rumination cycle kicks in. I'm quick to beat myself up, wishing I had been more considerate, said things differently, or hadn't said anything at all.

Rumination occurs when you replay a situation in your mind again and again and again and again, wishing you could go back in time and do things differently. As if watching a bad movie, you recall your dreadful actions while internally pleading for an alternate ending.

It happens to all of us. We expect people to uphold our mindset principle, but this time we're the one (gasp!) who is guilty of breaking our own rule. You may get triggered when people are rude, but now *you* behaved rudely to a cashier. You may feel frustrated when people don't make thoughtful decisions, but this time, *you* messed up and made a lousy recommendation. You may always need to keep things moving forward, but now *you* carelessly caused a setback.

As hard as we try, there are times we fail to uphold our own rule. The consequence is regret, remorse, guilt, and rumination. We become angry with ourselves and obsess about our wrongdoing.

Why did I do that?

Why did I say that?

Why didn't I catch that?

How could I have done that?

What's wrong with me?

You can ruminate for three hours, three days, or three weeks. Still, what's done is done. And however long you spend beating yourself up is time stolen from living out your principle, passion, and purpose because as long as you remain trapped in rumination, you stay misaligned.

When you catch yourself in a rumination cycle, you can continue to ruminate, despite it being highly unproductive, or you can accept responsibility by taking action to right a wrong and permit yourself to realign.

Ruminate or take responsibility and realign: the choice is yours.

Regret, remorse, and rumination act as warning signals—an illuminated check engine light—to reorient yourself and return to upholding your mindset principle. After all, when you break your own rule, it feels horrible. It reminds you: *I don't want to make that mistake again.*

Once you've learned this lesson, further rumination is futile. Berating yourself only keeps you trapped below the line. To invert the polarity, your attention must move above the line, into principle, purpose, and passion. If your mistake warrants action, then take responsibility, which might mean apologizing to someone for your misstep. If you've taken action or there is no action to be taken, give yourself permission to move on and realign.

That said, it's not always easy to snap out of the rumination cycle. It's like a dream that feels so vivid, you struggle to return to reality. Recently, I dreamt I helped someone by taking her cat with me while she cleaned a house she had rented. I put her cat in my car, drove to a gas station, brought the cat inside with me, and then sat at a table and worked. When the cat and I returned to the car, her two kids sat in the backseat screaming, enraged I had left them. The older child, maybe four years old, had called an adult and told him what I'd done. Despite the children magically appearing in the car, I was mortified. I knew the kids had been scarred by this experience. *What will I tell their mom? How will I ever fix this?* Then, the narrator of my dream chimed in: *It's a dream. You can stop. You don't have to give it your attention anymore.*

Like a dream, when we ruminate, we see and feel the events vividly. With our attention on our wrongdoing, we keep ourselves misaligned. We know we messed up, so it can feel downright careless to move on—as if the more responsible thing to do is to berate ourselves. However, when we try to make a case for rumination, it doesn't make any sense. After all, you generally do a stellar job of upholding your principle. This occurrence is the exception, not the norm. You feel more strongly about your principle than 96 percent of people, so of course, the occasional blip stings.

To break the rumination cycle, take action, if there is action to take, and then draw your attention back to your principle. Celebrate your principle and the fact that you uphold it so strongly. Acknowledge that it's okay to feel as you do and give yourself permission to realign. Focus on your principle and get back to living your true self. Let the narrator of your ruminating mind chime in and help invert the polarity: *You're ruminating. You can stop. You don't have to give it your attention anymore.*

HOW TO REVEAL YOUR BLIND SPOT

"Anything in excess is a poison."
—THEODORE LEVITT

What do ten teaspoons of salt, one hundred cups of coffee, and six liters of water have in common? All can be deadly when consumed in a short timeframe. As much as you might love salt, coffee, or water, it is possible to have too much of a good thing.

The same is true of principles. Your principle is good, but when it's upheld in excess, it creates a blind spot.

As a Synthesizer, I value being considerate. I want people to feel comfortable, and when I say something that's met with defensiveness, it tells me I didn't consider their perspective. To compensate, I learned it's safer to speak indirectly and tiptoe around certain subjects or people, always ready to reel back my words at the first hint of offending someone. Through my mindset lens, this cautious communication seemed justified; I was simply being considerate of others.

Except I wasn't merely being considerate. I was upholding my principle in excess. In doing so, I unknowingly triggered others.

In our need to stay above the line, we can inadvertently thrust others below it.

Herein lies your blind spot.

We all have blind spots because we all wish to avoid the discomfort of regret, remorse, and rumination. Upholding our principle in excess can thwart feelings of regret, but it propagates other issues. Because we are biased toward our own principle, we are blind to the fact that we may negatively impact others when we uphold it in an exaggerated way. The 25 Mindsets work together harmoniously, but this is true only when everyone upholds them in a balanced way—not in excess.

Blind spots emerge in several ways. To ensure preparedness, Protectors step in, take charge, and give orders, which triggers Progressors, who don't like being told what to do. To promote kindness, Cultivators may avoid giving negative feedback if it could hurt someone's feelings, triggering Integrators, who want prompt feedback so they can make changes. To ensure quality information, Optimizers demand statements be backed by proof and facts, which irritates Intuitors, who recognize their insights as a valuable source of information.

With a myopic focus on upholding my principle, I created a blind spot. I was completely unaware that I was triggering Captivators, among others, who value clear and direct communication. Not wanting to offend, I was oblivious to the reality that my indirect approach irritated others, and I was mortified to discover I was guilty of just about everything on a Captivator's trigger list.

You can't fix what you don't know is a problem, but once you see your blind spot, you can take action to address it.

You can reveal your blind spot by reading through the triggers for all 25 Mindsets and paying special attention to those mindsets you rated lowest, or least like you, in the *Discover Your Mindset* process (Step 2: Principle and Trigger Assessment). After you identify the mindset (or mindsets) you trigger, spend time learning about the principle this mindset upholds and do your part to avoid the triggering behaviors.

If after reading through the mindset chapters, you still don't see your blind spot (after all, it's called a blind spot for a reason), ask someone you trust and respect to offer feedback. It's possible you view your behavior as favorable when, meanwhile, others may view you as being a braggart, a complainer, arrogant, unapproachable, or someone who takes credit for other people's work.

By seeing my blind spot, I could see I was guilty of triggering Captivators. Then, by taking time to understand my blind spot, I could understand who Captivators are and why the principle they uphold is so important in the world. Captivators value directness because it's important to them that people get help when they need it, which can only happen if people speak up clearly—so if you're afraid of heights, they want you to speak up so you're not uncomfortable. They want people to speak freely and be free to be exactly who they are. It's not inconsiderate. It's beautiful and makes perfect sense. In contrast, when I upheld my principle in excess, I wrongly concluded it was safer to say nothing at all rather than risk offending or bothering someone. In doing so, I isolated myself because I could only rely on myself if I wasn't willing to speak up or ask for help. Captivators have taught me the value of speaking my truth clearly and not beating around the bush out of fear of offending someone.

As it turns out, the mindsets we inadvertently trigger can teach us the most. The big takeaway is this: we can learn from others who are different from us, keeping in mind that we are hyperfocused on upholding *one* of the 25 Mindset principles.

As we review the triggers and principles of different mindsets, part of working with our blind spot involves considering things through a different lens. For example, even if we think we know what a principle, such as "accountability," means, we may merely understand it through our own mindset lens. Being accountable is core to an Achiever mindset. And though I've always viewed myself as being accountable, given I consistently fulfill my commitments (even when it comes at the cost of myself), to Achievers, accountability means more than that. When I truly understood what accountability means to Achievers by looking through their lens, I revealed another one of my blind spots, which caused me to reflect on a time when I lacked accountability.

While working at Microsoft, our general manager asked me and my coworker to get an incentive program in place to reward account managers who sold our services to their customers. We delved in and met with several individuals, but we ultimately concluded the program incentivized the wrong behavior. When we shared these findings with our GM, he didn't hide his disappointment. He had not asked us to evaluate the incentive program; he had asked us to get it in place. For him, the program fits into a much larger vision—one that had many moving parts and counted on everyone executing their specific job. Through his mindset lens, he trusted us to do a job, but as it turned out, he couldn't count on us to get it done.

When we understand principles differently than the people who uphold them as their core principle, it can reveal another blind spot. On the other hand, when we make the effort to understand the mindset principles through the lens of the beholder, we can communicate better and work together better as a team. Had I understood accountability through the lens of an Achiever, I could have engaged my GM earlier, understood his vision, and we could have worked together to determine how to proceed.

A simple exercise, or mini workshop, you can do as a couple, team, group, or family includes letting each person share their mindset principle and trigger with the group. People can share in their own words or share excerpts from their mindset chapter; just make sure each person is heard. This typically only requires five minutes per person, which is also enough time for others to ask a question or two. The mini workshop involves a simple two-step process: teach and learn.

- **Teach**: Take turns "teaching" others about your mindset principle. Though upholding your principle is natural for you, it is not obvious to everyone else because they're upholding a different mindset principle. Along with helping people understand your principle, share your triggers while allowing people to see how they oppose your mindset principle. When talking about triggers, just be sure to keep the focus on yourself and avoid blaming others.

- **Learn**: Take turns "learning" as others share their mindset principle. Consider why their principle is important to you and in the world. When learning about others' triggers, keep in mind that they can't change the things that trigger them. Look for opportunities where you can do your part to uphold others' mindset principles.

I've facilitated numerous such workshops, and it's extraordinary to watch people's reactions as they listen intently to others. Behaviors that seemed outlandish suddenly make sense. You can watch the lightbulb go off when people understand their peers in a new way and former blind spots become apparent.

When we allow ourselves to look at our blind spots, we not only avoid triggering others, but we also strengthen our character and become more well-rounded in the process. We do our part to keep others aligned, which ultimately helps us remain above the line too.

ALIGNING WITH YOUR PASSION

"Nothing great in the world has ever been accomplished without passion."

—GEORGE HEGEL

I didn't burn out when I worked seventy-hour work weeks. I burned out while working thirty-hour work weeks. Working long hours wasn't a problem because I believed my efforts were worthwhile. I was aligned with my passion. When I was no longer aligned with my passion but, rather, in my void, mustering the energy to work half as many hours was a struggle. When you align with your passion, it gives you energy.

Just as you need to add logs to a fire to maintain it, you need to feed your passion to keep it burning strong. When you do things that align with your passion, it's like throwing a log on the campfire. It fuels you. Your passion requires your active participation because if you ignore it, it burns out.

A core passion resides in every one of us. It's not meant to remain a mystery. It's meant to be known, celebrated, and kindled. When you put energy into your passion, it, in turn, energizes you.

Aligning with your passion allows you to:

- **Bring your best effort to your work.** Doing things that naturally motivate you results in greater productivity, engagement, and an eagerness to get out of bed in the morning.

- **Bring your best self to your relationships.** Because you're living above the line, you feel lighter, clearer, kinder, happier, and more relaxed. Consequently, you're a more enjoyable person to be around.

- **Be productive with the least amount of effort.** We have come to associate "work" with being grueling and laborious. Yet, when you're aligned with your passion, work is much easier. Above the line, even difficult feats feel relatively effortless.

- **Experience a strong sense of self-worth.** It is through passion-aligned action that you experience a well-deserved sense of value. You build a stronger sense of self-worth when you align with your passion and see the satisfactory results of your actions.

- **Enjoy the natural highs of life.** Each time you see evidence that your actions have brought about a more desired after-state, you feel energized.

- **Experience true success**. If you make a million-dollar salary but feel miserable every day, that's not success; it's merely an *illusion* of success. True success involves living in alignment with who you are.

In this section, you will learn:

- How to prioritize your passion and use it as a filter to pursue work and activities that enliven you.
- Why you may not experience a high, even when you're aligned with your passion, and what to do differently.
- How to prevent and overcome burnout.

HOW TO PRIORITIZE YOUR PASSION

"Follow your own passion—not your parents', not your teachers'—yours."

—ROBERT BALLARD

In 2008, I read *The 4-Hour Work Week* by Tim Ferriss. The idea of living my life now, rather than waiting until I retired to do all the things I wanted to do, changed my life. Before Ferriss's book, I had accepted the notion that if I worked hard, I could enjoy my life later. With my expanded worldview, I hesitantly mentioned to my husband that "maybe" we could consider moving to the mountains full time. We lived south of Denver, in Parker, Colorado, but we spent our weekends in Keystone, where we enjoyed hiking, biking, fly fishing, skiing, and snowboarding. At the time, snowboarding energized me the most; I couldn't get enough of it. Moving ninety minutes closer to the mountain would allow me to do more of what I loved. Always moving forward, my husband wasted no time, and a few months later we settled in our new home at 9,200 feet in Keystone, Colorado. In voicing openness to make a change, I allowed myself to stop taking life so seriously and "let" myself pursue a life that fulfilled me.

Whether you've known your passion for decades or you just discovered it an hour ago, it's up to you to prioritize it. After all, your sense of vitality depends on it.

The best place to start, aside from jumping in and doing something that aligns with your passion, is to get to intimately know it. It's not enough to just read your mindset chapter. When you fully understand how your passion shows up in your life, you'll be better equipped to answer tough questions when they arise, such as: *What do I want to do as a career? What do I want to do in my spare time? What should I do in my retirement? Why do I no longer enjoy what I'm doing? What should I do next?*

What you do can either energize you or deplete you, so it's important you pursue aligned action whenever possible. To prioritize your passion, here are a few things to consider:

- Notice when you're aligned with your passion.
- Notice when you're in your void.
- Honor your passion in your way.
- Learn from others who share your mindset.

NOTICE WHEN YOU'RE ALIGNED WITH YOUR PASSION

Many of us have been coasting on autopilot. We align with our passion and feel motivated, but we don't necessarily know why some activities motivate us and others do not. When you know precisely what motivates you, you can pursue endless activities that fall under the umbrella of your passion. You also can tweak what you're doing so it better aligns with your passion.

Now that you've identified your mindset and know your passion, practice noticing it and naming it. Put words to the experience. When you're excited, ask, "How does this relate to my passion?" Intuitors, for example, may recognize they are looking forward to meeting with their clients because their work allows them to go within and follow their inner guidance.

Since most of us have been raised to think of passion as an activity, it's valuable to recognize the shift that transpires because of your actions. When you see beyond the activity and recognize what your passion accomplishes, you can use that information as a filter to help guide you on a path that honors your innate gifts. For example, in career planning, you can reflect on how your passion will show up in various roles and pursue what is right for you, not what is right for someone else.

Feel, or think about, the difference between the following statements, which compare an activity to the actual passion or what the actions *accomplish*:

- *My passion is sewing* (i.e., an activity), versus, *my passion is seeing my ideas and visions come to life* (i.e., what the action accomplishes).
- *My passion is skiing*, versus, *my passion is achieving new levels of mastery.*
- *My passion is writing*, versus, *my passion is igniting others' emotions.*
- *My passion is learning*, versus, *my passion is expanding horizons.*

- *My passion is traveling,* versus, *my passion is pursuing new experiences and adventures.*
- *My passion is teaching,* versus, *my passion is strengthening myself and others.*

Get clear on the shift that occurs as a direct result of your actions and then align with it whenever possible. Begin to identify the before-you state and the after-you state. For example, before you took action, your daughter didn't know how to change her tire; after you, she could do it on her own. Before you, an audience didn't understand cryptocurrency; after you, they understood it. Before you, the office supply room was a mess; after you, it's organized.

Whatever shift transpires because of you, pay attention to it and celebrate it. When you see the underlying shift that transpires because of your actions, you can align with your inner motivations no matter what comes your way—injury, boredom, or life changes—because your passion runs much deeper.

NOTICE WHEN YOU ARE IN YOUR VOID

Though your void lies below the line, it's helpful to fully understand it so you can spend more time above the line. In addition, it's better to respond to a subtle "*Ugh*," an indication you are in your void, early on, rather than waiting until it intensifies.

When you're doing something you don't want to do, ask, "How does this relate to my void?" Initially, it might be surprising: *Ah yes, I'm my void when I do boring things. No wonder I'm irritable.* In time, it will likely become shockingly predictable. You'll find yourself saying the same word again and again when referring to your void. For example, I find myself regularly using the word "waste."

Here are just a few words that other mindsets hear themselves saying repeatedly:

- Uninteresting
- Boring
- Unappreciated
- Trapped
- Unmeaningful
- Inefficient
- Slow
- Stagnating
- Disconnected
- Unoriginal

Anytime you recognize you're in your void, use it as an indicator to prioritize something that motivates you. If you find yourself procrastinating, there's a strong chance you're in your void. Procrastination is not a character flaw. You're just trying to avoid something that depletes your energy. The secret to overcoming procrastination is to align with your passion. That said, we all must do things, at least sometimes, that lie within our void. When that's the case, it's best to get in, get it done, and get out. That way it doesn't drain you so much.

HONOR YOUR PASSION IN YOUR WAY

We're not one-size-fits-all, so your passion may guide you to climb the corporate ladder or to stay away from management roles altogether. Your passion may lead you to run for political office or steer clear of politics. Your passion may guide you to remain in the same line of work for forty years or change careers every three years.

My passion led me to make a change during the height of my corporate career. Despite not knowing exactly what my passion was back then, what I did know was I wanted to work as long as possible—I just wanted to be doing something worthwhile. I didn't aspire to get my years in so I could retire and do less. I aspired to align with my passion and do more.

Your path needs to work for you, not anyone else. So resist copying anyone else who has a different mindset or projecting your passion onto others. If you are money-motivated, that's okay. Just don't assume everyone else is too.

LEARN FROM THOSE WHO SHARE YOUR MINDSET

Because people who share your mindset also share your passion, they can often provide a valuable perspective. You can glean insights from like-minded individuals by discovering what they enjoy, what they dislike, what activities fulfill or drain them, and the lessons they have learned along the way.

Of course, that doesn't mean you should follow someone else's exact path, even if they share your mindset. You can, however, leverage their perspective to help you in charting your own life because you will find many commonalities. Perhaps you are looking for a new hobby and discover that someone who shares your mindset loves pottery; it may spur you to sign up for an introductory class. It's also common to find similar career interests within people of the same mindset, for example, Intuitors pursuing careers as healers, Optimizers with PhDs, Producers as project managers, Achievers who are CEOs, or Integrators who are EMTs. That doesn't mean, however, if you're a young Integrator you need to pursue a career as an EMT. Yet, it could be extraordinarily valuable to learn what someone else with your mindset liked and disliked about their professional experiences.

Your mindset should never pigeonhole or limit you. You should simply honor it in a way that is compelling to you and that opens new worlds of possibility.

HOW TO ENSURE YOU EXPERIENCE A HIGH

"I can't change the direction of the wind, but I can adjust my sails to always reach my destination."
—JIMMY DEAN

My decade-long journey to learn about the mindsets played out like a rollercoaster ride filled with endless highs and lows. One day, I'd be on top of the world, exhilarated I had figured out something that could make people's lives easier, like how to identify your passion. A few days later, the solutions wouldn't come so easily, and I would question if my efforts would ever amount to anything useful.

In both cases I was aligned with my passion—I persisted because I believed my efforts were worthwhile—but sometimes I experienced a high, and other times, I did not. On the high days, I saw evidence that my efforts paid off because I had put one more puzzle piece together, while on the low days, even though I worked just as hard, I didn't see any obvious signs of my efforts being worthwhile.

Sometimes, even when we're aligned with our passion, we can still feel something is amiss. A Captivator may go out of his way to help a friend, but the friend isn't appreciative; an Intuitor may follow what she is led to do, but things don't go smoothly; a Perceiver may host an engaging webinar and then hear crickets after the fact.

Sometimes this is perfectly normal. In my previous example, I recognized that the highs and lows were all part of the process—something any entrepreneur could have told me. Yet other times, it's worth re-examining the Passion Shift.

When you align with your passion, remember there is an *opportunity* presented, *action* taken, and then a desired *outcome* resulting from your actions. You experience a high when you see evidence of this desired outcome.

On the other hand, when you fail to see evidence of the desired outcome, the Passion Shift is *not* completed, in which case, it all feels a bit anticlimactic. When we don't know if our actions made a difference, we sometimes conclude we've failed.

In such situations, the *Uncompleted* Passion Shift looks more like this:

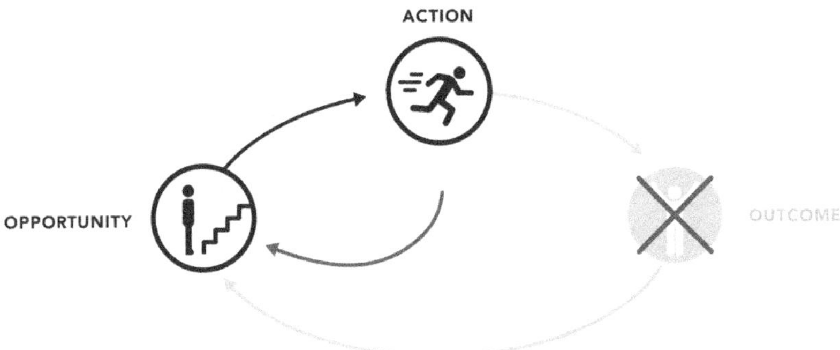

AN *UNCOMPLETED* PASSION SHIFT

Though aligned action does not guarantee a desired outcome, it can be worth taking a closer look when you find yourself missing out on the high. In some cases, a change may be in order.

An *Uncompleted* Passion Shift could indicate a *change of audience* is needed. If a Stabilizer chaired a fundraiser for a local nonprofit for the past three years and his efforts have become expected rather than appreciated, he will land in his void. He could continue doing the same thing and feel taken for granted, or he could look for opportunities to make a significant impact elsewhere. Rather than working on the fundraiser, the Stabilizer might opt to help with the school play. When we recognize a change of audience is appropriate, we need not feel guilty about it but instead recognize it as an opportunity to share our gifts in other areas.

For others, an *Uncompleted* Passion Shift could indicate the need for a *change in activity*. Some mindsets, including Integrators, Accomplishers, and Balancers, among others, regularly need new challenges and experiences. Balancers, for example, may find a once-enthralling activity, say climbing a particular mountain, no longer excites them after they've done it a few times. Perceivers may be drawn to an unconventional technology, but once it's mainstream, they may feel bored and ready to move on. Sometimes what motivated us in the past doesn't excite us in the present because the same activity no longer allows us to complete the Passion Shift.

Understanding the Passion Shift can help us recognize when a change in the audience or a change in activity is warranted and, as a result, feel more fulfilled. In my work as a coach, I found it less rewarding to work with people who already felt aligned in life and most rewarding when working with clients at a crossroads. By making a subtle shift in my audience, I was able to complete the Passion Shift more consistently because I saw evidence of my desired outcome—evidence that my efforts paid off by helping someone live a more fulfilling life.

What do you need to do to complete the Passion Shift?

For many, the high depends on other people's reactions. If your passion involves helping others, you'll naturally want evidence that your actions have, in fact, helped others. This has nothing to do with being needy or stroking your ego (though if you're helping others to make people like you, that would be a different story). Instead, it has everything to do with aligning with your passion in a way that keeps you engaged. Completing the Passion Shift helps sustain your motivation; therefore, it's worth examining the underlying mechanics when you don't realize your desired outcome so you can determine if some sort of change is appropriate.

To keep yourself rejuvenated, you can help others understand what motivates you. Since we're not all motivated by the same thing, it's beneficial if your manager, for example, knows what inspires you. Your boss isn't a mind reader, so it's up to *you* to tell him or her what makes you tick. When you're able to complete the Passion Shift more consistently, it can keep you engaged and energized, which benefits everyone.

Knowing we all crave evidence of our desired outcome, it's a good reminder for us to support others as they carry out their passion so they remain motivated. Something as simple as saying "thank you" could offer someone a boost. Appreciation is important to many mindsets, yet we sometimes overlook its importance. Your smile could be the difference between someone being refueled or feeling amiss.

Aligning with your passion doesn't guarantee you'll see evidence of your desired outcome every time, but if you find yourself regularly missing out on the high, it's worth taking a moment to reflect if a change—in the audience or the activity—can help you complete the Passion Shift and consequently feel more enlivened.

HOW TO OVERCOME BURNOUT

"A lot of the conflict you have in your life exists simply because you're not living in alignment; you're not being true to yourself."

—STEVE MARABOLI

Dr. Li, an Optimizer, found himself burned out after dealing with too much bureaucracy and not enough freedom to optimize his patients' health. Kristen, a Sensor, experienced burnout when a team reorganization caused her to feel siloed and disconnected from her teammates. Amelia, an Accomplisher, experienced burnout after winning competition after competition, yet she grew bored without new challenges in her life.

Burnout looks different from one mindset to the next, but the underlying cause is the same: spending too much time in your void.

Rather than aligning with your passion, burnout indicates you've been residing on the opposite end of the polarity, doing the very things that drain your energy. There's a price to pay for denying your motivations day in and day out. Eventually, your fuel reserves run out.

Burnout doesn't happen in an instant. It progressively worsens each day you deny your passion and instead attend to your void. Before burnout settles in, you experience discomfort stemming from misaligned actions. Integrators experience discomfort when working for micromanagers; Connectors, when disconnected from people and information; Inquisitors, when forced to memorize mundane facts.

Even as the discomfort intensifies, you may find reasons to ignore this inner nagging and rationalize why you need to keep doing what you're doing:

> I have to put food on the table and get the kids through college. I'm being paid well at this job and just need to keep at it.

> This is what I've worked so hard to achieve. Sure, I'm miserable, but at least I'm successful. Besides, it's too late to change my career now.

> I'm strong and can get through this. I just need to suck it up and make it through the end of the quarter.

Each time you accept such rationalizations, you commit to remain in your void. If you feel burned out, it means you've already endured a significant amount of time below the line. By doing more of the things that drain you, you can expect your discomfort to increase, rather than dissipate.

When you find yourself feeling burned out, or headed in that direction, some sort of change is necessary. If the idea of change feels unsettling, keep in mind that the change involves doing something you genuinely enjoy. It doesn't have to be drastic. If you think of your passion as a campfire, change simply means adding a couple of logs to the flame—something you haven't done for a while.

Though you have very real obligations in life—bills to pay, commitments to keep, and people to think about besides yourself—they shouldn't have to come at the price of burnout. With an understanding of your passion and void, you'll likely discover that you have more control over your circumstances than you may initially think.

The formula to end burnout is straightforward: maximize your passion and minimize your void.

In other words, do more of what enlivens you, and do less of what drains you. When you give your passion attention, you can invert the polarity and overcome burnout.

MINIMIZING YOUR VOID

Start by taking inventory of your void. What are you doing that depletes your energy? Observers: does your work lack meaning? Advisers: are you frequently interrupted? Authenticators: are you disengaged emotionally? Risktakers: are you maintaining the status quo? List all the things, personally and professionally, you're doing that fall into your void.

Once you have detailed your voids, brainstorm ways to reduce them. Look for creative solutions to spend less time doing the things that drain you and then take steps to eliminate them. Be wary of fixes that only temporarily anesthetize your void. A vacation can provide the necessary space to think about how to reduce your voids and give you renewed energy to make such changes. However, you can't overcome burnout by taking a vacation or sabbatical, only to return to your void, and expect to feel aligned.

A lasting solution requires you to address the underlying void. That said, you don't necessarily need to take extreme measures, like quitting your job. Explore the various options to reduce your void, be it outsourcing tasks, asking for help, turning off the news, or hiring a cleaning person. You can outsource your voids, but not your passion.

MAXIMIZING YOUR PASSION

As you eliminate tasks that thrust you into your void, you free up more space, and energy, for your passion.

Make a list of things you do—big or small, personal or professional—that motivate you. Resist the urge to be practical and instead allow yourself to brainstorm endless opportunities to align with your passion. Ask yourself: *If I could do one small thing for five minutes that aligned with my passion, what could that be?*

If you're having trouble answering that question, reflect on what you enjoyed doing as a child, or consider this: If someone handed you a million dollars, what would you do? If there were no rules or restrictions, and if anything were possible, what would you do with your precious time?

Next, choose at least one thing that aligns with your passion, commit to doing it, and then *do it.* This will launch you above the line. No matter how small the action, it can make a big difference. If you currently live in your void 90 percent of the time, a small action could reduce it to 85 percent. That's progress. And progress will eventually invert the polarity and land you above the line.

Remember: do what motivates you, whatever that is. Make cupcakes, host a dance-off, play board games with friends, set do-not-disturb hours, write a poem, or solve a problem. Each aligned action can help you overcome burnout.

A FINAL NOTE ON THE VOID

You have the recipe to overcome burnout: maximize your passion and minimize your void. But it's worth revisiting the void as a concept because our society doesn't acknowledge its existence. Our language shapes so much of our reality, yet we haven't had a word to describe this important aspect of our being until now.

An underlying challenge surrounding burnout involves our failure to acknowledge that *we all have a void.* None of us have what it takes to do it *all*, yet we—and society in general—often hold ourselves or others to such unreasonable expectations.

When we only acknowledge what motivates people, we miss half the equation. Because I didn't acknowledge my void before leaving my career at Microsoft, I couldn't make sense of my waning enthusiasm. *I should be happy*, I thought. Since I wasn't, I concluded something was wrong with me. Ashamed, I kept my struggles to myself. I remained misaligned and amplified my burnout. Had I understood the void as a very real concept, I could have made sense of my discomfort and addressed it immediately. Although I was surrounded by amazing people who always had my back and would have supported me, without understanding the existence of the void, I believed that quitting was my only viable option.

The void is real, and it's time we acknowledge it. Keeping it hidden has only hindered us as a society. When we find ways to justify spending time in our void, it breeds toxicity and can lead to poor relationships and a dysfunctional culture. When we acknowledge the void, we can accept the reality that no individual is meant to do it all. We're meant to complement each other's strengths. When we align with our passions, it breeds productivity and a healthy culture. Your passion—what you are innately motivated to do—is essential, yet it can't be expressed if you're caught up doing what you're *not* wired to do. Burnout is a call to realign and honor your passion.

Just as it takes more energy to get a new campfire burning than it does to throw a log into an already raging fire, overcoming burnout takes time. Be patient and continue to focus on decreasing the time spent in your void and increasing the time spent aligned with your passion. The initial highs may be subtle, but celebrate these small, incremental wins. Burnout didn't happen overnight, and overcoming it won't happen overnight either. Yet, it is doable, and you're worth it. Your gifts are important and necessary in the world. When you do more of what innately motivates you, you amplify passion and return to alignment. Isn't it time to throw another log on the fire?

ALIGNING WITH YOUR PURPOSE

"Just as ripples spread out when a single pebble is dropped into the water, the action of individuals can have far-reaching effects."

—DALAI LAMA

In January of 2022, I sat in my office where I, for the first time, clearly recognized that insecurities reside on the opposite pole of purpose. Until that day, I gave my insecurities a great amount of attention. For over four decades, I had tried to protect my ego by ensuring my insecurities never came to light. Yet at that moment, I saw insecurities and purpose as mutually exclusive, and my viewpoint—and actions—changed in an instant. I realized I no longer needed to attend to my insecurities. I suddenly understood the remedy: the secret to releasing insecurities lies in aligning with purpose.

This section, "Aligning with Your Purpose," delves deep into your insecurities because insecurities represent the nemesis of purpose. If you're like most people, there's a high probability you've spent a great deal of energy dealing with the opposite pole of purpose, hurt—which includes insecurities. As you understand this aspect of your being, you can tame it. For this reason, you will likely find this is one of the most important sections you read in this book.

We're each here for a purpose, and when we align with it, we give, and we gain, much. Purpose is the culmination of your multifaceted nature. While your principle represents *how* you expect people to behave and your passion informs *what* you're motivated to do, your purpose underscores *why* these two are so imperative: because it brings about the desired state of being you long for.

By knowing your purpose and understanding what lies at the other end of the pole, hurt and insecurities, you can take action to align. In this section, you will learn:

- How to identify your core insecurity.
- How to overcome insecurities.
- How to recognize when you are misaligned with purpose.
- How to pinpoint the area of misalignment that needs your attention when you feel misaligned.
- How to realize the sense of well-being you want most.
- How to see the gifts of misalignment.

HOW TO IDENTIFY YOUR CORE INSECURITY

"If you are insecure, guess what? The rest of the world is, too."
—TIMOTHY FERRISS

My first job was selling sweet corn on the side of the road. Looking back now, it was a fantastic job: I got to set my own hours, sit in the sun, and make a lot of money. But as an insecure high schooler, I felt embarrassed. I was convinced other kids would think I was a loser for setting up my roadside stand and signs, and I envied the cool kids serving ice cream at the local Dairy Queen. Not wanting to give anyone a reason to look down on me, I put a tremendous amount of energy into worrying about what my classmates would think of me.

We all have what we consider a dirty little secret. It's an insecurity dwelling deep within, masking a sense of shame, a feeling of not being good enough, or a fear people will find out we're not as great as they thought. We can't stand for that insecurity to see the light of day, so we work tirelessly to conceal it.

Your insecurity represents the things you cannot stand people to *do to you* or *think of you*. When insecurities bleed out of our nightmares and into the real world, it hurts.

So often, it feels as though you're the only person in the world who carries this uncomfortable burden. Whatever plagues you—perhaps a fear of being criticized, excluded, or made fun of—you notice that people around you don't seem to share the same concern.

But you're not the only one carrying around an insecurity. While we don't all share the *same* insecurity, *everyone* has an insecurity (even those who appear confident) embedded as deeply as our own. Just like us, others work hard to ensure people perceive them how they need to be perceived to feel comfortable. The burden of their insecurity is as unpleasant for them as it is for you.

We're conditioned to blame insecurities on traumatic life experiences—it's your mom's fault you're a perfectionist because when you were five, she reprimanded you for coloring outside of the lines, or it's your dad's fault you seek attention because he traveled too much for work. Your life experiences do, in fact, have a profound impact on you. But is it possible your distressing experiences highlight something already within you?

There's a very specific and perfectly logical reason for your core insecurity. It might not surprise you at this point to discover that your mindset influences your insecurity.

To understand the logic hidden within your insecurity, look closely at two of your innate tendencies.

First, think about a time when someone *severely* triggered you, a time when someone intensely activated your "*Grr!*" instinct. Now think about the person who triggered you and how you thought, felt, or acted *toward this person* (the wrongdoer). Because of what they did, you might feel differently about them (for example, you're disappointed in them) or treat them less favorably (for example, you talked badly about them behind their back).

In my case, when people belittle others (my trigger), I think less of them. I think they're scum. Is this thought flattering? No. Is it honest? Yes. We all punish those who trigger us most egregiously through our thoughts or actions, just as we punish ourselves through regret, remorse, and rumination when we fail to uphold our own principle.

What is true for you? Once triggered, how do you act toward wrongdoers? What do you think of them? Do you talk badly about them? Think they're stupid? Feel disappointed in them? Do you reprimand them? Exclude them? Criticize them?

> *Pause now and write down how you think, feel, or act toward those who have severely triggered you.*

Next, reflect on your main insecurity. What can't you stand for people to think about you? How can't you stand being treated? Think about how you would finish this sentence: "I work hard to make sure people don't ____________ me."

Consider what is most true for you. For example: Will you work hard to make sure people don't get angry with you? Don't judge you? Don't think you're incompetent? Don't abandon you? Don't disapprove of you?

> *Pause now and write down how you can't stand for people to treat you or perceive you.*

Now that you've answered both questions, consider them in tandem. What do your two answers have in common? Identify what your *punishment* (how you treat those who trigger you) and your *insecurity* (how you cannot stand for people to treat you) have in common. When examined closely, you'll find a direct link between punishment and insecurity.

When people severely trigger me, I think less of them (my punishment). Furthermore, I can't stand for people to think less of me (my insecurity). As it turns out, your punishment and insecurity are one and the same.

> Your dirty little secret, and your insecurity, is that you don't want to be treated by others in the same way you treat those who trigger you most.

If you can't stand for people to talk badly about you, there's a good chance you talk badly about others who trigger you. If it's unbearable to be excluded, you likely exclude those who trigger you. If you need people to think you're intelligent, you likely think those who trigger you are unintelligent.

You're not a bad person because you punish people who trigger you. And you're not weird or flawed because you have an insecurity. Insecurities are normal, and they run deep. They're insufferable because insecurities create your undesired state: hurt.

If people think less of Synthesizers (insecurity), Synthesizers won't feel safe to be themselves (hurt). If people feel let down by Stabilizers (insecurity), Stabilizers won't experience a sense of stability (hurt). If people are disappointed in Harmonizers (insecurity), Harmonizers won't experience a sense of peace (hurt). If people think Risktakers are irrelevant (insecurity), Risktakers can't realize success (hurt).

Whatever your mindset, you simply don't want to be treated the same way you reflexively treat those who trigger you.

Similarly, others reflexively punish you if you trigger them. Depending on their mindset, they may talk about you, criticize you, be disappointed in you, avoid you, or dislike you. If you want to prevent things like this, make efforts to uphold their mindset principle. It not only supports others; it also improves people's perception of you.

The Golden Rule, treat others how you want to be treated, needs an upgrade. The Golden Rule 2.0 tells us to treat others how *they* want to be treated. In other words, uphold their mindset principle, such as being decent, kind, effective, thoughtful, or well-intentioned. When we uphold all mindset principles, not just our own, we all win.

You also win when you make sense of your insecurity. You know your insecurity isn't random. You're not alone in how you feel.

Though your core insecurity may now make sense, it's also misaligned.

The good news is you can do something about it. Due to the mutually exclusive nature of polarities, you can even make it vanish—poof!

HOW TO OVERCOME INSECURITIES

"Too many of us are not living our dreams because we are living our fears."
—LES BROWN

When I was in seventh grade, I'd cover my face with my hair when I felt embarrassed or drew unwanted attention to myself. I guess I thought if I could hide, people couldn't see my flaws, and I could escape my insecurity.

To avoid our insecurities, we all create coping strategies. If you hate disapproval, you'll find ways to make sure people approve of you. If you don't want people to be disappointed in you, you'll make sure people don't have any reason to be disappointed. If you don't want people to reprimand you, you won't give them a reason to reprimand you.

All of us employ tactics to ensure our insecurities don't come to light. Conforming, intimidating, lying, shrinking, and people-pleasing are just a few of the strategies different mindsets use to avoid their insecurities.

Additionally, some of us put our energy into making sure people *see us how we want to be seen* (what I refer to as Insecurity Inversion). Others put more effort into making sure people *don't see us how we don't want to be seen* (Insecurity Suppression). The difference between the two concepts is bigger than you might think.

Consider the nuance of someone who needs people to think he's intelligent, as opposed to someone who needs to make sure people don't think he's unintelligent. The former is likely to be more outspoken, and the latter, more conscientious. Through Insecurity Inversion, people could come across as confident, even arrogant, and are more likely to experience imposter syndrome. This makes sense because they are trying to ensure that others see them in a favorable light (for example, as important, competent, or irreplaceable). When Insecurity Suppression is in play, people are more likely to come across as reserved, even insecure, and are more likely to withdraw. This also makes sense because they are trying to ensure people do not view them unfavorably (for example, as unimportant, incompetent, or useless).

Such tactics seem logical: if you can just show up in the right way, you can control others' perceptions of you. By sharing your successes, people will be impressed. By making yourself invisible, people can't criticize you. By doing the things you can do perfectly, people won't make fun of you. By refusing to do something you don't know how to do, people won't think you're stupid or incompetent. By giving up your preferences, people can't get upset with you.

For the most part, these strategies work. The problem is, even if we escape others' unwanted actions or perceptions, we rarely escape our own. You and I are our own worst critics. We examine our flaws aiming to fix them or conceal them because we can't stand it when others discover we're not good enough, smart enough, or capable enough. Internally, we lock our insecurities in a vault so no one will see what we see: our shortcomings. Externally, we play the game and act as needed. As a result, we end up spending precious energy focusing on what we don't want to have happen and ensuring we show up in just the right way. Every. Single. Day. It's exhausting, never-ending, unproductive—and it's below the line.

Ensnared by my own insecurities, but without the tools to know or act differently, I once made it my full-time job to try to fix myself. But this approach only amplified the problem. The more I worked to fix or conceal my insecurities, the more I fed them—and feared them.

The uncomfortable reality about insecurities is this: they're all about "Me." *Don't criticize me; don't reject me; don't humiliate me; do be impressed with me; do accept me, love me, want me, need me.*

What all insecurities have in common is *me, me, me.* In this sense, insecurities are selfish. They have everything to do with ego and self-preservation.

The good news is you can overcome your insecurities. When you invert the polarity by shifting your attention away from yourself and onto others, insecurities dissipate.

> Because your insecurities and your purpose reside on opposite ends of the same polarity, you can overcome your insecurities by aligning with your purpose.

Just as you cannot experience both brightness and darkness simultaneously, you cannot experience insecurities when you're aligned with your purpose. To overcome insecurities, shift your attention above the line. When you're consumed by your insecurities, your focus is on yourself. When you're aligned with your purpose, your focus extends beyond yourself. It's a heartfelt intention to create a more desirable state of being for others. With an intention to serve something beyond yourself, you break free from your insecurities. You no longer intend to control others' perceptions; rather, you unleash your potential so it may benefit others. Purpose isn't meant to be controlled, just allowed.

Where you place your attention—whether you aim to benefit yourself or others—matters. It's subtle, yet powerful.

Take, for example, a job interview. By focusing too much on what the interviewer thinks of you, you risk coming across as awkward. When your intention remains on benefiting the company and its customers, you are likely to shine. The difference between a mediocre interview and nailing it could be the difference between focusing on your insecurities or something beyond yourself.

As another example, think about students whose attention regularly revolves around themselves. This is not to say they are selfish but to acknowledge that they're regularly bombarded with worrying about their GPA, SAT and ACT scores, class ranking, making the team, college acceptance rates, popularity, and image. If we understand the mutually exclusive polarities, we shouldn't be surprised that this cohort often suffers from debilitating insecurities. Where insecurities exist, so, too, do defense mechanisms, which can include bullying. A campaign to stop bullying falls below the line. An above-the-line solution involves inverting the polarity to address insecurities and related defense mechanisms by shifting our focus beyond ourselves. It means we champion purpose-aligned students who help each other, teach one another, bring beauty into their communities through music or art, develop technical skills to help businesses thrive, or practice public speaking.

True confidence comes when you stop thinking about others' perceptions of you and instead focus on aligning with your purpose. As you shift your attention to your purpose, which benefits others, your insecurities dissipate because purpose conquers insecurity, just as light conquers darkness.

WHAT IS AN ALIGNMENT CRISIS?

"It is said that the darkest hour of the night comes just before the dawn."
—THOMAS FULLER

My coaching practice focuses on personal alignment and often helps professionals realign with some aspect of their lives using the 25 Mindsets as a tool.

During a coaching call on a Monday at 10:30 a.m., I met with Kim, an Accomplisher mindset. She joined the call right on time but rolled in hot. Her hair was uncombed, she didn't wear any makeup, and her desk was cluttered. I was a bit confused, sure I had made a mistake. *I thought I was meeting with an Accomplisher*, I thought to myself. *Who did I mistake her with?* Accomplishers are neat, tidy, and pulled together. This was not a typical Accomplisher sighting.

Kim shared how she was caught off guard that morning. It turned out the kids didn't have school, and she had a couple of extra kids staying with her, attending a nearby hockey camp. Recognizing she was having a rough go, I asked her if she wanted to reschedule, but she was all in. Kim keeps her commitments and is there for others, traits that contribute to her success as a realtor. A raw discussion ensued. We talked about purpose, and we talked about insecurities. At one point, she shared in a sobering tone, "I just don't have anymore f*cks to give, you know?"

Despite having a job she enjoyed and career success, she was tired of trying to do it all. She was tired of caring so much about what other people thought, tired of not feeling how she wanted to feel, tired of people-pleasing, tired of trying to impress everyone. So she showed up exposed. *This is me, girl. Take it or leave it.*

This attitude is familiar to many of us—especially in midlife—when we've pursued a path in life, only to find we don't feel how we thought we would. Whether we're struggling to get by, or even if we've realized success, something doesn't feel quite right. Life hasn't played out as we hoped or envisioned.

People often use the term "midlife crisis" to describe this phenomenon, but maybe a more accurate description is "alignment crisis."

An alignment crisis happens when we remain chronically misaligned with our purpose.

Whereas burnout stems from doing draining things that are in your void, an alignment crisis comes about when, instead of experiencing the state of being we desire most, we experience the opposite. For Accomplishers, rather than feeling they are reaching their fullest potential, they feel they're performing below their potential. For Integrators, rather than enjoying life, they feel they are stuck going through the motions. For Intuitors, rather than realizing their greatness, they feel no one understands them. For Balancers, rather than feeling they are living life to the fullest, they feel deficient in some area of their life.

This pattern occurs in all mindsets: our life experience is often the opposite of what we seek most. Supporters yearn to feel supported, yet they go through life feeling unsupported. Stabilizers wish for stability, but they experience much instability. Protectors want to feel protected in the face of uncertainty and risk, yet they find themselves feeling vulnerable or at risk.

This below-the-line absence of our desired state of being eventually takes its toll.

We may try to satiate our desire by buying things, doing stuff, and achieving more, but it doesn't feed the underlying hunger.

Despite all we've faced and overcome, despite all we've been blessed with, something is still missing.

When we reach the point where enough is enough, we're likely to stop catering to our insecurities. It can even feel like our personality has changed—you used to be a nice person who gave a damn about what other people think and wanted to make a good impression, but now you don't.

We're also apt to sabotage relationships we perceive as threatening to our desired state of being. If you yearn to reach your full potential, you may sever relationships with those who seem to limit you. If you yearn to be happy, you may cut ties with those who take life too seriously. If you yearn to feel safe to be yourself, you may sabotage a relationship if you don't feel you can be yourself around someone. If you yearn to experience a sense of stability in life, you may sabotage a relationship after someone rattles your foundation. If you yearn to feel secure, you're likely to sever relationships with people who threaten your sense of security.

So much of this happens at an unconscious level. We generally don't know exactly what we want or don't want; we just know something isn't working. Having tried so hard to right the ship, we feel beaten down. Little did we know that to overcome our misalignment, we needed to extend our intention beyond ourselves.

The road to alignment involves focusing on your purpose. Living your purpose is not about getting what you want for yourself, but about giving it to others. To overcome an alignment crisis, extend your intention beyond yourself. As you create a more desirable state of being for others, you too will soon begin to feel how you hoped to feel. So if you want to feel safe, bring a sense of safety to others. If you want to experience wealth and security, help others experience wealth and security. If you want to feel peace of mind, bring peace of mind to others.

Do that, and there is no crisis, only alignment.

SIX AREAS TO CONSIDER WHEN YOU FEEL MISALIGNED

"Balance is not something you find; it's something you create."

—JANA KINGSFORD

Despite having tools to help me align, I still find myself feeling misaligned. I may have discovered my passion, but after working long days for weeks on end, I feel the impact of having neglected my relationships and eaten too many quick, unhealthy meals. Even though I'm aligned with my passion and doing what I enjoy, I can end up being misaligned socially and physically.

It happens to all of us. An excess in one area of life, such as passion, leads to a deficiency in some other area. An Optimizer obsessed with her current project may get so focused, she forgets to eat. A Balancer in an endless pursuit of adventure might overlook his professional obligations. An Adviser chasing a challenge may neglect his relationships. As good as passion is, you can have too much of a good thing.

Like Goldilocks, we seek the "just right" balance—not too much, not too little. A deficiency in passion can result in burnout, but an excess can take a toll on your relationships, health, or emotional well-being. Therefore, in addition to aligning with your principle, passion, and purpose, overall alignment recognizes the need to align socially, physically, and emotionally.

Achieving balance is a dynamic pursuit. To realign when you're misaligned, it's important to identify the source of your misalignment. Are you misaligned with your principle, passion, or purpose? Or are you misaligned socially, physically, or emotionally? *The Six Areas of Alignment* can help you pinpoint where you are misaligned so you can focus your attention where it's needed most.

	Principle	**Passion**	**Purpose**	**Social**	**Physical**	**Emotional**
Aligned						
Misaligned						

The objective of acknowledging these six areas is not to help you stay aligned 100 percent of the time—that's simply not realistic. Instead, the goal is to help you identify where you are misaligned so you can get back above the line.

The summaries below detail the six areas of alignment and provide examples of what *aligned* and *misaligned* look or feel like for each area. As you read through them, you may wish to make note of any that jump out at you as needing your attention the most.

THE SIX AREAS OF ALIGNMENT

Principle

Uphold Collective Principles ⟷ *Do Not Uphold Collective Principles*

The objective of the first area is to work toward upholding all twenty-five principles in a balanced way. For example, if you notice increased bickering between you and your fiancé, it points to an opportunity to better understand and uphold one another's principles.

WHEN YOU ARE *ALIGNED*

- You acknowledge your mindset as one of many and recognize the importance of all twenty-five principles.
- You help others understand your mindset principle using a non-defensive approach.
- You learn about the mindset principles of the people closest to you and take small actions to uphold them, thereby helping others remain aligned.
- You know you may be inadvertently triggering others when you uphold your principle in excess and take steps to uphold your principle in a balanced way.
- You strive to better understand and uphold all 25 Mindset principles.

WHEN YOU ARE *MISALIGNED*

- You are frequently triggered by other people.
- You expect people to be mind-readers and automatically understand your principle.
- You uphold your principle in excess and intentionally or unintentionally trigger others as a result.
- You don't take time to understand others' principles and instead judge people as unreasonable.
- You ruminate incessantly when you inadvertently fail to uphold your mindset principle rather than taking accountability for your actions or allowing yourself to move on and realign.

Passion

Align with Your Passion ⟷ *Do Not Align with Your Passion*

The second area recognizes the importance of aligning with your passion. For example, if you hate your job, your opportunity is to do more of the things that enliven you.

WHEN YOU ARE *ALIGNED*

- You prioritize your passion.
- You recognize that different people with different mindsets have different motivations.
- You do your part (as opposed to doing it all) and let others use their gifts.
- You understand that different passions complement each other and see the value of each person doing what motivates them.
- You feel motivated, engaged, and energized.
- You have a strong sense of self-worth.
- You invest in yourself and continue to develop skills that amplify your passion and purpose.
- You do hard things.
- You align with your passion in a way that adds value to others and is sufficiently rewarded, thus enabling you to meet your personal and financial needs.

WHEN YOU ARE *MISALIGNED*

- You spend a significant amount of time doing things that drain your energy or leave you feeling burned out.
- You do whatever it takes to meet demands; you get things done, but it comes at the cost of something else (for example, sleep, exercise, time with family, peace of mind, etc.).

- You loathe what you are doing or dread going to work.
- You do it all yourself without asking for, or accepting, help when you need it.
- You feel unmotivated, disengaged, and lack a sense of self-worth.
- You look down on people who aren't motivated by the same things as you.
- You are not sufficiently rewarded for your actions and are therefore unable to meet your personal and financial needs.

Purpose

Intend to Serve Beyond Yourself ⟷ *Intend to Serve Yourself*

Purpose focuses on the intention behind your actions and whether you intend to serve yourself or someone or something beyond yourself. When you're consumed by personal insecurities or a need to inflate your ego, it signals an opportunity to align with your purpose.

WHEN YOU ARE *ALIGNED*

- You know your purpose.
- You take steps to align with your purpose and serve something bigger than yourself.
- You serve a purpose that benefits others, as well as yourself.
- Your intention is clear and aligns with your purpose.
- You allow life experiences, including misalignment, to guide your purpose.
- You recognize yourself as an integral part of the whole.
- You advance your purpose.
- You experience your desired state of being by bringing it to others.

WHEN YOU ARE *MISALIGNED*

- You obsess about your insecurities.
- You focus on protecting or inflating your ego.
- You go to great lengths to ensure people perceive you in the way you desire.
- You shame yourself for being flawed, or you see everyone else as flawed.
- You serve yourself at the cost of others, or you serve others at the cost of yourself.
- You regularly expect people to do more with fewer resources so that things get done, even though it predictably creates misalignment in others' lives.
- You care more about your agenda than the success of your team, family, or friends.
- You seek money to control, or have power over, others.
- You focus only on yourself in your effort to meet your desire (for example, by compulsively "fixing" yourself or obsessing about money or accolades).
- You stay awake at night dwelling on something bothering you (the things that keep you up at night typically relate to a misalignment with purpose).
- You view yourself as separate.

Social

Cultivate Nourishing Relationships ⟷ *Lack of Nourishing Relationships*

This area acknowledges the importance of people, connections, community, and belonging. When misaligned, our opportunity is to focus on fostering healthy relationships.

WHEN YOU ARE *ALIGNED*

- You prioritize nourishing relationships in your life.
- You experience a sense of belonging and connection.
- You are engaged in your community.
- You honor differences, recognizing that people are meant to complement one another, not be like one another.
- You support others in aligning with who they are.
- You cherish the people in your life and celebrate the memory of those who were in your life.
- You foster mutually supportive relationships that honor individuality, authenticity, and alignment.

WHEN YOU ARE *MISALIGNED*

- You lack nourishing relationships.
- You demand consensus and uniform thinking, needing people to think like you.
- You resist human interaction and instead have relationships with video games, technology, busyness, etc.
- You isolate, go it alone, or deny support from others.
- You divide people.
- You put energy into harboring resentment and holding grudges.

Physical

Prioritize Self-Care ⟷ *Neglect Self-Care*

This area focuses on aligning your physiology. If misaligned, your opportunity is to focus on self-care. For example, if you've been taking on more work while sleeping less, eating whatever is convenient, and forgoing exercise, your opportunity is to prioritize rest, nourishment, and a level of fitness suitable for you.

WHEN YOU ARE *ALIGNED*

- You prioritize self-care.
- You support and nourish your physical body.
- You regularly engage in physical activity and movement that support you.
- You nourish and hydrate your body and breathe fresh air.
- You maintain adequate sleep, recovery, and restoration in your life.
- You have the physical stamina required (and within your capability) to actively align with your passion.
- You are an active participant in life.
- You develop healthy habits.

WHEN YOU ARE *MISALIGNED*

- You neglect self-care.
- You have a sedentary lifestyle and lack activity and movement within your physical limits.
- You have an unhealthy obsession with physical activity.
- You neglect nourishment, hydration, sleep, and restoration.
- You continue unhealthy habits.
- You rely on stimulants to provide energy to get you through your day.
- You operate under chronic stress or adrenaline and put yourself last.

Emotional

Allow Emotions to Guide You ⟷ *Control Emotions or Let Emotions Control You*

The final area focuses on honoring your emotions and understanding what they are telling you. Your emotions provide you with an abundance of information—if you're willing to listen. Your opportunity is to not judge emotions as good or bad but use them as a tool to help you align with who you are.

WHEN YOU ARE *ALIGNED*

- You recognize feelings and insights as valuable sources of knowledge, including so-called negative emotions, which provide you with information to help you be your best self.
- You allow yourself to be quiet, and even bored, to get in touch with what you're feeling.
- You feel the fullness of your emotions (for example, allowing yourself to express excitement, show gratitude, or take time to grieve).
- You tune into your emotions, including the painful ones, and ask, "What are these emotions telling me?"
- You use your emotions to guide productive action.
- You live in the present.

WHEN YOU ARE *MISALIGNED*

- You tolerate only "good" emotions and suppress, numb, judge, or deny uncomfortable feelings.
- You seek distractions, such as constantly looking at your phone, when you experience lulls.
- You do not acknowledge the messages your emotions are telling you and instead view them as a nuisance and seek to get rid of them.
- You believe you are supposed to feel happy and be aligned all the time.
- You live in the future or past.
- You live in fear, feed your fear, or become paralyzed by fear, stress, or other emotions.

To avoid the trap of sustained misalignment, it's important to differentiate the six areas—principle, passion, purpose, social, physical, and emotional—so you can identify what needs your attention most. If you find you're misaligned across many or all areas, it doesn't mean you are flawed. It simply means you are misaligned and, perhaps, that you have been for some time now. The good news is this: you now have a roadmap that points the way back to alignment.

If you are an employer, it's useful to be mindful of these six areas because they affect your culture and employee engagement. The February 2023 "U.S. Employee Engagement Trend" *Gallup* poll showed 33 percent of US employees are engaged, 51 percent of employees are disengaged, and 16 percent of employees are actively disengaged. This suggests that 33 percent of employees are aligned with their passion, 51 percent are not aligned with their passion, and 16 percent of employees are in their void and misaligned with purpose. When people are misaligned with purpose, they not only quit, but they might also sabotage, which could mean telling others not to work there, smearing your brand, or involving an attorney. On the flip side, the effort you make to help employees align with their passion and purpose will result in a more engaged workforce, greater productivity, better attitudes, and a healthier culture. It's nearly impossible for people to work hard if they hate what they do, yet they will go to bat for you when they're aligned. Whether you have a healthy or toxic culture is directly related to whether your employees are aligned or misaligned.

Alignment, as an individual or a team, is a dynamic process. It changes, teaches, and it provides opportunities to expand and grow. Use the six areas of alignment to help you see what needs your attention most. Your next step is to simply pick one area and then start there to help you get back above the line.

HOW TO GET WHAT YOU WANT MOST

"Life is an echo. What you send out comes back."

—ZIG ZIGLAR

When I was ten, I spotted the biggest teddy bear I'd ever seen in our small-town Ben Franklin store. It was love at first sight. I *needed* this bear in my life. But regrettably, I didn't have enough money saved to buy him. I was thirty dollars short, so I had to find a way to quickly make up the difference.

When you want something as badly as I wanted that bear, you'll try your darndest to get it. I had collected a few two-dollar bills and saved some change in a jar; using that would get me a little closer. I had some sought-after stickers I decided to sell to a friend. I begged my siblings to give me their chores so I could earn their allowances, and then I negotiated with my parents to pay me in advance. With the money I needed in hand, I returned to Ben Franklin to buy my bear and beamed as I brought him home.

When you want something, you go after it.

But what if what you want most is not a thing, but a desired state of being? What if you want to feel happy, secure, successful, or safe? What if you want to feel content, prosperous, or like you're living life to the fullest?

You go after that too.

If we want to feel happy, we ask: What will make me feel happy? *Ice cream.* What will make me feel secure? *Money.* What will make me feel successful? *A promotion.* What will make me feel safe? *A security system.* What will make me feel comfortable to be myself? *A teddy bear.*

Our inclination is to look for, and find, ways to help us feel the way we want to feel.

This approach seems logical and direct, but for too many of us, it eventually fails us. Rather than finding a lasting sense of satisfaction, we instead receive a hit of dopamine and are left wanting more. We even hear stories of the rich and famous who seemingly have it all but are, nonetheless, dissatisfied. Perhaps you're feeling unfulfilled, despite attaining the things you believed would bring satisfaction.

So how do you get what you want most? How do you feel content and satisfied?

The most direct way to get what you want is to give it to others.

Perhaps you have heard someone say, "It makes me happy to see them happy." This is the simple secret to your well-being. If you want to feel happy, intend to make others happy. If you want to experience success, seek to help others succeed. If you want to live in peace, aspire to bring peace into others' lives. Just approach it in a way that aligns with *your* mindset.

By giving others what you yearn for most, an uncanny alchemy unfolds. You receive it in return. In this aligned state, you get what you desire most—you experience your desired state of being.

It sounds too simple, and yet, it is one of the most powerful things you can do for yourself. We don't give others what we want because it's not what we're naturally led to do. After all, if you're hungry, you don't give someone else a sandwich to satiate your hunger; you eat a sandwich yourself. The nuance makes sense only when understanding the polarity: when aligned with purpose, your intention is directed beyond yourself; when misaligned with purpose, your intention is self-serving.

Therefore, to invert the polarity when you lack your desired state of being, the opportunity is to align with your purpose. If you are a Cultivator, for example, you would focus your attention on bringing peace into the world and to others—not to yourself. In doing so, however, you will find peace of mind yourself.

Doing this is easier said than done, so let's break it down into three steps, which will help you experience your desired state of being. First, get to know your purpose. Next, practice aligning with your purpose. And finally, connect your passion and purpose.

1. KNOW YOUR PURPOSE

To align with your purpose, it's important to have a clear purpose statement that resonates deeply with you. You may remember from Part 1 of the book that purpose stems from your innermost desire for yourself. To clarify your purpose, you must first be clear about what you want most for yourself.

The purpose stated in your mindset chapter reflects a common theme shared by individuals who share your mindset. For example, the Inquisitor's purpose reads: *so that we can enjoy life and be happy*. And, as you learned, that's what Inquisitors want most for themselves: *to enjoy life and be happy*.

So what do you want? What is your innermost desire for yourself? Speak the words, "I just want to...," and then listen to the deep yearning in your heart and complete the sentence. For example, an Inquisitor may write down: *I just want to feel happy*. You may find your answer is identical to the purpose statement in your mindset chapter, or you may find it differs slightly. What's most important is that your purpose statement feels true to you. So if you're an Inquisitor and your inner yearning is to *have fun*, then roll with that.

Once you clarify what you want most for yourself, write it in a way that focuses on others. For example, *I just want people to enjoy life and feel happy*. This statement, with a focus on others, should feel equally true for you as the prior statement, which revolved around yourself. It should feel true that you want others to experience this state of being as much as you want to experience it yourself.

Take time to create a purpose statement that completely resonates when you apply it to both you and others because you will, ideally, return to it again and again.

2. PRACTICE YOUR PURPOSE

Once you have written your purpose statement in a way that resonates deeply when it refers to both you and others, the next step is to practice it.

When you put it into practice, you will synchronize your heart and mind. For example, before you head into a meeting, reflect on your purpose statement and set your intention for the meeting in a way that aligns with your purpose. A Producer might set his intention to make people feel secure despite the changes the company is going through. A Balancer might set her intention to help her client live life to the fullest. Be deliberate in your intention, and practice applying it in various situations, such as when you are giving a speech, talking to your kids, playing a sport, starting a new project, or going on a vacation.

Putting your purpose into practice requires you to turn off autopilot and consciously consider: *Is my intention to benefit myself, or is my intention focused beyond myself?* Even when your actions help others, your *intention* may be self-serving. Pause to clarify your intention and where you are directing it. If you are giving a speech, are you primarily worried about what the audience will think of you, or are you focused on helping your clients? If you discover your intention is self-serving, that's okay. It just means you have an opportunity to redirect your intention beyond yourself so you can practice fully aligning with your purpose. When insecurities creep up, think of it as an alert on your dashboard reminding you to align with your purpose.

When you align with your purpose, you likely will notice it feels expansive (unlike insecurities, which feel restrictive). It's as though you are releasing your intention out into the world. When practicing my purpose, I consciously take time before a coaching session to think *and feel* my intention. I will feel in my heart and say in my mind something like: *Thank you for this opportunity to meet with this client so she may see the brilliance of who she is and share her extraordinary gifts.* For some people, it may feel like a prayer or a request sent out into the universe. For others, it feels like gratitude, and still, for others, it's like a strong intention or certitude. Purpose is a heartfelt intent to bring about a more desirable state of being to others. Put it into practice, and you'll experience your desired state of being too.

3. CONNECT YOUR PASSION AND PURPOSE

Each passion pursuit has a definitive beginning and end, and you experience a high when you see evidence of your desired outcome. Purpose, in contrast, does not require that you see evidence of the desired state of being because purpose has no definitive end. It emanates and radiates. It outlives the moment.

Passion is what you do; purpose is why you do it. But when passion meets purpose, they become force multipliers. Connecting passion and purpose means you are doing things that allow you to fulfill your *Why*. You do what you do to bring your desired state of being to others. When your actions and intention are aligned, it's a recipe for success and fulfillment. You not only enjoy what you do, but you also experience your desired state of being as you offer it to others.

My friend, Melissa, a Harmonizer, sprinkles random acts of kindness throughout her day. She's motivated to make a positive impact. It's her passion, but she's occasionally met with a confused look after giving flowers to a stranger. Though she doesn't necessarily see evidence of her desired outcome, she's okay with that. Her passion and purpose—her actions and her intention—are aligned. In this state, we're less attached to the outcome and more open to honoring the potential of our aligned actions and intention.

When you align passion with your purpose, your influence continues, like a ripple in the water. It's a place where magical things happen—as though the universe is conspiring to support you. The place where passion and purpose coincide is the underpinning of legacy. When you leave a legacy, your influence carries on long after your actions have ended. Martin Luther King Jr. gave his *I Have a Dream* speech, yet sixty years later, King's powerful influence lives on. Purpose is expansive and holds the power to influence future generations.

Impulses that tell us to obtain the feeling we want only for ourselves are often misguided. There is something even greater than experiencing your desired state of being, which is to experience fulfillment while also sharing it with others.

Your purpose serves someone or something beyond yourself, but it also serves and rewards you. Your sense of well-being hinges on being aligned with your passion and purpose. So do what you love and do it in a way that benefits others.

HOW TO SEE THE GIFTS OF MISALIGNMENT

"What is to give light must endure burning."

—VIKTOR E. FRANKL

As unpleasant as misalignment feels, it is also normal and necessary, and, yes, it can even be a gift. If not for my own experiences with burnout and insecurities, I would not have found the motivation to discover my passion, untangle our multifaceted nature, and write this book. My work is only possible *because* I was misaligned. The gift of my misaligned experiences is that they allowed me to serve something larger than myself. Only through suffering and pain did I eventually find my purpose—and purpose found me.

How we align with our purpose is often influenced by past mistakes, pain, disappointment, injustice, or loss. Consider the songs born of heartbreak, the nonprofit organizations created after witnessing unmet needs, the inventions born of frustration, or memoirs written after an author's struggles. The angst, hardship, and discomfort accompanying misalignment also can inspire growth and productive action.

During the most trying times in your life, you plant seeds of purposeful action. Our challenges create the opportunity for us to be the hero in our own story: because of hardships, you're able to serve others facing similar challenges. The unbearable angst you experience today can serve you, and others, in the future.

Your experiences—even the misaligned ones—shape and serve you. No mindset comes with a challenge-free life. Ups and downs are all part of the journey. They prepare you for what's next. Then, when we look back, we see how our experiences took us where we needed to be.

"Life can only be understood backwards, but it must be lived forwards." These beautiful words expressed by philosopher Søren Kierkegaard ring true, despite the natural tendency for many of us to want to have everything figured out and under control. Purpose has a way of connecting the dots of past challenges to present opportunities. Looking back, we can often see how even difficult experiences served us. Yet, there is a time to connect the dots and a time to collect the dots. We can't always make sense of our life experiences, so collect the dots by living your life and allowing new experiences. Your most important job right now may be to make mistakes, learn from them, and honor the mystery.

So what's next? I don't know. What I do know, however, is that if you are misaligned right here, right now, it may mean you're exactly where you are supposed to be. If you have experienced hardship in the past, your life may have prepared you for this very moment. Wherever you are, let the moment inspire you to take action and keep going.

CONCLUSION

"Tell me, what is it you plan to do with your one wild and precious life?"

—MARY OLIVER

In the stirring book, *Five Regrets of the Dying*, author Bronnie Ware shares common themes people express at the end of their lives. The core of each regret revolves around looking back and recognizing they had not lived a life in alignment with who they were. They had spent much of their lives below the line.

Living a life in alignment with who you are is the nonnegotiable ingredient for living a satisfying, rewarding, and fulfilling life. It's not enough to *know thyself*. You must also *be thyself*.

By discovering your mindset, you have gained clarity of *who* you are by understanding your individual *How, What, and Why*.

- Your principle specifies *how* you expect people to behave.
- Your passion specifies *what* you are motivated to do.

- Your purpose specifies *why* it's imperative you honor your principle and passion.

The opposite of your principle, passion, and purpose—trigger, void, and hurt, respectively—show you who you are not (and how not to spend your time and attention) and, in that way, also provide clarity about who you are.

Using the Mindset Framework, which is comprised of these six facets—principle and trigger, passion and void, purpose and hurt—you can understand not only yourself but also others. You no longer need to limit yourself to seeing others' perspectives only through your mindset lens; you can now understand them through their lens. Suddenly, even people quite different from yourself make sense.

As we get to know all 25 Mindsets, it becomes apparent that all of us are part of something much larger—an integrated system dependent upon everyone being who they are. When aligned, every individual from every mindset contributes to a more perfect humanity. We can see how diverse principles, passions, and purposes serve the united whole.

PRINCIPLE

Quite incredibly, all 25 Mindset principles work harmoniously with one another. And because every single principle is essential, we've each been entrusted to uphold one principle above all others. We each have an opportunity to share the importance of our mindset principle and to learn about and uphold other mindset principles. Together, these principles provide the moral fabric of humanity. When humanity collectively upholds all principles, our society is more stable, our efforts are more fruitful, and our relationships are more peaceful.

PASSION

No single person is meant to do it all. Collectively, however, we *can* do it all. Through diverse passions, people feel motivated by different things, which ensures our vast variety of needs may be met. Passion is not simply an activity. Rather, it represents a shift to a more-ideal state that comes about when people do what they are motivated to do. Our voids show us we're meant to support one another. We are better together when each person honors what they are motivated to do, and not do. When we accept and explore our passion, we can do our part to strengthen ourselves and each other, and we are rewarded with the energy to do more.

PURPOSE

Our purpose aims to bring about a more desirable state of being to others and to make the world a better place. This intention to steward and serve others unites us in our shared humanity and benefits future generations. Though we long for this desired state of being for ourselves, we discover it is by giving it to others that we receive it for ourselves. Purpose shows us we aren't separate; we are connected, a part of something greater. By honoring our purpose with an expansive focus beyond ourselves, we can overcome our insecurities and be rewarded with a solid sense of well-being.

The strength of humanity resides in our differences, not our similarities. We were never meant to be just like each other. On the contrary, we are exquisitely designed to complement one another. We are an integral part of the whole.

You are perfectly designed.

Your mission is to align with who you are.

So now that you know who you are, go out and be exactly who you are meant to be, and together we'll help create a better world.

ACKNOWLEDGMENTS

This book would not be possible without the hundreds of people who were willing to share more about themselves in depth with me. I thank each one of you.

To Dr. Carolyn Mein, Jolina Karen, Dr. David Martin, and Scott Whitten: this book would not be what it is without your influence.

Carolyn, thank you for your decades dedicated to this body of work and for providing the foundation for *The 25 Mindsets*. I am forever grateful for you, your support, your patience, and all you continue to do. Thank you for putting your trust in me to carry the torch that you have lit. May it shine brightly for many generations to come.

Jolina, thank you for planting the seeds so I may see the duality in our lives and how all experiences serve us. I know you will continue to expand the horizons of myself and so many others. I can't wait for the world to know you.

David, thank you for sharing your immense wisdom. Though our connection was brief, your impact—on me, and the book—was profound. Your teachings to "invert the polarity" can help all of us align with who we are and serve the whole we are a part of. I am deeply grateful for you and your persistent commitment to serving humanity.

Scott, thank you for your support, for believing in me, and for the regular push to share my work before I felt ready. You've always been my biggest fan. Thank you for providing our family stability as I followed a path with no guarantee of success. You made this work possible. And though our differences have made for a wild ride, it has also taught us both so much. I wouldn't have it any other way.

Kai Whitten, thank you for being an incredible teacher to me, for offering feedback, and, most of all, for being who you are. You are extraordinary, and I'm so very proud of you.

To Mom and Dad, thank you for your support over the decades. I'm so very blessed to have you as my parents and grateful for the foundation you gave us. It's been a joy and a gift to learn more about you through your mindset.

My sincerest thanks to Dawn D'Alessandro, Paul Austin, Melissa Kjonaas, Deb Schindele, Laura Pettett, Kyle Peterson, Justin Peterson, Karen Darst, Allyson Keller, Amy Nakos, Ashelyn Larson, Chad Rempfer, Eric Rosswog, Iris Fang, Gail Shoeman, Kathryn Grohusky, Kerri Karcz, Kristin Amenson, Lena Wessel, Matt McLaughlin, Mike Russo, Murray Fife, Peggy Stafsholt, Pele Pasquesi, Raymond Devine, Robin Stahl, Ryan Klima, Sean Corrales, Travis Pullen, Tristan Larson, Alan and Stacy Anderson, Vern and Bev Whitten, the Tribull Ladies, and too many others to name. I am so very grateful for your support and patience to help me understand your mindset and help me put the pieces together to better understand you. I can only do what I do because you were kind enough to share with me. Thank you.

Thank you to my extraordinary coworkers at Microsoft and beyond—in SoCal, Fargo, Texas, across the US, and around the globe. I miss working with your brilliant minds day in and day out, but also know my path took me exactly where I needed to be, then and now. Thank you to everyone who was a part of that journey. I have fond memories and hope our paths may cross again.

Thanks to so many others who have inspired me. Thank you, Stan Slap, for taking the time to mentor a stranger. Thank you, Marcus Buckingham, Tim Ferriss, Neil Strauss, Rich Roll, Simon Sinek, Susan Cain, Adam Grant, Elena Cardone, and her husband for your influence.

Thank you, Kimberly Nicoletti, for having my back and being a most incredible editor and coach. I am sincerely grateful to have found you, worked with you, and learned from you.

Thank you, Ori Anderson, for your design creations featured throughout this book.

I have learned when you write a book, life will throw you all the experiences you need to learn, for better and for worse. Case in point: to understand sabotage, it means I hurt some people along the way. I've had a plethora of misaligned experiences, and when misaligned, it doesn't bring the best out of anyone, including me. For those whom I have hurt, you know who you are. I am sorry, and I am also deeply grateful to you. Without such experiences, I could not have learned what I needed to learn so that I could share it here. May our misaligned experiences be transformed into something more beautiful that serves others.

And finally, my deepest thanks to all those who choose to pursue a life living in alignment. You are the reason I wrote this book. Together, we can do great things and serve others. Though you have reached the end of the book, I know this is only just the beginning. Go get 'em.

GLOSSARY

One of the best ways to keep yourself and others above the line is to use the 25 Mindsets language. Here are some frequently used terms as they relate to the 25 Mindsets.

Above the Line: Refers to being in an aligned state (for example, with your attention focused on your principle, passion, or purpose).

Alignment: Refers to the satisfactory state of living congruently with your nature. When aligned, you are honoring the essence of your mindset.

Alignment Crisis: A gnawing state of being chronically misaligned with your purpose resulting from catering to your insecurity (i.e., catering to others' perception of you).

Below the Line: Refers to being in a misaligned state (for example, with your attention focused on your trigger, void, or hurt).

Blind Spot: Represents one or more principles you fail to uphold (and, therefore, trigger others), often as the result of upholding your own principle in excess.

Burnout: The predictable consequence that results from chronically inhabiting your void by doing things that drain your energy.

Essence: The aligned state, where you honor your innate gifts and share these gifts with others.

Facet: Represents one of the six key elements of a mindset: principle, trigger, passion, void, purpose, and hurt. Each facet represents one end of the three polarities.

Grr: A description of the universally felt sensation—*grr!*—experienced when someone is triggered.

High: A burst of energy or feeling of excitement, which signifies you have completed the Passion Shift (i.e., you have evidence you have achieved your desired outcome).

Hurt: The agonizing state of being that you can't stand experiencing and that you can't stand for others to experience. It includes your insecurities because insecurities cause the agonizing state of hurt.

Insecurity: Represents how you cannot stand for people to treat you or to perceive you because it causes you to experience the agonizing state of hurt.

Insecurity Inversion: A tactic used to deal with an insecurity by putting effort into making sure people treat you how you want to be treated or perceive you how you want to be perceived (for example, acting in a way to make sure people think you are intelligent).

Insecurity Suppression: A tactic used to deal with an insecurity by putting effort into making sure people don't treat you in ways you don't want to be treated or don't perceive you in a way you don't want to be perceived (for example, acting in a way to make sure people don't think you are unintelligent).

Insecurity-Punishment Link: Acknowledges that your insecurity and your punishment are one and the same.

Mindset: An innate disposition governing *how* you expect people to behave (and not behave), *what* you are motivated to do (and not do), and *why* you do what you do (and the consequence if you do not).

Mindset Framework: A model depicting the three polarities (*How, What, and Why*) of each mindset and their respective facets: principle and trigger, passion and void, purpose and hurt.

Misalignment : The uncomfortable state of going against your nature (for example, focusing your attention on your trigger, void, or hurt).

Multifaceted: Acknowledges that your mindset is made up of six facets (principle, trigger, passion, void, purpose, and hurt), and yet you do not occupy all facets simultaneously.

Mutually Exclusive: Refers to opposing behaviors, actions, or states-of-being that cannot take place simultaneously. Polarities are mutually exclusive because you cannot experience both ends of a mindset polarity, simultaneously. For example, you cannot be doing what you love (passion) and doing what you loathe (void), at the same time.

Passion: Represents what you are innately motivated to do, and by doing it, you bring about a desired outcome.

Passion Pursuit: A specific project, task, goal, challenge, endeavor, or activity with a distinct beginning and end that you are motivated to pursue because it aligns with your passion. It recognizes that the three steps—opportunity, action, and outcome—repeat each time you align with your passion and complete the Passion Shift.

Passion Shift: Depicts a transformation from a less-ideal state (opportunity) to a more-ideal state (outcome), which transpires when you take action that aligns with your passion.

Polarity: The distinguishing of two opposing attributes (for example, accountable and unaccountable). Within the Mindset Framework, three distinct polarities are defined. They distinguish (1) *How* someone should and should not behave, (2) *What* someone is and is not motivated to do, and (3) *Why* they are important, as well as the consequence if not honored.

Principle: An innate expectation of how someone expects people to behave. Also referred to as a "rule" we need others to abide by.

Punishment: An instinctive shift in how you perceive or treat those who severely trigger you. For example, because someone triggered you, you may dislike or avoid them.

Purpose: Represents a heartfelt intention to create a more desirable state of being—a *Why* behind what you do—that is focused on someone or something beyond yourself.

Regret, Remorse, Guilt: Common feelings experienced when you have failed to uphold your own mindset principle. It's like a trigger, except it is you, not someone else, who broke your mindset rule.

Rumination: The persistent focus on your regretful actions, in which you play a scene over and over in your mind, wishing you could go back in time and do things differently.

Six Areas of Alignment: Recognizes that in addition to aligning with your principle, passion, and purpose, overall alignment also requires social, physical, and emotional alignment, and an excess in any one area can create a deficit in another.

The *How* Polarity: One of the three mindset polarities that distinguishes *how* you expect people to behave, and how you expect people to not behave. It is also known as the Principle-Trigger Polarity.

The *What* Polarity: One of the three mindset polarities that distinguishes *what* you are naturally motivated to do, and what you are not motivated to do. It is also known as the Passion-Void Polarity.

The *Why* Polarity: One of the three mindset polarities that distinguishes *why* you do what you do, and the consequence if you do not. It is also known as the Purpose-Hurt Polarity.

Trigger: Represents an expectation of how people should not behave because it opposes your mindset principle.

Void: Represents what you are not motivated to do because it depletes your energy when you do it.

Well-Rounded: Refers to people who are aware of their blind spots and strive to uphold all mindset principles in a balanced way.

MINDSETS OF PEOPLE I KNOW

Use this section to record the mindsets of friends, family, and coworkers.

Name	Mindset
Elon	Inquisitor
Elvis	Cultivator
Enrique	Authenticator

Name	Mindset

Made in the USA
Middletown, DE
19 July 2024